Tipton County, Tennessee

Marriages

1840 – 1874

Byron and Barbara Sistler

JANAWAY PUBLISHING
Santa Maria, California

Tipton County, Tennessee, Marriages 1840-1874

Originally published, Nashville, 1987

by

Janaway Publishing, Inc.
732 Kelsey Ct.
Santa Maria, California 93454
(805) 925-1038
www.JanawayPublishing.com

2006, 2013

ISBN: 978-1-59641-056-5

Made in the United States of America

TIPTON COUNTY, TN MARRIAGES

1840-1874

Where two dates appear on an entry, the first one is the date license was issued, the second (in parentheses) the date marriage was solemnized. If only one date, it usually means that the date of execution was the same as the date of license issuance.

Sometimes the execution of the marriage was not reported to the courthouse, and occasionally the clerk failed to note in the marriage book that the license was returned. We would usually make a notation in the entry to indicate the non-execution of a marriage if the book so stated.

The marriages are arranged alphabetically, the first half of the book by groom--the second by bride.

The records included in this book were transcribed by us directly from microfilm of the original marriage books. Error, where it occurs, may be attributed to us, or to the clerks of the period, many of whom did an appallingly sloppy job of entering the information.

If the bride and groom were black, a B is placed at the end of the entry.

It should be remembered that this and other marriage books we have prepared are indexes, and do not include all the information to be found in the original marriage book. Such data as names of bondsmen, ministers, justices of the peace, churches etc. are omitted. Often such information is helpful to the researcher. Consequently the serious researcher, to obtain this additional information as well as to check on the accuracy of the transcriber, should examine the original marriage record if at all possible, or at least another transcription which may contain this data.

Byron Sistler
Barbara Sistler

Nashville, TN
February, 1987

Abnathy, Richard A. to Nancy Sample 3-8-1873 (3-9-1873)
Ackin?, Samuel J. to Sallie J. Chapman 4-18-1865
Adams, Anderson to Martha Wilson 9-21-1870 (9-22-1870)
Adams, Andrew to Leah Sherrell 3-17-1866 (3-25-1866)
Adams, David to Margaret Ralph 9-30-1873 (10-1-1873)
Adams, Green to Jane Franklin 3-3-1874
Adams, Ira to Sarah Winston 11-4-1865 (11-14-1865)
Adams, J. G. to Isa L. Sherrill 12-4-1873
Adams, James Goodram to Martha Susan Hopper 2-9-1849 (2-15-1849)
Adams, John to Amanda Densford 4-6-1866 (4-7-1866)
Adams, Migugol? to Ella? Faucett 10-30-1869
Adams, Richard to Milley Strong 9-30-1865 (10-28-1865)
Adams, Taylor to Mary Ann Cup 10-21-1869 (10-22-1869)
Adams, W. H. to Fannie Calhoon 1-4-1857 (1-6-1857)
Adams, W. H. to Martha Brown 2-12-1873 (2-13-1873)
Adkins, Albert to Elizabeth Trobough 4-14-1866
Adkins, Benj. Tho. to Margaret Miller 10-2-1850
Adkins, Charles Howell to Harriet L. Wooton 9-11-1853 (9-13-1853)
Adkins, Charles to Martha Weaver 7-26-1852 (7-27-1852)
Adkins, F. B. to Elizabeth McLennan 3-7-1860 (3-8-1860)
Adkins, James L. to Jane Hill 2-3-1847 (2-10-1847)
Adkins, John to Annie Bledsoe 8-18-1874 (8-8?-1874)
Adkins, Moses to Ann Payne 1-7-1874 (1-8-1874)
Adkins, Nathan to Louisa Coward 10-22-1874 (10-23-1874)
Adkins, Phillip to Harriet Holmes 4-2-1866 (4-7-1866)
Adkins, Sam to Amy Robinson 2-14-1867
Adkins, Saml. Will to Lennie Thompson 12-29-1870
Adkins, Saml. to Matilda Gillum 1-11-1873
Adkinson, John to Margaret E. String no date (with 1862)
Adkison, Bynum to Eliza Easley 5-31-1858 (6-1-1858)
Adkison, James to Mary Easley 11-20-1869 (11-23-1869)
Adkisson, Isaac to Charlotte Cooper 3-6-1843 (3-9-1843)
Admas?, Saml. to Judia Walker 3-17-1866
Aikens, R. E. to Mattie C. Hurt 1-1-1866 (1-4-1866)
Akin, John J. to Sallie J. Chapman 4-18-1865 (4-20-1865)
Akin, John W. to Martha H. Stroud 11-21-1870 (11-23-1870)
Akin, John to Easter Boyd 11-2-1868
Akin, John to Easter Boyd 11-7-1868
Akin, N. T.? to Tennessee E. Grimes 11-10-1874 (11-11-1874)
Aldridge, Thos. to kSina Sanford 1-11-1866 (1-13-1866)
Ales, Charly to Cylvia Anderson 10-13-1871
Alexander, Barney to Emina Wilson 12-7-1874?
Alexander, Jack to Elizabeth Alexander 10-8-1873 (10-20-18730
Alexander, James R. to Fannie S. Sanford 12-8-1858
Alexander, Milus to Pleasan Small 2-28-1867
Alexander, P. C. to Lavina Delashment 11-11-1862 (11-13-1862)
Alexander, Thadeus A. to Mary C. Howerton 1-19-1858 (1-20-1858)
Allen, Archer to Lucinda Adams 2?-17-1867 (3-26-1867)
Allen, C. A. to Sarah Jane Kluigh 10-29-1856 (10-30-1856)
Allen, Carlton to Rebecca Vaughan 4-3-1843 (4-4-1843)
Allen, Cyrus A. to Jane Richardson 2-27-1849
Allen, Edward G. to Ann Vaughan 12-14-1844 (12-19-1844)
Allen, George to Ellen Betten 9-16-1871 (9-21-1871)
Allen, James to Setta Allen 10-29-1870 (11-2-1870)
Allen, Saml. to Jane Williams 12-28-1870
Allen, Samuel to Martha Phillips 1-17-1868
Allen, Thomas Jefferson to Mary Robinson 1-17-1843 (not executed)
Allen, W. M. to Elizabeth J. Nelson 12-22-1858
Allen, W. M. to Elizabeth Nelson 12-22-1858
Allen, William to Ann Bledsoe 1-25-1871 (1-26-1871)
Allison, Henry to Kate Vaughn 9-21-1867 (9-21-1867)
Alsten, Sandy to Emerlin Watter 1-10-1867
Alston, Aaron to Jannie Avery 7-10-1869 (7-13-1869)
Alston, Ben to Mary Johnson 1-24-1870
Alston, Furgus to Harriet Sherrill 1-7-1874
Alston, George to Ellen Evans 1-4-1871
Alston, George to Julia Smith 11-29-1866 (11-30-1866)
Alston, Lawrence to Ellen Phelps 3-28-1874
Alston, Mat to Sarah Wilson 1-16-1871
Alston, Phil to Maria Angus 3-8-1867 (3-10-1867)
Alston, Richard to Mary Alston 12-27-1867 (12-2-1868?)
Alston, Sandy to Jennie Gray 12-16-1873
Alston, Thos. to Agnes Alston 12-30-1867 (12-2-1868?)
Alston, Thos. to Martha J. English 3-3-1874 (3-26-1874)
Alston, Washington to Malissa Brown 7-8-1873
Alston, Whit F. to Isabella Smith 2-10-1873 (2-12-1873)
Alston, William to Duley Taylor 5-6-1867
Alston, Wylie to Katie Alston 9-28-1872 (9-29-1872)
Anderson, Anderson J. to Sarah E. Townsend 7-12-1869 (7-13-1869)
Anderson, Andrew J. to Sarah E. Townsend 7-12-1867
Anderson, Burrel to Jane Webb 12-24-1869 (12-25-1869)
Anderson, Edwin to Malinda Malone 1-13-1869
Anderson, Gabriel M. to Rachel Talbot Barker 1-2-1855 (1-3-1855)
Anderson, George to Eliza Coe 1-21-1874
Anderson, Green to Fannie Smith 12-22-1869
Anderson, Wash to Sarah Lawthon 3-13-1869 (3-14-1869)
Anerson?, Stark to Sarah Mosby 8-16-1870 (9-4-1870)
Angel, Calvin to Laura A. Robinson 2-12-1866 (2-1?-1866)
Angus, Jacob to Ellen Hemphill 1-17-1871 (1-18-1871)
Angus, Thomas L. to Eliz. Ann Corisar? 10-12-1846 (10-13-1846)
Angus, Thomas Lowry to Eliza Jane Bowers 3-22-1851 (3-25-1851)
Angus, Thos. to Sue Goodman 1-23-1869 (1-26-1869)
Angus, William Werter to Jane Ralph 7-16-1849 (7-17-1849)
Anthony, Thos. C. to Mary A. Adams 4-11-1866
Applewhite, Jesse to Piety Killingsworth 4-10-1843 (4-12-1843)
Applewhite, John to Nancy Jane McFerin 2-16-1841 (2-20-1841)
Archer, C. T. to Sarah B. Penny 2-20-1869 (2-24-1869)
Archer, Charles W. to Susan Ann Walk 6-20-1855
Archer, Richd. to Susan Howard 2-25-1869
Archer, W. H. to Margaret J. Corder 11-27-1861 (11-28-1861)
Archer, W. H. to Matilda C. Manasco 2-8-1871
Archer, W. to Fannie Hitower 4-8-1874 (4-5?-1874)
Archer, Wm. Franklin to Margaret Ann Smith 12-5-1849
Archey, Matt to Famy Trigg 7-2-1872 (7-13-1872)
Armstrong, Abe to Fanny Alston 11-20-1871 911-23-1871
Armstrong, James Harvey to Juliann Minerva Clark 1-29-1842 (2-?-1842)
Arnold, James to Virginia Stewart 10-6-1845
Ashurst, Wm. to Mildred A. Jarson? 3-6-1873 (3-7-1873)
Atkins, G. P. to Margaret S.? Waters 12-13-1871
Atkison, John to Margaret E. Strong 3-18-1862 (3-20-1862)
Avant, Nelson to Martha Ann Person 1-23-1872 (1-28-1872)
Avery, Albert to Rachal Moore 12-17-1869 (12-18-1869)
Aycock, A. A. to Martha V. Farris 10-22-1864 (9-26-1864)
Ayers, James L. to Mary E. Yarbro 5-12-1858
Ayers, Wm. F. to Gray Howell 4-15-1858
Baenbridge, William B. to Jane Dean Campbell 11-15-1847 (11-16-1847)
Bailey, Benjamin C. to Nancy Wade Sullivan 12-8-1845 (12-10-1845)
Bailey, George to Matilda Cage 1-8-1874
Bailey, James L. to Sarah Hartsfield 12-20-1851 (12-21-1851)
Bailey, Joshua to Elizabeth Cannon 1-3-1867
Bailey, R. W. to T. J. McCullough 12-1-1873
Baily, Henry to Jane Wiley 12-24-1872
Baines, B. F. to Susan Keller 2-25-1874 (3-1-1874)
Baird, J. Linsey to M. Bettie McQuiston 12-6-1870 (12-8-1870)
Baird, John to Eliza Miller 1-29-1868
Baird, William to Nancy Jane McQuiston 3-5-1844
Baird, Wm. C. to M. M. E. McDaniel 8-25-1873 (9-4-1873)
Baker, H. D. C. to D. E. Young 9-9-1867 (9-11-1867)
Baker, Henry to Tabitha Boyd 10-13-1866
Baker, Phinias G. to Sallie E. Bergman 6-13-1874 (6-14-1874)
Baker, T. S. to Mary Logan 10-24-1874 (10-25-1874)
Baldock, Derastus to Mary Jane Hill 12-26-1853 (1-2-1854)
Bales, Fed to Sarah Feild? 2-9-1867
Ballard, D. M. to Elizabeth Brinkley 1-6-1868 (1-8-1868)
Ballard, Henry M. to Eliza Williams 7-16-1861 (8-17-1861)
Ballard, J. A. to Dicy Culbreath 2-23-1860
Ballard, J. A. to Dicy Galbreath 2-23-1860
Ballard, J. W. to S. M. Johnson 6-29-1868 (7-1-1868)
Ballard, John D. to Martha E. A. Ballard 7-26-1858 (7-18-1858)
Ballard, John to Carolin Ballard 9-18-1865 (9-19-1865)
Ballard, John to Margaret Lewellen 7-9-1866 (7-12-1866)
Ballard, Milton Jackson to Arrianna Pernett Talley 4-5-1848
Balley, J. H. to Sallie B. Hunn? 12-12-1868 (12-10?-1868)
Bambridge, A. A. to J. V. Beaver 8-6-1870 (8-9-1870)
Banden, J. C. to Florence E. S. Motley? 8-21-1869
Bandy, Josiah Washington to Mary Vanburen Driver? 8-28-1852
Bandy, Smith M. to Caroline Feezor 12-20-1851 (12-28-1851)

Banks, H. O. to Frances Strong 4-25-1871 (4-26-1871)
Banks, Jno. D. to Jane E. String 12-13-1864 (12-14-1864)
Banks, Ro. M. to Louisa Elmira Strong 1-10-1853 (1-12-1853)
Banner, George W. to Jane E. McCalley 12-30-1868 (1-2-1869)
Bannon, Edward to Susan Lyon 12-23-1873
Baptist, N. Wilson to Belle H. Boyd 1-11-1871 (1-18-1871)
Barker, G. L. to Amanda J. Tate 4-29-1871 (4-30-1871)
Barker, L. A. to Catherine A. Tims 6-3-1871
Barman?, Charles to Sallie Smith 7-8-1867 (7-9-1867)
Barmer?, Coleman to Harriet Grigsby 3-12-1874
Barnell, James to Matilda Alston 1-28-1870
Barnes, C. L. to Margaret English 1-8-1873 (1-9-1873)
Barnes, Tho. J. to Mary Catharine Akin 3-12-1856 (3-13-1856)
Barnet, J. W. to Nancy Larimore 2-11-1868 (3-3-1868)
Barnett, G. W. to Mollie Green 8-11-1874 (8-13-1874)
Barns, Anderson J. to Nancy Rooks 1-26-1842 (1-?-1842)
Barret, George Washington to Catherine Boyd 12-27-1870 (12-28-1871?)
Barret, John H. to Isabella F. Smith 12-14-1870
Barret, Ned? to Maria Lippman 10-9-1868 (10-12-1868)
Barret, Richard S. to Mary Matilda Harris 12-22-1847
Barrett, James M. to Ann Jane Sharp 4-3-1861
Bashears, J. S. to S. J. Muligin 12-23-1874
Basheres, Rufus T. to Martha Helen Davis 7-24-1843
Baskin, Turby to Eliza J. Baskin 2-26-1867 (2-28-1867)
Baskins, David J. to Sallie Freeman 7-12-1864 (7-13-1864)
Baskins, J. H. to M. J. Wallis 7-13-1864 (7-14-1864)
Baskins, John B. to Malinda J. Kelly 12-16-1868
Baskins, W. L. to Elizabeth Jane Dawson 8-1-1866 (8-10-1866)
Bass, Shade to Mollie Avery 3-14-1874
Bate, H. H. to N. D. Simpson 11-24-1873 (11-25-1873)
Batey, J. C. to C. C. Stewart 1-2-1871 (1-5-1871)
Batte, Robert B. to Mary E. Dickerson 10-17-1866 (10-25-1866)
Baugh, John R. to Fannie Baugh 4-6-1858
Baugh, Thos. J. to Frances Stokes 7-26-1854 (1-?-1854)
Baxter, Jno. Edwin to E. J. Tacket 11-13-1872
Baylam?, J. to Hellen Taylor 2-26-1869
Bayley, Robt. to Lucinda F. Sneed 1-10-1872 (1-11-1872)
Bays, W. S. to Aceneth E. Aikin 4-10-1861 (4-17-1861)
Beadls?, Dick to Martha Bledsoe 1-12-1868
Bean, George to Hamar Taylor 1-1-1872 (1-7-1872)
Beasley, Rubin to Fannie Harden 3-30-1867 (4-2-1867)
Beats, Elijah to Fannie Garland 12-23-1873
Beauty, William to Harriet Weatherington 1-19-1860
Beaver, H. W. to Julia C. Smith 10-29-1873 (11-3-1873)
Beaver, H. W. to Margaret Long 5-1-1862
Beaver, Michael to Mildred J. Ralph 4-21-1853
Beaver, Thomas to Emaly Howard 11-8-1873
Beavers, Henry to Mary Ann Ralph 12-19-1846 (12-25-1846)
Beavers, L. J. to Martha E. Fuller 9-21-1872 (9-22-1872)
Beavers, Macal to Harriet Long 1-14-1868 (1-16-1868)
Beaves, R. L. to Tersa McIlwaine 2-20-1873
Becksterling, John to Jane Adams 8-18-1863 (8-20-1863)
Bedingfield, S. W. to Sallie McClenahan 11-9-1874 (11-11-1874)
Bell, Aaron S. to Susanna W. Townsend 2-11-1851 (2-13-1851)
Bell, Alexander to Sarah Roberts 9-16-1871
Bell, Ben to Cohaly? Bumpas 7-28-1866 (7-29-1866)
Bell, George W. to Martha Bragg 10-2-1845
Bell, George to Emma Tinsley 9-7-1872
Bell, Henry to Martha Neel 11-1-1869
Bell, M. to Sue H. Ligon 5-16-1865 (5-17-1865)
Bell, Robert to Mary Owen 8-10-1870 (8-11-1870)
Bell, S. M. to A. L. Cotheran 2-17-1874 (2-18-1874)
Bell, Samuel H. to Sarah C. Bigham 9-28-1865 (10-22-1865)
Bell, William to Sarah Alston 4-25-1872 (4-27-1872)
Bellar, Mosel? to Missouri Elder 3-1-1869 (3-3-1869)
Bennett, Ezekil to Rebecca Guardner 6-4-1855 (6-7-1855)
Bennett, John to Margaret Shaw 5-8-1840 (5-12-1840)
Bennett, William to J. C. Laxton 7-19-1873 (7-20-1873)
Benson, Benjamin B. to Rosa P. Farrar 8-14-1848 (8-?-1848)
Benson, H. W. to M. E. Jamison 12-16-1873 (12-17-1873)
Benson, Jessee C. to A. A. Byrd 2-14-1868 (2-20-1868)
Benson, Pleasant Davis to Catharine Sharp 1-11-1850 (1-16-1850)
Benton, J. F. to Mattie P. Sullivan 12-22-1874 (12-23-1874)
Berges, E. G. to M. J. Hightower 12-15-1873 (12-16-1873)
Beriam, Robert to May Eller Hill 11-28-1871 (11-29-1871)
Bernard, Anthony to Alice Hall 3-27-1869 (3-28-1869)
Bernard, Benj. to ___ane Hall 9-9-1865
Bernard, Frank to Hager Murphy 2-6-1871 (3-5-1871)
Bernard, Johnson to Felia Lowe 8-7-1872 (1-16-1872?)
Bernard, Mingo to Lucy Harris 12-27-1871 (12-28-1871)
Bernard, Saml. P. to Nancy Cotton 2-13-1854
Bernard, Wm. to Rachel Booker 12-24-1867
Berry, W. J. to Angeline Williams 12-21-1868 (12-23-1868)
Beson, James M. to Carolin Thomas 12-22-1869 (12-25-1869)
Best, J. W. to Sarah Wiseman 2-5-1868
Bettis, Jno. to Martha Ann Julian 6-4-1864 (6-5-1864)
Billing, F. T. to M. R. Roan 11-25-1868 (11-26-1868)
Billings, David M. to Martha E. Williams 1-13-1866
Billings, G. W. to Sarah F. Walker 12-11-1865 (12-19-1865)
Billings, George W. to Jane L. Walker 11-6-1847 (11-18-1847)
Billings, George to Keziah Barnes 5-26-1873 (5-27-1873)
Billings, Henry Y. to Nancy Smith 8-1-1855
Billings, Jas. Abner to Elizabeth Roe 11-21-1855 11-21-1855
Billings, John to Martha Witherington 12-5-1846 (12-6-1846)
Billings, Spinia? to Sharlott Roe 9-3-1856
Billings, William H. to Amanda Shankle 7-17-1868 (7-19-1868)
Billings, Wilson to Eliza Violet Grace 5-3-1851 (5-4-1851)
Bird, J. H. to P. F. McNat 11-8-1872 (11-12-1872)
Bird, M. T. to A. J. Hamilton 11-20-1871
Bird, Robert S. to Sarah O. McMin 12-16-1867 (12-18-1867)
Bius?, John J. to Martha Lummicons 6-24-1868 (6-25-1868)
Bivens, Jack to Elizabeth Epps 3-15-1871 (4-10-1871)
Black, C. R. to R. J. Irby 12-12-1866 (12-20-1866)
Black, James M. to Sarah E. Adams 12-29-1858 (12-30-1858)
Black, R. J. to Fannie M. Somerville 4-12-1869 (4-14-1869)
Blackburn, John C. to Ardinia? Reese 4-28-1841 (5-4-1841)
Blackwell, Jack to Caroline White 6-22-1868 (6-25-1868)
Blackwell, John to Katy Granderson 11-17-1873
Blalock, Richard A. to R. C. Winford 12-10-1870 (12-14-1870)
Blanchard, J. H. to Mrs. M. A. McCreight 6-21-1866
Bland, Newman to Nancy Trobough 12-9-1865
Blasingame, Columbus to Mary J. Smith 4-14-1874
Blaydes, James to Georgeanna Payne 12-25-1873
Bledsoe, Aaron to Mary Witherington 9-11-1854
Bledsoe, Anthony to Ann Weathington 2-26-1857
Bledsoe, Bart to Elizabeth Green 2-12-1873 (2-13-1873)
Bledsoe, Granderson to Freesave? Yarbro 3-10-1873 (3-11-1873)
Bledsoe, Sandy to Amanda Rose 12-20-1867 (12-27-1867)
Blescot(Hescot?), B. J. to M. J. Adams 12-2-1874
Blount, Jesse F. to Martha Jane Ewill 1-11-1851 (1-12-1851)
Bloyde, James E. to Malinda E. Payne 4-33-1866
Bolton, John J. to Anna Reid Waller 11-10-1874 (11-11-1874)
Bond, Annias to Mattie Smith 3-15-1873
Bond, Antelpes? to Minerva Smith 5-5-1871 (5-7-1871)
Bond, Cornelius to Eliza McQuister 1-23-1866
Bond, Lewis to Fannie Boyd 12-3-1873 (12-5-1873)
Bond, Noah to Tempa Sherrod 2-10-1866 (2-15-1866)
Bond, Peter N. to Olivid? P. Branch 5-8-1865 (5-10-1865)
Boner, Wm. to Julia Moore 12-23-1858 (12-30-1858)
Bonne, P. A. to Virginia M. Boswell 8-6-1857
Bonner, Georg W. to Olivia Mason 2-6-1854 (2-7-1854)
Bonner, George W. to Mary E. Newsom 7-21-1865
Booker, C. T. to E. R. Clements 11-16-1874 (11-18-1874)
Booker, Edmund to Eliz. Anderson Perkinson 6-29-1846 (7-2-1846)
Booker, William Branch to Alethia Munford Jones 9-18-1852 (9-23-1852)
Booker, William to Mary Bernard 12-27-1870
Booker?, Edmond J. to Mary Ann White 8-3-1842 (8-4-1842)
Booser, Ivason to Mary Smith 9-28-1871
Booth, David C. to Mary L. Menascoe 5-7-1866 (5-11-1866)
Borum, Joseph H. to Ann C. Brooks 2-9-1841
Boswell, Daniel Buford to Frances Dacus 9-27-1848 (9-28-1848)
Boswell, John D. to Amanda Dacus 9-3-1859
Boswell, John Davis to Martha L. Dacus 12-28-1854
Boswell, John to Elizabeth Jane Dacus 2-11-1847
Boswell, N. H. to Catharine Merrit 10-12-1865 (11-6-1865)
Boswell, Nicholas H. to Eliza Jane Baskins 6-9-1842
Boswell, W. C. to Eliza McCarroll 10-1-1864 (10-2-1864)
Bough, Johnathan to Sarah Maye 8-25-1866

Bourn, P. A. to Lucy E. Moss 10-11-1870 (10-12-1870)
Bowden, A. J. to Eliza Leach 11-20-1853
Bowden, Jeremiah to Maria Myers 11-15-1853
Bowden, Thomas P. to Mary Ellin Bonigle? 12-26-1866 (12-27-1866)
Bowden, Thos. P. to Mary J. Erwin 7-1-1874
Bower, James A. to Mary C. Jones 1-12-1867 (1-15-1867)
Bowers, Henry C. to Fanny E. Newton 8-22-1865 (8-23-1865)
Bowers, James Henry to Cordelia Ann Joice 1-12-1846 (not executed)
Bowers, S. T. to J. F. Chapman 3-19-1874 (3-20-1874)
Bowers, W. F. to Frances V. Tucker 11-24-1856 (11-25-1856)
Bowers, W. H. to Amerca J. Brown 10-2-1865 (10-3-1865)
Bowles, J. S. to E. M. Turnage 3-21-1871 (3-23-1872?)
Bowles, Philip D. to Sarah Virginia Heart 10-27-1846 (10-28-1846)
Bowles, Wm. B. to M. T. P. Ferrell 12-3-1864 (12-4-1867)
Boyaknir, Lynn to H. J. McLennahan 1-20-1871 (1-22-1871)
Boyce, Robt. to Amanda Harris 10-28-1871 (11-2-1871)
Boyd, Armistead to Violet Ann Fults 2-2-1869
Boyd, Burril to Fannie Thomas 12-22-1866
Boyd, George to Vina Hill 8-8-1873
Boyd, James to M. J. Farmer 12-20-1858 (12-22-1858)
Boyd, John George to Harriet Sitner 3-19-1872
Boyd, John to Margaret Turnage 8-13-1873 (8-14-1873)
Boyd?, Adam to Nancy Peter 12-1-1865 (12-3-1865)
Boykin, Thadius H. to S. J. Hilliard 10-10-1860
Boykin, William to Lida Catten 11-26-1868
Braden, Edward to Martha H. Taylor 11-7-1871
Bradford, Dick to Agnes Jackson 12-7-1870
Bradford, James C. to Arrilla Kelly 9-2-1868 (9-31-1868)
Bradley, John Q. to Martha A. Page 11-17-1869
Bradshaw, Jacob to Parthina Bowers 9-28-1867 (9-29-1867)
Bragg, Albert to Louise Jackson 1-11-1871? (2-11-1872)
Bragg, J. M. to M. D. Moore 1-7-1873 (1-9-1873)
Bragg, Jas. Dick to Violet Holloway 8-3-1871 (8-4-1871)
Bragg, M. to A. C. Howard 5-21-1870 (5-22-1870)
Bragg, Robert to Eliza Harwell 8-6-1868
Bragg, Robt. J. to Luticia Bell 11-19-1845
Bragg, William to Martha M. Howard 12-29-1869 (12-30-1869)
Branch, Danil to Mary Trusdile 11-4-1871 (11-5-1872?)
Brandon, Henry to Lusinda Walker 3-23-1867 (3-24-1867)
Brasher, Lomax to Tabitha Casey 6-6-1853 (6-7-1853)
Brassell, John to Mary C. Smith 10-24-1871
Breck?, James B. to Nancy Jane Willhellmis 3-20-1873
Briggs, T. J. to Elisa Ladd 2-19-1870 (2-24-1870)
Bright, James B. to Emma P. Adams 10-29-1873 (10-30-1873)
Bright, Malica C. to Dilly Dinwoody 1-24-1848
Brimley, Wm. J. to Elizabeth Parsons 2-23-1857 (3-8-1857)
Bringle, C. A. to Rosa J. Rich 1-2-1871 (1-5-1871)
Bringle, James H. to Nancy J. White 11-11-1868 (11-12-1868)
Bringle, James to Mollie Maxwell 2-14-1872
Bringle, John Nicholas to Margaret Billings 7-14-1846
Bringle, S. J. to Elizabeth J. Owen 4-28-1860 (4-29-1860)
Briseman, Wm. E. to C. C. Woods 6-21-1859 (6-22-1859)
Brisentine, Wm. to Bettie Browne 5-16-1868 (5-17-1868)
Brodnax, Jacob M. to Nancy Stevens 12-7-1874
Brodnax, Richard T. jr. to Sallie H. Taylor 1-18-1867 (1-23-1867)
Brodnax, William F. to Mollie Bet. Taylor 12-24-1862 (12-25-1862)
Brodnax, Wm. F. to Eliza S. Maclin 5-15-1865
Brooks, Aganza? Benton to Cynthia Jane Wright 11-27-1848 (11-30-1848)
Brooks, Edwin to Charlotte Baker 9-2-1840
Brooks, James to Matilda Wooten 3-16-1861
Brooks, Joseph C. to Louisa Cobb 11-14-1861
Brooks, Tob? to Lucy Alston 7-10-1868 (7-11-1868)
Broomly, Alfred to Mildrid C. Stevens 12-23-1868 (12-24-1868)
Brough, Giles to Ellen O. Byram 8-12-1863 (8-16-1863)
Brown, Andrew to Eliza Scott 3-7-1872
Brown, C. M. to Sarah P. Adams 2-12-1872 (2-13-1872)
Brown, Clark to Martha Richardson 1-3-1871 (1-5-1871)
Brown, Cornelius to Rosanna Campbell 9-5-1872 (9-14-1872)
Brown, David to Julia Berry 12-24-1874
Brown, Dolphus to Polly L. Smith 9-23-1867
Brown, Elijah to Eliza Kitchen 2-26-1855 (2-27-1855)
Brown, Henry to Mary Smith 12-30-1871
Brown, Hosea Carroll to Harriet Ford Leach 9-22-1852
Brown, Jesse G. to Louisa C. Daniels 2-27-1871 (2-22?-1871)
Brown, Jesse G. to Mary E. Corbet 9-23-1868 (9-24-1868)
Brown, Jesse to C. A. Clement 2-7-1861 (2-12-1861)
Brown, Jo to Nancy McCuller 12-30-1873
Brown, John T. to Susan Whitlock 4-16-1857
Brown, Noah to Matilda Wiseman 12-26-1865 (12-28-1865)
Brown, S. H. to Elizabeth Yarbro 6-5-1856
Brown, W. P. to M. T. Siler 8-2-1873 (8-3-1873)
Brown, William to Louisa Brooks 7-23-1867
Brown, William to Sallie Wiseman 1-7-1874 (1-10-1874)
Brown, Wm. to Penni? Moore 1-11-1871 (1-15-1871)
Brown, Wm. to Sarah Flaniken 7-3-1841 (10-17-1841
Brown?, Thomas to Ella Bumpass 12-11-1869
Browning, James to Kate Eddie 4-27-1872 (4-29-1872)
Brunson, David Alexr. to Mary Coffy McClellan 1-12-1846 (1-13-1846)
Brunson?, Joshua N. to Susan A. M. S. Easley 9-14-1840 (9-15-1840)
Bryan, N. to Elizabeth M. Petty 11-26-1853 (11-27-1853)
Bryant, James S. to Mary Jane Freeman 8-7-1843
Bryant, John D. to Nancy M. Hall 8-19-1867
Bryant, John J. E. to Susan Ann Stevens 8-1-1853 (8-3-1853)
Bucham, John W. to Mary E. Plumley 5-30-1872
Buckley?, James to Elizabeth Culbreath 12-4-1843 (12-?-1843)
Budgett?, Jonathan to Margaret? Alfred 12-29-1862
Buford, Smith to Mattie A. Hall 2-6-1866 (2-7-1866)
Buford, W. L. to H. A. Hall 8-2-1859 (8-3-1859)
Buggs, Phillip to Kate Fields 8-30-1873 (8-31-1873)
Buhse?, Leopold to Mary E. Pugh 8-22-1874 (8-26-1874)
Bulger, James to M. E. Hays 1-30-1862
Bull, William to Mary H. Bandy 11-16-1869
Bullington, Richard E. to Sallie Peete 12-27-1869
Bullock, Billey to Mary Ann Taylor 2-27-1868
Bumpas, Anderson to Fannie Binam 11-11-1871 (11-24-1871)
Bumpbass, Julian to Lovy Coe 4-23-1870
Bumphass, Monroe to Matilda Wright 2-16-1874 (2-24-1874)
Burch, B. D. to Sallie B. Turner 5-12-1860
Burchet, P. to A. Burchet 7-27-1870 (9-1-1872?)
Burchett, Henry to Cora Hays 5-7-1870
Burdick, James L. to Dicy A. Sullivan 5-10-1861 (5-14-1861)
Burgess, James to Susan Markham 9-8-1855 (9-10-1855)
Burgitt, Wm. Porter to Sarah Ann Withington 12-17-1855 (12-20-1855)
Burkhart, J. F. to J. M. Reeves 8-29-1860 (9-4-1860)
Burkhart, James Miles to Mary Ann Henderson 8-15-1843 (8-18-1843)
Burks, William to Bell Badwell 12-24-1866 (12-25-1866)
Burlerson, Wm. L. to Eurind Holsouser? 12-20-1853
Burlison, Henry to Catharine Hemphill 2-15-1868 (2-6?-1868)
Burlison, J. H. to Jennie Ballard 12-21-1873
Burnett, Wesley A. to Susan F. McFadin 10-12-1858
Burns, W. M. to Eliza M. Koonce 12-18-1859 (12-21-1859)
Burrel?, David to Sina Maclin 12-23-1872 (12-26-1872)
Burrell, John to Henrettia Corss 2-15-1873 (2-16-1873)
Burrell, Peter to Rachell Moss 11-12-1873
Burrell, Richmond to Fannie Cage 5-9-1874
Burris, William J. to Martha Ann Campbell 11-7-1844 (11-9-1844)
Burtis, Theodore to Nancy E. Chapman 6-15-1866 (6-19-1866)
Burton, Hezekiah to Mary Jane Bakers 11-15-1843 (11-16-1843)
Burton, J. B. to Franca? J. Drummond 4-3-1868 (4-5-1868)
Burton, James Thos. to Ellen Akin 11-5-1867 (11-6-1867)
Bushins?, David J. to Louisa Adkisson 8-5-1846 (8-6-1846)
Busic, Thomas to Catherine Warthwait? 7-20-1872 (7-21-1872)
Butler, Ezekal to Catherin Eaton 4-3-1872 (4-4-1872)
Butler, George to Irene Reed 10-12-1866
Butler, George to Parthena Ann Taylor 3-13-1856
Butler, John Madison to Mona Agnes Rice 7-17-1843 (7-19-1843)
Buttery?, James to Margaret Miller 12-16-1871 (12-17-1871)
Butts, Bob to Martha Green 3-2-1872 (11-20-1872)
Byers, James to Mary Jane Vincent 5-15-1851
Byford, Irvin to L. J. Brady 1-9-1866 (1-10-1866)
Bynan, Guy to Frankie Tipton 11-4-1872 (11-5-1872)
Bynum, Guy to Laura Burchett 11-9-1871
Bynum, Patrick to Mollie Owen 3-26-1868
Byrd, C. C. to S. F. Timms 8-11-1874 (8-13-1874)
Byrd, Jesse S. to Minirva Reynolds 11-21-1860
Byrd, Jesse to Mary Margaret Williams 6-14-1855
Byrd, Neapolheo? D. to Frances Jane Tam? 12-24-1846 (12-30-1846)

Byrnes, Wilson to Cornelia Wetherington 8-17-1867 (8-18-1867)
Cage, Hibrey? to Miss Peggy Hill 12-2-1865
Cage, Hilary to Pecella Lauderdale 3-5-1869
Calaway, Adam to Charlotte Adkins 6-15-1873
Caldwell, John to Elizabeth Markham 10-4-1851
Calhoon, Boyd to Becky Harris? 12-29-1865 (1-14-1866)
Calhoon, James A. to Elsey Larimore 9-17-1840 (10-15-1840)
Calhoon, William S. to Eliza Bacyas? 4-2-1867
Calhoun, Ben to Jane C. Harris 1-5-1871
Calhoun, Dan to Rena Belford 5-16-1870 (5-18-1870)
Calhoun, Grandison to Minerva Clement 12-29-1865 (12-30-1865)
Calhoun, John W. to Sallie A. Barret 1-19-1870
Calhoun, Pomp to Ellen Hawood 8-15?-1871
Calhoun, Pompey to Mary Yarbroh 9-29-1866 (10-29-1866)
Calhoun, Thos. to Sarah Bernard 6-5-1869 (6-6-1869)
Camel?, John to Virginia F. Craig 4-10-1871 (4-11-1871)
Campbell, Adam Dean to Eleanor B. Davis 12-3-1855 (12-4-1855)
Campbell, Erasmus Sydenham to Eliza Jane Mariner 6-1-1844 (6-4-1844)
Campbell, J. W. to Mollie J. Miller 10-20-1871 (10-26-1871)
Campbell, Jno. Boyd to Eleanor Valentin Bambridge 2-1-1843 (2-7-1843)
Campbell, John to Frances Jane Hite 3-6-1869 (3-7-1869)
Campbell, Lemuel M. to Eliza Jane Bowles 12-1-1841 (12-2-1841)
Campbell, Thomas C. to Eliz. Mary Isabella Archer 12-5-1849 (12-6-1849)
Campbell, William F. to Mary Bartlett 12-31-1849 (1-2-1850)
Campbell, William to Kezir? Smith 1-30-1866 (1-31-1866)
Cannon, C. C. to M. L. Wages? 3-13-1873
Cannon, Haywood to Louiza Stevens 10-29-1856
Cannon, Henry to Sarah Ann Glass 8-12-1858
Cannon, Levi to Smith Ann Maclin 2-27-1867
Cannon, Spencer to Indiana Wortham 1-10-1870
Cannon, William to Mary Brown 12-31-1866
Capehart, William to Elizabeth Joiner 11-28-1853
Caraway, James Henry to Mary Love Edwards 12-28-1844 (1-2-1845)
Carn?, James Irwin to Ann Savanna? Gustins? 1-5-1843 (1-5-1843)
Caroway, Lewis to Eliza Strong 1-27-1872 (2-6-1872)
Carr, C. C. to Susan W. Smith 5-26-1866 (5-29-1866)
Carriston?, William to Mariah A. Chaney 3-4-1871
Carson, Thomas to M. C. Davis 10-11-1865
Carson, Wm. to Martha A. Freeman 2-2-1859 (2-3-1859)
Carter, Edmond to Emaline Dowell 12-4-1873
Cary, John A. to Anna E. Sherrill 12-22-1874 (12-23-1874)
Cash, G. B. to S. E. Pennel 12-7-1868 (12-9-1868)
Cash, James L. to Mary J. Crain 6-24-1873 (6-26-1873)
Cash, W. D. to M. E. Pennel 1-21-1874 (1-24-1874)
Cash, W. D. to S. E. Hunt 3-23-1869 (3-24-1869)
Caskey, James to Hellen Hindman 12-8-1861
Cassan, Alexander to Margaret Williams 10-12-1867
Castles, J. C. to E. W. McQuiston 12-12-1870 (12-15-1870)
Cates, George S. to Margaret E. Myers 12-23-1873
Cates, William to E. S. Wilson 8-29-1871 (8-30-1871)
Caughein, John C. to Mrs. Byrd 10-2-1869
Caulbreath, J. C. to Sarah J. Cockrill 4-11-1868 (4-12-1868)
Cavenar, J. W. to Amanda E. Clifton 12-26-1870 (12-27-1870)
Chamber, Daniel Webster to Maney Gracey 1-27-1866
Chamber, George to Susan Harper 10-16-1874 (10-17-1874)
Chambers, Edwin to Sylva Samuels 10-10-1868
Chambers, Geo. to Jane Young 11-30-1872 (12-1-1872)
Chambers, Guss to Bettie Alexander 12-13-1873 (12-15-1873)
Chaney, W. A. to Ann Verser 12-5-1857 (12-6-1857)
Chapman, Francis M. to Mary Ann Biggs 11-12-1842 (11-13-1842)
Chapman, J. B. to C. P. Bowers 11-10-1874 (11-11-1874)
Chapman, Jessee R. to Nancy S. Sanders 5-8-1873 (5-14-1873)
Chapman, John A. to Narcissa Carter 2-24-1869
Cheek, Jacob to Sallie Calhoon 1-20-1866 (1-21-1866)
Cheek, Jacob to Sallie Calhoun 1-20-1866
Cherry, David A. to Eliza C. Knox 5-31-1854 (6?-1-1854)
Cherry, G. W. to Miss A. S. Butler 7-18-1861 (7-19-1861)
Childress, L. A. to Martha B. Sanders 4-15-1865 (5-28-1865)
Chisam, George to Nancy Roberts 12-4-1869
Churchill, Charles C. to Mary A Rivers 7-8-1857 (7-15-1857)
Claiborn, Jas. Henry to Amelia Vanclaire? Ryan 10-26-1852
Claiborn, Jesse M. to Elenor H. Markham 5-4-1859
Claiborne, Thomas to Laura Ann Clark 9-24-1849 (10-4-1849)
Claiburne, Charles to Charlett Harrison 3-22-1869 '
Claiburne, Harry to Emaline Bragg 9-11-1865 (9-14-1865)
Clark, B. L. to Delia Elizabeth Calhon? 5-25-1872
Clark, Isaac to Elizabeth Hart 12-27-1866 (12-13?-1866)
Clark, Isaac to Lizzie Hart 12-29-1866
Clark, Isaac? to Rosa Clements 9-7-1872 (9-8-1872)
Clark, James S. to Nancy A.? Smith 2-6-1869 (2-10-1869)
Clark, John Wesley to ____ Vanhook Darby 11-24-1842 (12-?-1842)
Clark, L. W. to Miss Minerva Childress 11-4-1874 (11-8-1874)
Clark, Logan to Amanda Richardson 3-2-1869 (3-3-1869)
Clark, Wallace to Matilda Barret 2-4-1870
Clark, William to Indiana Miller 1-20-1866
Clay, Albert to Mary Harris 12-28-1870 (12-29-1870)
Clayton, J. C. to Marth E. Davis 10-21-1865 (10-25-1865)
Clement, James to Anne Belle Strange 10-29-1874
Clement, Lenard to Rhody Ann Peete 6-1-1866 (6-2-1866)
Clements, A. J. to Susan L. Galbreath 4-4-1870 (4-5-1870)
Clements, Abner to Caroline Galbreath 8-2-1858 (8-3-1858)
Clements, Adam Dabney to Martha Ann Sherrod 5-3-1847 (5-6-1847)
Clements, Charles A. to Ann Henry Williams 12-21-1847 (not executed)
Clements, Claiborn to Winnie Bolton 10-4-1870 (10-8-1870)
Clements, Jame J. to Nancy W. Smith 3-6-1871 (3-16-1871)
Clements, Paul to Alice Winford 8-31-1866 (9-13-1866)
Clements, Saml. to Sarah Benton Dodson 8-9-1851 (8-10-1851)
Clements, William E. to Drucilla D. Drummons 12-19-1843 (12-21-1843)
Clements, Wm. R. to Mary Jackson Hunt 9-9-1854 (9-14-1854)
Clifton, Ridley to Mary O. Robertson 4-30-1860
Cloud, Robert Evans to Angeline J. Mounts 1-17-1843 (not executed)
Coachman, Robt. to Harriet Rice 6-28-1867
Coates, J. B. to Mary M. Roe 11-18-1871 (11-21-1871)
Coates, J. H. to A. E. Roe 7-21-1871 (7-26-1871)
Coats, Alan to Elizabeth Boswell 12-24-1843 (12-26-1843)
Coats, Berry to Gilly Eglentine Coats 11-1-1850 (11-3-1850)
Coats, Boston to Kysiah Somervill 7-2-1866
Coats, Felty to Frances Jane Boswell 9-18-1845
Coats, Geo. Gideon to Frances America Harrison 9-2-1846 (9-3-1846)
Coats, George to Martha Peeler 1-23-1866
Coats, Henry to Charlotte Frances Bibb 2-23-1847
Coats, Henry to Martha Coats 10-4-1845 (10-15-1845)
Coats, James to Charlotte Hytower 1-24-1860 (1-26-1860)
Coats, Milton A. to Jerusha Ann Jane McGuice 11-7-1857 (11-10-1857)
Coats, Newt to Scyntha Woods 1-15-1866
Coats, Solomon to Sarah Ann Oliver 12-8-1853
Coats, Thomas W. to Susan Jane Campbell 8-24-1841 (8-26-1841)
Coats, Wilson Wm. to Mary Cathrine Oliver 3-18-1854 (3-19-1854)
Cobb, Benjamin to Jenny Stokes 5-25-1841 (5-27-1841)
Cobb, Henry to Margaret E. Bragg 3-11-1844
Cobb, Hesekiah to Eliza J. P. Angus 11-2-1857 (11-3-1857)
Cobb, John to Rebecca Bell 9-4-1866 (9-15-1866)
Cocke, W. H. to Mattie E. Hudson 12-18-1871 (12-19-1871)
Cockrell, James Henry to Martha Ann Haynie 10-13-1847
Cockrill, Blunt to Mary Clements 1-10-1869
Cockrill, William G. to Laura J. Mayo 3-18-1867 (3-14?-1867)
Cocrum, John C. to Sarah Woods 2-23-1867 (3-11-1867)
Coffman, James to America Stake 11-17-1874 (11-18-1874)
Coldwell, Dave to Margaret Walker 10-5-1872 (10-6-1872)
Cole, Logan T. to Matilda Beasley 6-14-1873 (6-17-1873)
Coleman, J. C. to A. D. Ore 3-22-1873 (3-25-1873)
Coleman, Thomas to Emily Owen 9-23-1871
Coleman, Walter Archer to Massey Lavinia Pennell 10-30-1849 (11-2-1849)
Collier, Joseph to Narcissa Caraway 5-27-1859 (5-28-1859)
Collier, Joseph to Narcissa Carraway 5-27-1859 (5-28-1859)
Collier, Robert P. to Mary E. Feezor 5-29-1845
Collins, Andrew to Annie Miller 5-21-1874
Collins, Saml. to Sallie Goodman 12-24-1874 (12-25-1874)
Collinsworth, George P. to Amanda Rose 9-6-1873
Colman, Henry to Harriet Coward 12-23-1867 (12-27-1867)
Colwell, James to Elizabeth F. Culbreath 5-4-1860 (5-5-1860)
Combs, David to Evaline Stevens 3-2-1869
Conelly, Alfred to Emeline Harmon 12-26-1874 (12-27-1874)

Conner, Jeff to M. Hadly 1-4-1872
Connor, Lewis to Mollie Brooks 12-13-1872 (4-24-1873)
Cook, Geo. Washington to Sophia C. Flowers 12-21-1851 (not executed)
Cook, Jas. H. to Harriet V. Deakin 11-14-1856 (11-19-1856)
Cook, Ned to Victoria Taylor 8-1-1868
Coonts, Jas. W. to Susan C. Byrns? 10-15-1856 (10-16-1857?)
Cooper, Albert to Bell McConnell 10-30-1872 (11-1-1872)
Cooper, Colemon to Lucy Culbreath 6-18-1870
Cooper, Derry to Mary Grimes 11-23-1870 (11-27-1870)
Cooper, Garrett to Judith Ann Kent 8-18-1849 (8-22-1849)
Cooper, J. N. to L. J. Robertson 7-27-1874 (7-29-1874)
Cooper, James L. to M. A. Whitley 5-21-1867 (5-23-1867)
Cooper, John to Eliza Glover 1-24-1868 (1-25-1871?)
Cooper, Mansel to Malinda Sexton 4-25-1844 (5-28-1844)
Cooper, Richard to Minerva Peete 2-21-1867 (2-23-1867)
Cooper, Robert to Leanah Moore 11-18-1861
Cooper, Saml. to America Gibson 3-6-1869 (3-9-1869)
Cooper, ____ Addison to Margaret Murphy 5-22-1843
Copland, Isaac to Nelley A. Powell 12-23-1867 (12-31-1868?)
Coppedge, William L. to Mary A. Armstrong 9-21-1844 (9-?-1844)
Corbet, John to S. H. Packard 10-5-1858
Corder, Joseph to F. J. Bell 6-29-1872 (6-30-1872)
Cotheran, Henry to Hannah Flower 1-13-1866
Cotherane, Jos. to Sallie Minor 1-5-1866 (1-27-1866)
Cotherum, Richmond to Jane Walk 12-7-1869 (12-8-1869)
Cothran, Dick to Loveann Bumphass 12-25-1873
Cothran, Esquire to Sallie Edwards 2-20-1873 (2-21-1873)
Cothran, James to Elmira Butler 12-18-1843 (12-21-1843)
Cothran, Jesse S. to Ann Rebecca Howard 11-14-1840 (11-19-1840)
Cotten, Jason to Fannie Cotten 12-26-1868
Cotten, Lee to Milly Jones 7-2-1872 (7-13-1872)
Cotton, Henry W. to Julia Ann Gornet? 6-28-1869
Cotton, Henry Washington to Julia Ann Graham 6-28-1869 (7-1-1869)
Cotton, James Hooper to Ann Elizabeth Purvis 4-2-1853 (4-4-1853)
Cotton, Tom to Sarah Saunders 2-10-1872 (2-11-1872)
Cousar, J. F.? to S. E. Campbell 5-9-1870 (5-10-1870)
Covdy?, A. J. to Nancy Harris 10-15-1874
Covington, John A. M. to Melvina Davis 6-11-1857
Cowan, Henderson to Lucy Fields 2-14-1874
Cowan, Lewis to Maria Thompson 9-18-1872
Cowan?, Thomas to Leanna Moore 5-5-1842 (5-12-1842)
Coward, Anthony B. to Mary Wooten 12-14-1841 (12-15-1841)
Coward, Cal to Harriet Moffit 12-30-1874 (12-31-1874)
Coward, Henry to Louisa Chamber 11-17-1865 (11-18-1865)
Coward, William S. to Mary N. Hall 10-10-1865 (10-11-1865)
Coward, William to Angeline Thomas 1-7-1874 (1-8-1874) B
Cowen, W. F. to L. A. Jones 12-20-1871
Cowser, Thos. to Margaret A. Faulkner 12-24-1866 (12-25-1866)
Cowser?, Prichard to Elizabeth A. Wright 3-25-1843
Cox, Franklin to Eliz. Burns 11-13-1871
Cox, George W. to Mary Johnson 6-23-1855 (6-26-1855)
Cozby, William to Mary N. Montgomery 5-5-1866
Craig, Alfred to Aggny? Maclin 12-14-1867 (12-21-1867)
Craig, J. D. to S. M. P. Blackwood 10-21-1871 (10-25-1871)
Craig, John to Martha D. McCraw 6-26-1866 (6-28-1866)
Craig, John to Sarah Margaret Delashmet 8-2-1871 (8-3-1871)
Craig, Saml. S. to Jennie T. Wright 3-13-1862
Cranbury, Isaac to Bettie Sasser 3-7-1868 (3-8-1871?)
Crawford, Thos. C. to Eliza P. Marshall 2-9-1871
Crawley, Isaac to Mary Cothran 2-8-1873 (2-9-1873)
Crenshaw, C. to Catharine Waller 2-18-1874 B
Crenshaw, David K. to Clara A. Jackson 10-19-1853 (10-20-1853)
Crenshaw, Josephus to Elizabeth J. Hendron 1-28-1850
Crenshaw, Ned to L. A. Trosdale 9-8-1874
Crenshaw, Yeatman to Amanda Crenshaw 2-24-1870
Crider, G. C. to Mary E. Probusaugh? 10-2-1871 (10-?-1871)
Crofford, ____ to Louisa A. Simon? 6-19-1864 (6-21-1864)
Crosby, Saml. to Henrietta Grimes 12-28-1868
Crouch, Edward Radford to RAchel Miller 8-12-1844 (8-15-1844)
Crouch, George W. W. to Serilda Ann Jones 5-7-1860 (5-8-1860)
Crouch, James E. to Emily A. Stokes 1-14-1846 (2-24-1846)
Crouch, John Hendin? to Ann Elizabeth Hurt? 3-7-1853 (3-8-1853)
Crouch, William Anthony to Catharine Murphy Stokes 4-12-1845 (4-15-1845)
Culbreath, Cowell? to Eliza Clewellyn Smith 8-3-1841 (8-5-1841)
Culbreath, Henry to Janie Ann Roil 3-31-1870 (4-1-1870)
Culbreath, J.R. to S. M. A. Davis 6-20-1874
Culbreath, James Jefferson to Susan Eliz. Slaughter 1-20-1851 (1-23-1851)
Culbreath, William to Sarah Christmas Power 4-23-1849 (4-26-1849)
Culbreth, James J. to Mary E. Stewart 1-22-1844 (1-?-1844)
Cullam, Wm. J. to Susan D. Delashmet 12-13-1869 (12-14-1869)
Cullen, Z. C. to Julia C. Davidson 8-27-1860 (8-28-1860)
Cullens, J. D. to Luler Harper 10-28-1868
Cullim, William H. to Isadora Harper 12-21-1871
Cullison?, Mathew to Adeline Pyles 10-26-1867 (11-4-1867)
Cullum, Marcus H. to Elizabeth Jane Davis 1-27-1845
Cummins, David Hays to Emma Holmes 8-14-1843
Cummins, John to Lucinda Kelley 3-24-1851 (4-3-1851)
Cup, Wesley to Martha Jane Odom 6-25-1857
Cup, William to Eliza Ann Adams 10-21-1869 (10-22-1869)
Curlin, James M. to Sarah L. Traylor 4-10-1861
Curtis, Andrew J. to Sarah J. Scales 1-25-1870
Custer, John Cox to Margaret Jane Moore 12-3-1850 (12-8-1850)
Dacus, Alexander to Rebecca Starnes 8-15-1850 (8-18-1850)
Dacus, H. C. to L. A. Huffman 11-7-1874 (11-10-1874)
Dacus, Henry Jackson to Hester Ann Hamilton Rigsby 1-20-1852 (1-22-1852)
Dacus, Joseph A. to Elizabeth C. Upchurch 7-25-1866 (7-26-1866)
Dalin, John to Julia Boner 5-17-1867
Daniel, Byrd to Betty Griggs 5-3-1873 (5-4-1873)
Daniel, E. B. to Larisa A. W. Maley 6-8-1858
Daniel, G. W. to L. C. Aldridge 12-26-1864 (1-2-1864?)
Daniel, J. B. to Cornelia W. Hall 12-20-1865
Daniel, Thomas M. to Mary Louisa James 8-28-1849 (9-6-1849)
Daniels, J. M. to Sarah Maley 1-31-1871 (2-2-1871)
Danniel, Byrd to Bettie Grigg 5-3-1873
Danniel, J. B. to Carolin W. Hall 12-20-1865
Danniel, James A. to Martha M. Baker 12-13-1867 (12-15-1867)
Danniel, Mosel C. to Ann E. Baker 12-13-1867 (12-15-1867)
Dannil, James W. B. to Frances Owen 1-29-1868
Davenport, David to Maria Amanda Starnes 4-25-1849 (4-26-1849)
David, Felix Robertson to Nancy McKenon 1-25-1842 (1-26-1842)
David, J. W. to Ruth Ann Kitchum 7-4-1870 (7-7-1870)
Davidson, Minor B. to Eleanor K. Moore 1-4-1842
Davidson, Thos. to Sarah Dumis 12-2-1874
Davidson, W. T. to Martha E. Marsh 12-28-1869 (12-30-1869)
Davidson, thomas to Lucinda Tims 11-2-1847 (11-3-1847)
Davie, W. S. to Katie E. Hall 9-29-1874 (9-30-1874)
Davis, Calvin to Nancy J. Blasingame 1-17-1872 (1-18-1872)
Davis, D. A. to C. D. Mason 10-25-1865 (10-26-1865)
Davis, Davie to Cordie Kindle 4-16-1873 (4-17-1873)
Davis, Edward to Louise Tamey? no date (with 12-1874)
Davis, F. F. to Anna Yarbro 7-15-1874
Davis, Henry Clay to Lucey Field 9-22-1874
Davis, J. W. to Nancy Jane Mayfield 12-12-1859 (12-13-1859)
Davis, J.E. to Christinea Shoaf 11-25-1874
Davis, Jacob M to Caroline Jones 3-2-1866 (5-30-1866)
Davis, Jacob to Maryetta Burrel 12-17-1873 (12-20-1873)
Davis, James F. to Mary E. Marsh 10-23-1866 (10-24-1866)
Davis, John B. to Sarah Simpson 10-12-1846 (10-15-1846)
Davis, Jonathan Calvin to Martha Jane McCain 9-13-1854
Davis, Laudin to Frances McLinn 5-5-1871
Davis, Richard to Emaline Sanders 1-8-1870 (1-9-1870)
Davis, Rubin to Siller Davis 11-5-1874 (11-8-1874)
Davis, Samuel to Nancey Hanly 4-5-1861
Davis, Stevens to Adalin Hall 1-7-1865 (6-10-1865)
Davis, W. A. to Louisa V. Proctor 11-22-1873 (11-27-1873)
Davis, W. C. to Namie? Sullivan 3-12-1866 (3-15-1866)
Davis, W. H. to Susan Lane 1-19-1871
Davis, William H. to Frances M. Kinney 7-23-1857
Davis, William to Caroline Buise 10-28-1842
Davis, Willis to Caroline Treadaway 10-24-1874 (10-25-1874)
Davis, Wm. Carroll to Sarah Adiline Davis 9-4-1854 (9-6-1854)
Dawson, Jessee F. to Martha A. Mills 1-18-1871 (1-19-1871)
Dawson, Perry to Mary Jane Cox 10-14-1872 (10-16-1872)
Dawson, W. D. to Rosa Ann Jane Mills 12-?-1869 (12-19-1869)
Day, Riland to Lucey Tarry 4-15-1867 (4-27-1867)
DeVries, Gerrit to Rosa Fisher 8-12-1872 (9-1-1872)

Deakins, Henry to Matilda Champion 8-27-1866 (8-28-1866)
Deakins, John Henry to Eliza M. Lamb 9-19-1849 (9-20-1849)
Dean, W. B. to M. S. Putman 8-5-1870 (8-7-1870)
Dearing, John to Sarah Eliza Clark 1-7-18557
Dearing, Joseph to Iva Ann Winn 6-24-1856
Dedrick, Home? to Lidia A. Wooten 12-24-1866 (12-27-1866)
Delashmeit, Joseph G. to Julia E. Morrison 7-1-1865
Delashmet, Chas. to Mildred Davidson 11-18-1867 (11-21-1867)
Delashmet, George W. to Verlinske B. Turnage 12-7-1867 (12-10-1867)
Delashmet, William to Margaret C. Turnage 12-1-1840 (12-2-1840)
Delashmet, Wm. to Mary Walker 2-14-1855 (2-15-1855)
Delashmit, M. L. to Miss L. G. Turnage 12-16-1874 (12-17-1874)
Delashmut, M. L. to V. C. Jenkins 10-14-1871 (10-19-1871)
Demar, Luby? to Martha Ann Young 12-20-1873
Dennis, Alexander to Easter Webb 10-14-1871
Dennis, Alexander to Josephin Cockrill 1-14-1869 (1-18-1869)
Densford, James O. to Caroline Clements 4-2-1862 (4-3-1862)
Densford, William B. to Mary Bryant Dehart 10-13-1849 (10-14-1849)
Deson, Clark C. to Elizabeth Mila 11-27-1844 (11-28-1844)
Devaughn, James to Mariah Winn 11-1-1873 (11-5-1873)
Dewees, S. A. to Jones Glass 11-2-1874 (11-4-1874)
Dick, Sam to Ester Jones? 1-5-1869
Dickens, Anthony to Charity Williams 12-23-1872
Dickens, Geo. to Missouri Alston 12-23-1872 (12-25-1872)
Dickens, W. H. D. to Emeline Smith 1-12-1868 (1-2-1868)
Dickerson, A. W. to Emmer Fitzgerill 2-14-1872
Dickerson, George to Mollie Gilham 1-19-1872
Dickerson, Robt. to Mary Cotton 6-22-1867 (6-23-1867)
Dickerson, Thomas to Emmer Ford 1-8-1873
Dickerson, W. M. to Lottie T. Hanley 1-26-1858
Dickerson, W. T. to M. E. Haye 12-10-1867
Dickery?, Joseph to Mary J. Brown 2-15-1858 (2-16-1858)
Dickey, Gaml.? C. to Catherine E. Smith 4-3-1871 (4-20-1871)
Dickey, James to Margaret Moore 12-25-1861
Dickey, Jas. to Fannie C. Moore 5-12-1869
Dickson, Ben to Adaline Caldwell 6-3-1871 (6-5-1871)
Dickson, Charles S. to Lucetta Bernard 9-1-1846 (9-2-1846)
Dickson, Charles Strong to Margaret Leventen Hill 1-31-1849 (2-1-1849)
Dickson, Christopher W. to Henrietta S. Barrett 12-7-1846
Dickson, Ed to Sallie Rose 3-21-1872
Dickson, James F. to Rachel S.? Payne 11-22-1865 (11-23-1865)
Dickson, John to Rachel Litus 7-20-1867
Dickson, Joseph A. to Mary C. McCain 9-15-1855
Dickson, Newton to Mary Elder 2-28-1850
Dickson, Saml. Dunn to Sarah Isabella McQuiston 10-9-1850
Dicus?, Robert Lessley to Sarah Wilkins 6-21-1853
Dill, James to Mary J. Willis 3-27-1874 (11-29-1874)
Dillahinty, William H. to Amanda A. Walton 12-17-1866 (12-18-1866)
Dillon, Richard to Jane E. Shaw 2-20-1867
Dinwoody, Thomas Washington to Fidelia James 5-19-1842
Dobson, J. E. to N. M. McGuire 1-3-1865
Dodson, James to Sarah E. Gibson 9-8-1846 (9-9-1846)
Dodson, __thas W. to Julia A. Parham 8-11-1868
Donelsen?, Wm. Jefferson to Mary Louisa Toddy 11-13-1855 (11-15-1855)
Donely, John to E. A. R. Rose 6-29-1870
Donnaway, A. W. to Nancey Carracle? 12-19-1868 (12-20-1868)
Dorch, Henry to Holly Owen 12-28-1868 (12-31-1868)
Dorsey, Jerome to Mary R. Crouch 5-10-1855 (6-12-1853?)
Douglas, Adam to Susan Parker 6-14-1873 (6-15-1873)
Douglas, Andrew J. to Mary L. Taylor 12-17-1866
Douglass, Andrew Jackson to Louisa Ann Smith 12-21-1846
Douglass, John T. to Evaline H. Smith 1-21-1842
Douseford, John T. to Amanda J. Lamb 2-17-1858 (2-18-1858)
Dover?, Anthony to Josephine ____ 4-24-1873
Dowell, John T. to Nancy Simpson 3-13-1843 (3-15-1843)
Dowell, Lorenzo to Lizzie Somerville 12-25-1871
Downing, Am? to Fannie Shankle 1-17-1867
Downing, E. M. to Elizabeth A. Vaughn 6-10-1868
Downing, Granderson to Georgetter Adkins 5-14-1874 (4?-15-1874)
Downing, Sandy Wilson to Bettie Haynes 5-13-1874 (5-14-1874)
Downing, Washington to Sallie Montgomry 1-6-1869 (1-8-1869)
Doyle, Zachariah J. to Margaret M. White 11-11-1868 (11-12-1868)
Draffin, John to Margaret S. Craig 2-24-1855
Drane?, Prit to Rachel Polk 12-3-1868 (12-4-1868)
Drappin, Robt. H. to Elisabeth Wright 7-17-1856
Drappin, W. F. to Amelia Ann Hays 10-7-1856
Drappin, Wm. M. M. to Margaret A. Tarbish 5-13-1856 (5-14-1856)
Drennon, M. to Julia Ann Strayhorn 12-17-1861 (12-22-1861)
Dreums?, William to Cordia Woods 5-10-1873
Driver, Simon dP. to Annie E. Melugin 10-18-1869 (10-19-1869)
Driver, Wody to Betty Ross 5-13-1871 (5-15-1871)
Druffin, John to Mary L. Craig 11-19-1851
Drummon, J. W. jr. to M. L. Roberts 6-2-1873 (6-4-1873)
Drummonds, James to Arminta H. Leach 1-4-1862 (1-5-1862)
Drummonds, S. K. to Elizabeth A. Wright 2-22-1871 (2-23-1871)
Drummons, James to Nancy Walker 1-15-1842 (1-16-1842)
Drummons, Mack to Elizabeth Moore 12-4-1843 (12-13-1843)
Drummons, Robert M. to Laura Hunt 8-4-1865 (8-5-1865)
Druse?, A. W. to Alva Miller 1-24-1871 (1-25-1871)
Ducast, A. F. to Rebecca Ann Oliphant 2-2-1859 (2-3-1859)
Dueast, A. F. to Rabecca Olipshaw 2-22-1859 (2-3?-1859)
Dueast, William to M. Adline Budget 10-12-1857 (10-16-1857)
Dugget, Mack to Caladonia Baptist 1-21-1871
Duke, John to Martha Boyd 12-28-1870
Dumas, A. W. to Margaret E. King 1-27-1869
Duncan, A. M. to Nancy Emily McBride 3-12-1856 (3-13-1856)
Duncan, John L. to Charlotte J. McCullough 2-18-1873 (2-20-1873)
Duncan, Tillman to Eveline Turner 7-27-1874
Dunham, Joseph Henry to Sarah Carolin Cotten 12-12-1848
Dunlap, Henry to Ann Blackwell 10-25-1871
Dunn, G. A. to E. V. Riley 12-14-1874 (12-15-1874)
Dunwood, Regis to Fredonia Olivia Freeman 2-16-1853 (2-17-1853)
Durant, John W. to Caroline V. Sherrod 11-2-1844
Dyer, Billy to Mary Wortham 8-9-1869
Dyson, Isaac to F. Clements 12-5-1871
Dyson, Isaac to F. Clements 12-5-1871 (1-6-1872)
Dyson, Jack to Ellen Wortham 8-28-1869
Dyson, Jacob to Mary Elam 5-21-1866 (5-22-1866)
Dyson, Jonas to Eliza Jackson 12-27-1870 (12-28-1870)
Dyson, Peyton jr. to Harriet A. Green 7-16-1870 (7-17-1870)
Dyson, Peyton to Mary Ann Bradford 10-11-1872 (10-26-1872)
Dyson, William to Sue Murphey 3-31-1873 (4-1-1873)
Ealver?, Moak? to Alice Williams 12-27-1869
Earwood, Joseph W. to Sarah E. Delancey 9-18-1867 (9-22-1867)
Easley, J. D. to Mary J. Pickard 2-13-1860 (2-14-1860)
Eaton, Aleck to Louisa Hart 2-15-1867
Eaton, Isaac to Emmer Shepard 4-10-1871
Eaton, Robert to Lu Morgan 11-23-1869
Eckford, Becton to Mollie Warmack 12-12-1866
Eckford, W. W. to Annie Warmath 12-12-1865
Edings, Thomas P. to Allice A. Tucker 10-15-1859 (10-18-1859)
Edmonds, Jerry to Mary Parker 12-25-1874
Edward, Anderson to Ellen Young 2-18-1868
Edwards, Erasmus Darwin to Charlotte Dowdy 8-27-1844
Edwards, John W. to Mary Femins? 5-10-1861
Edwards, Richard to Indy Macklin 12-20-1867
Edwards, William to Cardelia Luckado 8-21-1868
Elam, D. B. to Mollie A. Benson 1-25-1873 (1-29-1873)
Elam, Geo. to Rachel Cotton 7-2-1870
Elam, Jefferson to Margaret Tennant 1-21-1852 (1-25-1852)
Elam, Robert to Cordelia Wood 3-29-1858 (4-1-1858)
Elcan, A. L. to Bettie T. Swayne 11-3-1869 (11-4-1869)
Elcan, H. H. to Martha A. Hunt 7-10-1865
Elcan, Henry L. to Mary H. Kennon 9-1-1865 (9-7-1865)
Elcan, Junius H. to Heurin C. Carter 3-2-1865
Elcan, Junius H. to Heurin? C. Carter 3-2-1865 (3-7-1865)
Elcan, N. H. to Virginia E. Clements 7-4-1859 (7-6-1859)
Elcan, Preston to May Bennet? 11-11-1871
Elder, John to Nancy Burress 4-27-1842
Elder, Joseph to Emily Mildred Talley 7-2-1849 (7-5-1849)
Elder, William to Louiza Schrigs? 7-6-1861 (7-9-1861)
Elder, Wm. Franklin to Lorania C. Elder 8-18-1851 (8-19-1851)
Eldridge, Wesley to Catharin Woodley 7-1-1869
Eldridge, Wm. M. to Mary F. Delashment 1-23-1865
Elison, Wm. to Ann J. Dunlap 1-27-1868 (1-30-1868)
Ellam, Jno. C. to Alice J. Harley 11-20-1871
Elliett, John to Mary Ballard 3-5-1866 (3-8-1866)

Ellis, Ben to Eveline Meeler 2-14-1874 (2-15-1874)
Ellis, E. S. to M. E. Miller 1-17-1872 (1-18-1872)
Ellis, Griffin to Harriet Elliot 1-5-1866 (1-27-1866)
Elmore, Richard Thomas to Martha Jane Brooks 12-9-1841
Elmore, William E. to Julia F. Cannon 7-18-1840
Englihs, J. B. to Martha E. Prince 11-27-1858
English, Arche to Mary McCommack 9-23-1868 (9-24-1868)
Ennis, Peter D. to Mary C. Thompson 2-8-1871 (2-9-1871)
Enochs, F. A. to Catharine R. Scott 8-30-1869 (9-16-1869)
Ensley, R. G. to Amanda Starnes 10-23-1869 (10-24-1869)
Eperson, R. F. to O. C. Farmer 10-24-1868 (10-25-1868)
Epperson, Richard Morning to Julia C. Jackson 5-27-1843 (5-30-1843)
Erwin, John D. to Susan Land 9-29-1847 (9-30-1847)
Erwin, John P. to Nancy Wilson 12-24-1866 (12-25-1866)
Erwin, R. P. to R. T. Bowden 6-8-1874
Erwin, Robert P. to Mildred C. Bowden 9-2-1867 (9-5-1867)
Erwin, William T. to Elizabeth M. Read 11-25-1869
Erwin, Wm. D. to Julia Densford 6-4-1866 (6-12-1866)
Erwood, W. S. to M. E. Proctor 1-8-1872 (1-9-1872)
Estes, Moreau P. to Catharin Sherrod 11-27-1867
Etherly, Joseph to Mary L. Rose 4-15-1868 (4-18-1868)
Evans, Absolam Hendricks to Eliza Janie Dawson 10-8-1853 (10-9-1853)
Evans, Absolum H. to Martha Kelley 6-30-1847 (7-1-1847)
Evans, George to Mary McIntyre 9-6-1841
Evans, George to Tennessee Baskins 1-4-1870 (1-6-1870)
Evans, Jerry to Angeline Johnson 8-19-1872 (8-5-1873)
Evans, John to Rose Payne 12-21-1867 (12-26-1867)
Evans, W. R. to Elizabeth Stevens 12-27-1865 (12-28-1865)
Evritt, F. W. to Martha F. Myers no date (with 12-1861)
Ewart, James to Sarah E. Starnes 6-30-1857
Ewell, John to Amanda Crawford 1-2-1854 (1-7-1854)
Faires, W. J. to E. C. Pickard 4-28-1857
Fallin, James R. to Lucy A. Slaughter 1-18-1871
Fallin, John W. to Sallie Hill 1-7-1874
Fallon, Chas. W. to Sarah E. Tally 10-6-1840
Faris, Jas. McWherter to Martha V. Harris 2-4-1856
Faris, Jesse Thomas to Elvira Lake 10-23-1848 (10-24-1848)
Farmer, Henry K. to Amand L. Wiseman 9-21-1867 (9-24-1867)
Farmer, James K. to Elizabeth Ralph 7-30-1841 (8-3-1841)
Farris, Oliver B. to Frances E. Townsend 12-29-1865 (12-31-1865)
Faulk, Allen to Aggy Robinson 5-7-1869
Faulk, Allin to Aggy Robinson 5-7-1868
Faulk, James to Charlott Adkins 1-2-1872
Faulk, James to Henrietta Christmas Power 10-28-1843 (11-2-1843)
Faulk, Jessee to Julia Crenshaw 12-20-1865
Faulk, Johnathan B. to Margaret J. Grant 11-24-1874 (11-25-1874)
Faulk, S. W. to Emma Shenault 10-19-1872 (10-24-1872)
Faulkner, Jas. J. to Mary E. Moore 10-7-1856
Faulkner, John J. to Martha A. McCain 11-25-1867 (11-26-1867)
Faulkner, John J> to Jane Strain 11-8-1871 (11-9-1871)
Faulkner, John to Martha Frances Franklin 3-24-1854 (3-29-1854)
Faulkner, T. L. to Mary A. E. Kelley 10-7-1873 (10-9-1873)
Feazur, Ephriam to Matilda Jones 6-15-1867 (6-16-1867)
Feezor, E. A. to Elizabeth C. Cooper 11-27-1867 (11-28-1867)
Feezor, O. S. to M. C. Huffman 2-23-1874
Feezor, Otho S. to Mary Elizabeth Clark 12-21-1854
Feezor, Peter L. to Sarah A. E. Yount 7-27-1854
Feezor, Smith M. to Purlina M Tennant 3-5-1849 (3-8-1849)
Feezor, Smith Miller to Peggy Owen 6-18-1846
Feezor, William Henry to Dora Bledsoe 10-17-1867
Fellows, Joseph J. to Sarah Robinson 2-6-1847 (not executed)
Fenton, Robt. W. to Sarah J. Shaw 2-20-1867 (2-21-1867)
Fenton, Robt. W. to Sarah J. Shaw 2-26-1867 (2-27-1867)
Ferbury, Phillip to Malissa Jackson 10-12-1867 (10-13-1867)
Ferrell, Hubbard to Mary R. Flanikin 5-26-1855 (5-31-1855)
Field, Caleb to Lucy Ann Bragg 12-27-1872 (1-1-1873)
Field, Sip to Luvenia Owens? 11-15-1869 (11-15-1869)
Field, William to Laura Green 12-27-1870
Fields, Davy to Hester Webb 6-15-1867 (6-18-1867)
Fields, Henry to Margret V. Barret 8-9-1865
Fields, Jack to Anna L. Macklin 12-26-1868 (1-20-1870)
Fields, Jordan to Nancy Joiner 11-14-1872 (11-15-1872)
Fight, E. W. to Annie E. Pennington 12-23-1865
Fisher, A. J. to N. J. Stroud 10-7-1874 (10-8-1874)
Fisher, Charles J.? to Martha W. Smith 12-3-1868 (12-9-1868)
Fisher, Louis to Emaline Dickens 3-20-1866 (3-24-1866)
Fisher, Shirley to Mary Sanford 2-14-1874 (2-15-1874)
Fisher, W. H. to Bettie Davenport 7-22-1871
Fisher, William Dunham to Sophia Cotten Flowers 1-19-1852 (1-20-1852)
Fitch, William to Isabla? Neel 11-27-1874
Fite, David L. to Ellen Banks 10-14-1857 (10-15-1857)
Fitze, George to Caroline Smith 3-15-1873
Fitzgerald, Thomas to Caroline Hooks 10-11-1853 (10-12-1853)
Flanakin, C. W. to Eliza J. Smith 1-23-1858 (2-4-1858)
Flanakin, Robert J. to Nancy Griffith 9-9-1867
Flanigan, John D. to Martha F. Rodgers 3-13-1867
Flanigan, R. J. to Laura Jones 8-26-1874 (8-27-1874)
Flanigan, Z. A. to Marth Ford 2-13-1867 (2-15-1867)
Fleming, Downey to M. E. Fleming 12-25-1871
Fleming, Napolian to Cynthia M. Bledsoe 12-11-1868
Flemming, F. to S. L. Feezor 10-12-1870 (10-13-1870)
Flemming, J. M. to Hanna? Martin 2-8-1870
Flemming, Wm. Cannon to Laura Ann Kenney 4-13-1854 (4-15-1854)
Flerms?, L. to Elisabeth Ticon 7-7-1856
Fletcher, Ephran P. to Bettie Turnage 5-27-1867 (6-2-1867)
Fletcher, J. B. to Sarah E. Acock 8-4-1873 (8-7-1873)
Fletcher, M. to S. T. Ivey 12-14-1864 (12-18-1864)
Fletcher, Moses to Mary Ann Maddocks 10-12-1852 (10-14-1852)
Fletcher, William to Emily Claiburne 1-15-1868
Fletcher, William to Louisa Allen 1-19-1871 (1-22-1871)
Flower, Andrew Davis to Dicy A. Covinton 2-19-1869
Flowers, Andrew D. to D. A. Carrington 2-19-1869 (2-20-1869)
Flowers, J. H. to R. H. Rice 11-13-1860
Flowers, W. P. to Mary E. Cummins 5-8-1871
Foley, Andrew to Annie Davis 10-14-1874 (10-15-1874)
Forbess, A. L. to S. A. Easly 1-8-1872
Forbess, John C. to Mary W. Howell 5-23-1845 (5-25-1845)
Forbess, Samuel to Rhoda Duveast 12-18-1854 (12-26-1854)
Forbess, Solomon R. to Sarah P. Turnage 1-26-1870 (1-27-1870)
Forbess, T. J. to J. A. Miller 12-21-1870 (12-22-1870)
Forbess, Thomas to Louvina A. McBride 7-16-1866 (7-18-1866)
Forbiss, A. L. to P. Ann McCraw 12-6-1859 (9-8-1859)
Forbiss, James B. to C. H. Houston 2-25-1859 (2-28-1859)
Forbiss, James P. to Clerisa H. Houston 2-25-1859 (2-28-1859)
Forbiss, L. A. to Penelopee Ann McCraw 12-6-1859
Ford, J. A. to L. P. Watson 2-3-1873 (2-5-1873)
Ford, Jerre to Minerva Walton 1-20-1870
Ford, John C. to Jane C. Roberson no date (with 1861)
Ford, John to Betsy Ann Lauderdale 4-14-1866
Ford, R. S. to S. L. Delancey 2-23-1874 (2-26-1874)
Ford, Wm. Thos. to Dorcus Melissa Thompson 1-28-1851
Forrest, Benj. F. to Mary E. Bibb 11-11-1871 (11-12-1871)
Forsyth, Joseph to Elizabeth M. Sherrill 11-13-1866 (11-15-1866)
Fortner, James H. to Safronia Evaline Burkhart 8-27-1846 (9-3-1846)
Fortner, Robert T. to Martha Mickelberry 3-29-1851 (3-30-1851)
Fortner, William A. to Sallie E. Myers 12-17-1866 (12-16?-1866)
Fortune, Frank to Ann Liza Yarbro 11-21-1867
Foster, James to Patsey Whitley 11-15-1870
Foster, Robert Thompson to Louisa A. P. Hill 12-20-1847 (12-23-1847)
Foster, Robt. Thompson to Louisa Townsend 12-1-1851 (12-4-1851)
Fowler, George to Ann E. Hall 2-11-1867 (2-17-1867)
Fowler, John Fell to Clarisa Aldridge 9-14-1868
Fowler, John to Bettie Rhodes 3-13-1873
Fowlkes, Benj. to Dora Brooks 4-1-1870 (4-3-1870)
Fradle?, Alex. W. to Emly McGuire 5-18-1854
Fraizar, Ephran to Matilda Jones 6-15-1865
Fraley, Phillip to Laura Campbell 12-30-1869 (1-7-1870)
Francis, W. H. to L. A. Myers 8-8-1866 (8-9-1866)
Frazier, Charles to Matilda Smith 8-21-1869 (8-23-1869)
Frazier?, Henry to Emily McIntosh 3-24-1870 (3-30-1870)
Freeman, Charles C. to Eliza Pace 1-16-1860
Freeman, Charles Christopher to Prefom? Mathis? 7-17-1843 (8-18-1843)
Freeman, John A. to Mary E. Lane 8-25-1866 (8-28-1866)
Freeman, John P. to Elizabeth Curtis 6-3-1844
Freeman, Joseph O. to Indiana Parsons 5-14-1859 (5-16-1859)
Freeman, William to Maryana Patterson 1-17-1870 (1-18-1870)

French, William M. to Sarah J. Easley 1-1-1874
Friel, Daniel to Mary Ann Richarson 4-2-1870 (9-29-1872?)
Frierson, John S. to Harriet N. McCormick 2-5-1855 (2-8-1855)
Fry, Anderson to Cynthia P. Prince 6-1-1870 (6-9-1870)
Fry, Henry to Mary Luellen Livingston 8-22-1874 (8-23-1874)
Fuller, William H. to Elizabeth B. George 12-29-1844
Fuller, Wm. H. to N. Catharine Totty 7-9-1855 (7-19-1855)
Fultin, Charles W. to Mary A. McFarland 6-7-1848 (6-?-1848)
Furgerson, James J. to Margaret Jane Owen 10-10-1855 (10-11-1855)
Furguson, James J. to Martha J. Owen 1-15-1867 (1-22-1867)
Futhey, James to Margaret J. Kilpatrick 11-17-1869 (11-18-1869)
Gacy, John to L. P. Murrin 11-24-1867
Gaines, Alexander to Synthia Tivool? 9-4-1872
Gaines, Harrison to Adalin Read 1-15-1872 (1-18-1872)
Gaines, Thomas T. to Sue A. Bandy 2-27-1873
Gaines, Wade to Hannah Smith 4-16-1874 (4-23-1874)
Gaise, Frank to Emily Sadler 4-4-1867 (4-6-1867)
Gaither, Andrew to Louisa Futhey 12-20-1870
Galbreath, W. W. to Ann Traylor 5-6-1867 (5-7-1867)
Galbreth, James H. to Lucinda C. Lasseter 2-5-1866 (2-18-1866)
Gardener, David A. to M. J. Bledsoe 1-11-1866
Gardner, Joseph Lewis to Louisa Lavinia Prewett 2-1-1846
Gardner, Swinson? to Louisa Henry 4-13-1843 (4-15-1843)
Gardner, William M. to Martha Killingsworth 3-24-1847 (3-?-1847)
Garland, John C. to Mary C. Slaughter 4-21-1868
Garland, Thomas L. to Julia C. Crenshaw 2-23-1865
Garret, Isham to Jane Henderson 3-8-1867 (3-9-1867)
Garret, J. J. to E. J. McCormack 12-17-1872
Garret, Robert F. to Mary M. Hamilton 1-23-1871 (1-25-1871)
Garrett, John to Frances E.? Rhodes 5-16-1865 (5-17-1865)
Gatewood, Wm. to Rhoda Winn 10-17-1866 (10-20-1866)
Gay, Columbus F. to Nancy J. Dickerson 6-22-1867
Gee, Robert to Susan Dillihunty 6-15-1859 (6-?-1859)
Gehen, John B. to Louisa Chapman 12-13-1859 (12-15-1859)
Gehen, John B. to Louisiana Chapman 12-13-1859 (12-15-1859)
George, John C. to Margaret C. Forbess 12-19-1870 (12-22-1870)
Gerred?, Hugh to Easter Adams 3-15-1853
Gibbs, Alfred to Violet Clements 3-23-1872 (3-31-1872)
Gibbs, Cyrus to Emer Harrison 2-15-1867 (2-16-1867)
Gibbson, William to Mary Holland 1-17-1851 (1-20-1851)
Gibson, Elijah to Lucretia Ann Boothe 9-11-1848 (9-14-1848)
Gibson, George to Claway? Smith 4-29-1868
Gibson, William to Mary Read 5-8-1871
Gillespie, William to Rebeca Allen 8-7-1845 (8-8-1845)
Gist, Chas. to Lucy Bailey 9-28-1869 (9-29-1869)
Givin, James Lycurgus to Sarah Clark 11-11-1843 (11-?-1843)
Glakin?, John D. to Martha T. Rodger no date (with 1867)
Glass, Charles to Harriet Cook 12-25-1869 (12-28-1869)
Glass, D. L. to Matilda J. Roe 8-31-1859 (9-1-1859)
Glass, J. C. N. to Lucy Ann Roe 11-11-1858
Glass, James Knox Polk to Barbara Luticia Billings 12-8-1859
Glass, Peter to Betsey Grant 10-8-1869 (10-9-1869)
Glass, S. F. P. to N. J. Hightower 12-20-1871 (12-21-1871)
Glenn, Edward to Amanda Allen 9-28-1867 (9-29-1867)
Glidewell, Wm. to Susana Timens 11-6-1861 (11-7-1861)
Goad, John H. to M. J. Young 12-17-1874
Goforth, J. C. to Jiffy R. Trobough 1-3-1866 (1-1?-1866)
Goforth, John to Nancy Owen 1-19-1867
Goforth, John to Nancy Owen 1-19-1867 (1-20-1867)
Goforth, Josiah to Eliza Whitlock 1-7-1850 (1-16-1850)
Goforth, Josiah to Louisa B. Bently 1-1-1873 (1-2-1873)
Goforth, Russell to Susan R. Myres 3-16-1859
Golston, Geo. to Amanda? Smith 12-15-1866 (12-16-1866)
Gooch, John B. to Charlotte Ann McCalla 1-11-1870
Good, John P. to Elizabeth Hightower 4-21-1873 (5-1-1873)
Gooden, Jas. to Ellen Green 12-1-1869 (12-4-1869)
Goodman, Albert to Cathrine Ralph 4-11-1872
Goodman, Alfred H. to Mary E. Murphy 10-29-1866
Goodman, Isham to Anner Smith 11-28-1868
Goodman, Kelley to Mary Smith 11-3-1866 (11-4-1866)
Goodman, R. G. to Eleanor H. Roulker? 8-7-1866
Goodman, R. G. to S.B. Murphey 11-18-1869
Goodman, Rufus to Clarisa Ann Johnson 12-19-1866
Goodman, Spencer to Donna Smith 3-29-1871 (4-4-1871)
Goodman, William V. to Ellen C. Clark 9-26-1865
Goodram, Washington to Louisa Yarbro 11-20-1867 (11-21-1867)
Goodrum, William to Caroline Elizabeth Townsend 7-12-1849
Goodwin, James to Ann Smith 6-20-1870
Gorden, George to Amanda Boyd 8-23-1872 (8-20?-1872)
Gordon, Jacob to Margaret Mitchell 1-20-1870
Gordon, Robert to Lizzie Richardson 5-8-1872
Gordon, Solomon to Candis Grishom 9-14-1846 (9-17-1846)
Gorin?, George W. to Frances Jane Sweney 4-19-1842 (5-2-1842)
Goss, David to Ellen C. Ternas 9-6-1873 (9-11-1873)
Goss, David to Nancy J. Quinby 7-12-1859
Goss, John A. to Nancy Catharin Fleming 2-4-1857
Goss, William W. to Sarah A. Hutchinson 12-22-1847 (12-25-1847)
Grace, William Gillom to Eliz. Caroline Rebec Cullum 1-13-1846
Grace, Wm. G. to Martha A. E. Davis 5-1-1855
Gracy, J. Barnett to Margaret J. Calhoun 12-9-1868 (12-10-1868)
Graham, Ned to arion Dickason 11-26-1869 (11-27-1869)
Granbury, Gabril to A. Vertun? 12-28-1869 (12-30-1869)
Grant, Wm. P. to Julia M. Anderson 11-7-1871 (11-8-1871)
Grattum, Lewis to Sarah Coats 3-3-1842
Graves, George to Janie Henderson 8-5-1867 (8-6-1867)
Gravy, Aux? W. to Miss Jane Finty? 3-13-1869 (3-17-1869)
Gray, Armstead to Alace Avery 6-28-1872
Gray, John Lenoir to Mary Goforth 8-10-1852
Gray, Louis to Laura Smith 12-10-1870
Gray, Tho. Evans to Mary Kulbeth 9-16-1851 (9-17-1851)
Gray, Thomas to Maria Mabene 5-4-1872
Gray, Thos. J. to Sallie E. Brown 11-23-1867 (11-24-1867)
Gray, Young to Nancy Owen 10-21-1851 (10-23-1851)
Grayham, Jessee to Mary Walker 5-5-1873 (7-4-1873)
Green, Edward Holister to Catharine Clamentine Hall 7-17-1851
Green, Fras. M. to Mary Catherine Field 11-15-1853 (11-16-1853)
Green, John Uriah to Mary Jane Sanford 4-7-1853
Green, John Uriah to Sallie Ann Green 3-29-1865 (3-30-1865)
Green, Joseph Allen to Elizabeth Frances Newman 3-4-1845
Green, June to Harriett Boyce 11-9-1870 (11-11-1870)
Green, M. J. to A. L. Blackwell 10-1-1872 (10-2-1872)
Green, Marcus C. to Sarah Ann Sanford 3-23-1848
Green, Mike to Mary T. Flower 12-25-1868 (12-26-1868)
Green, R. to Phoebe Calhoun 12-15-1866 (3-30-1867)
Green, Richard to Adaline Miller 11-9-1872
Green, Richard to Laura Hill 3-2-1872 (3-5-1872)
Green, Richard to Nancy Miller 4-18-1874
Green, Robert M. to Rachel L. McBride 9-7-1867
Green, Robert to Susan Peete 3-22-1869 (3-?-1869)
Green, S. P. to Kate Aubry Somerville 10-13-1869 (10-20-1869)
Green, T. W. to Catherine T. Somervill 10-26-1869 (10-27-1869)
Green, Thos. to Charity Strange 2-18-1873 (3-25-1873)
Gregory, Thomas to Sarah Jane Gregory 10-13-1870 (10-14-1870)
Griffee, William to Nancy C. Flanakin 1-11-1860
Griffin, A. B. to M. M. Macke? 8-7-1871 (8-8-1871)
Griffin, Chas. F. to Sarah F. Smith 12-27-1871 (1-25-1872)
Griffin, Isaac to Milly Mitchell 1-20-1870
Griffin, John to Letty Butler 9-16-1871 (9-21-1871)
Griffith, C. G. to Martha H. Smith 12-13-1858 (12-15-1858)
Griffith, Charles G. to Indiana M. Burkhart 11-12-1866 (11-13-1866)
Griffith, Wm. H. to Sarah E. McGuire 10-20-1860 (10-21-1860)
Grigg, J. L. to Manerva C. Wade 1-26-1858
Grigsby, W. H. to Nancy Ann McCullough 11-16-1872 (11-19-1872)
Grimes, George F. to Pattie E. Grimes 2-25-1873 (2-26-1873)
Grimes, N. W. to C. A. French 1-17-1861 (1-20-1861)
Grimes, W. C. to Eliza Orr 4-22-1873 (4-23-1873)
Grizzard, Mark to Henrietta Turnage 3-10-1873 (3-13-1873)
Gross, James to Sarah Lathan 1-10-1855 (1-11-1855)
Gross, John to Joice Hunley 2-16-1841 (2-17-1841)
Gross, John to Leana Moore 5-30-1865
Gross, Thomas to Nancy J. Innis 4-7-1870
Gunter, James to Lizzie E. Petit 5-18-1872 (5-22-1872)
Gurley, William H. to Polina C. George 11-12-1840 (11-18-1840)
Gutherie, Robert to Colorado Harris 11-4-1854 (11-5-1854)
Guthrie, Robert to Amanda Harrison 11-26-1855 (11-29-1855)
Guthrie, W. H. to Amanda Hitower 6-17-1871 (6-22-1871)
Hafter, Charles W. to Martha E. Hafter 4-16-1872
Haines, John A. to Catharan E. Dale 10-15-1870 (10-16-1870)
Halaway, Henry to Ann Eliza Twisdale 12-26-1859
Haley, Henry to Sarah Smith 12-27-1872

Hall, A. C. to Mariah L. Clark 5-8-1866
Hall, Alex to Dilcey Douglas 2-14-1866
Hall, Andy to Frances Smith 6-6-1873 (6-14-1873)
Hall, Billy to Mary Robertson 4-1-1867 (4-3-1867)
Hall, Coleman to Amanda Yarbro 10-15-1873 (10-16-1873)
Hall, Farris to Elizabeth Williams 1-16-1874
Hall, Frank to Mary Catten 6?-15-1867 (6-16-1867)
Hall, Geo. W. to Laura] Sherril 12-29-1865 (1-3-1866)
Hall, George to Feebe Calhoun 10-29-1870
Hall, Henry to Caroline Green 1-7-1869
Hall, J. F. to C. E. Ligon 2-4-1873 (2-9-1873)
Hall, James Iredell to Sarah Irene Lemmon 12-26-1849 (12-27-1849)
Hall, James J. to Mary E. Hall 1-2-1866
Hall, Jas. J. to Mary E. Hall 1-2-1866
Hall, Joe to M. Larrimoore 12-17-1874
Hall, John G. to Ermine Munford 5-29-1872
Hall, John Green to Patti W. Rose 12-21-1871
Hall, John J. to Margaret J. Sharp 3-15-1841 (3-18-1841)
Hall, John N. to Hollen Applewight Green 3-5-1842 (3-8-1842)
Hall, Martain to Elizabeth Williams 10-8-1870
Hall, Peter E. to Elizabeth E. Fry 8-16-1860
Hall, Peyton to Sophronia Tweedle 12-29-1874 (12-28?-1874)
Hall, R. S. to A. E. Stitt 11-10-1858 (11-11-1858)
Hall, Sidney to Elizabeth Smith 4-4-1870 (4-10-1870)
Hall, Thomas? to 'Amanda? Sanford 1-20-1869 (1-21-1869)
Hall, Wash to Catharine Anderson 3-2-1874
Hall, William J. to Eliza W. Collier 7-9-1850 (7-10-1850)
Hall, William Minor to Sarah Rebecca Holmes 8-7-1849 (8-8-1849)
Hall, Wm. to Gracy Hanlin 12-30-1871
Hall, Wm. to Martha Sherill 10-14-1865 (2?-14-1865)
Hall, Wm. to Martha Sherril 10-14-1865
Hallum, Relix Grundy to Patsey Safroney Quinaly 10-22-1846 (10-26-1846)
Hamby, J. H. to M. A. Loyd 5-24-1873 (5-25-1873)
Hamelton, William to Narcissa Caroline Smitheal 9-11-1867
Hamilton, Henry to Eliza Hayley? 1-18-1871
Hamilton, J. R. to H. J. Bird 2-23-1869 (2-25-1869)
Hamilton, James B. to Annie L. Fisher 10-24-1867
Hamilton, L. W. to M. R. Byrd 2-15-1870 (2-20-1870)
Hamilton, O. E. to M. E. Rhodes 10-26-1868 (10-29-1868)
Hamilton, Thomas to Margaret Evans 12-30-1873 (1-1-1874)
Hamilton, Thomas to Martha Montgomery 5-16-1857 (5-18-1857)
Hammers, John F. to Josephine Wilkins 1-24-1871
Hammers, John to Nancy Tims 5-22-1867
Hankison?, Thomas to Martha King 6-29-1852 (7-1-1852)
Hanks, Hugh T. to Eliza G. Rice 3-17-1865 (3-18-1865)
Hanley, James G. to Frances W. Adams 5-24-1842 (5-25-1842)
Hanna, John E. to Mary O. Faussett 1-10-1867
Hanner, Abner J. to Mary E. Wylie 1-3-1857
Harding, Jno. Mesina to Frances Eliza Coward 12-22-1855 (1-2-1856)
Hargrove, William to Mary Bond 3-14-1868
Harper, Jack to Susan Jones 2-7-1870
Harper, James Franklin to Elizabeth Susannah Johnston 4-3-1844 (4-4-1844)
Harper, Parriss? to Hanna Alexander 3-13-1869 (3-14-1869)
Harper, Robert B. to Martha McQLuiston 9-9-1847
Harper, Robert P. to Martha H. McClerkin 5-17-1841 (5-18-1841)
Harper, William H. to Margaretta A. T. Caruthers 11-19-1847
Harrel, R. N. to E. Dillahunty 11-6-1865 (11-15-1865)
Harrell, Joseph B. to L. A. Dellahunty 11-17-1868 (11-18-1868)
Harris, A. J. to E. A. Feezor 10-2-1865 (10-3-1865)
Harris, A. to Matilda Morrison 1-4-1869 (1-8-1869)
Harris, Amanuel to Catharine Brown 12-10-1873 (12-11-1873)
Harris, Bob to Drusilla Smith 12-15-1871
Harris, C. R. to Columbia W. McGregor 1-4-1865
Harris, Calvin to Jane Hughleette 6-18-1870
Harris, Edward Thomas to Elizabeth Ann Williams 1-6-1849 (1-7-1849)
Harris, F. M. to Nancy J. Huffman 4-3-1871 (4-4-1871)
Harris, Henry L. to J. W. McGuier 12-23-1874
Harris, Hughlut to Lucy Boswell 2-16-1870 (2-22-1870)
Harris, Ira to Permelia Winston 5-5-1874 (5-6-1874)
Harris, J. N. to Annie E. Somerville 1-18-1869
Harris, J. W. to Elizabeth McGregor 7-15-1851
Harris, Jas. A. to Elizabeth O. Tucker 12-15-1866 (12-6?-1866)
Harris, Jas. O. to Mary L. Adams 1-3-1853
Harris, John M. to Angaline Smith 10-25-1872 (10-27-1872)
Harris, John to Easter Richards 6-27-1866
Harris, Joseph S. to Mary R. Bain? 11-11-1850 (11-12-1850)
Harris, Joseph to Sarah A. Murphey 9-1-1869 (9-9-1869)
Harris, Lewis to Mary Jane Cotheran 3-6-1872 (3-7-1872)
Harris, M. V. B. to Susan A. Downing 5-5-1871
Harris, Moses to Silvia Glass 7-17-1869 (7-18-1869)
Harris, S. C. to A. P. Clay 10-30-1867
Harris, T. H. to Mary E. Murphey 10-24-1874 (10-5?-1874)
Harris, Tyler to Mitty McGregor 1-3-1867
Harris, W. T. to Caladonia Cooper 2-7-1874
Harris, William G. to Mary Huffman 1-7-1867 (1-13-1867)
Harrison, Henry to Sarah Elizabeth Walker 1-2-1842 (1-3-1842)
Harrison, John E. to Nancy Jane Wilkins 5-17-1853 (5-?-1853)
Harrison, M. B. to Sarah E. Goforth 1-19-1870
Harrison, R. H. to Mattie V. Towell? 5-5-1856
Harrison, William Henry to Elizabeth Winney Stevens 11-22-1845
Harrison, Wm. H. to Mariah J. Smith 4-3-1868 (4-4-1868)
Harrison, Zachariah to Manerva Daniel 1-31-1857 (2-5-1857)
Hart, Charles Henry to Ann Faris 1-31-1844 (2-8-1844)
Hart, Jordon to Lizzie Smith 5-28-1870
Hart, Spencer Thomas to Martha Caroline Hoffler 6-1-1844 (6-6-1844)
Hart, William C. to Eleanor C. Davis 1-28-1850
Hartfield, M. F. to Hariet L. Max 1-3-1870 (1-5-1870)
Hartsfield, Benjamin F. to Nancy Ann Leach 8-8-1855
Hartsfield, Jacob to Martha F. Hartsfield 1-3-1873 (1-5-1873)
Hartsfield, James to Abigail Williams 3-12-1849
Hartsfield, M. H. to M. F. Myers 9-29-1866 (9-30-1866)
Hartsfield, Marcus H. to Susan Myers 11-30-1853 (12-1-1853)
Hartsfield, Marcus Henry to Emily Leach 12-26-1849
Hartsfield, W. A. J. to Rebecca Ewell 3-5-1857
Harvell, Allen to Amanda? S.? Rhodes 11-28-1867
Harvell, W. R. to Mary Williams 9-7-1874 (9-9-1874)
Hastings, Henry to Lucy Lacy 7-6-1867
Hastings, Simpson to Susan A. Fortner 8-21-1844 (8-?-1844)
Hatch, E. R. to Jane Grooms 6-28-1841
Hatchel, E. L. to Martha Wilson 9-6-1871 (9-12-1871)
Hawk, Ephreham to Judy Shelton 12-16-1871 (12-17-1871)
Hawkins, S. H. to ____ Dinkins 5-6-1868
Hawze, W. D. to Bettie J. Adkins 6-18-1874 (6-25-1874)
Hay, Moses to Luciller Wood 12-10-1870 (12-11-1870)
Hayden, Daniel to Maggie Payne 9-21-1869 (9-24-1869)
Haynes, Solaman to Bettie Walton 12-11-1866 (12-13-1866)
Haynes, Solomon to Lizzie Clark 12-9-1874
Haynie, David E. to Maggie Saddler 1-10-1871 (1-11-1871)
Haynie, George W. to Martha A. Delashmet 5-29-1852 (5-30-1852)
Haynie, Jesse R. to Paulina S. Walker 8-13-1850
Haynie, John L. to Mary G. Sadler 12-19-1872
Haynie, Thomas J. to Susan J. Douglas 12-31-1866 (1-1-1867)
Hays, J. W. to Elizabeth Sharp 9-26-1870 (9-27-1870)
Hays, Thos. to Nannie Gay 1-4-1871
Haywood, Lewis to Clarissa Hall 6-16-1867
Helm, Saml. to Laura Dillahenty 2-24-1872
Hemp, Bill to Lusten Fisher 1-5-1869 (not executed)
Hemp, Henderson to M. J. Dyer no date (with 12-1874)
Hemp, Jim to Annie Johnson 12-24-1874
Hemphill, Wm. to Jane Smith 12-20-1871
Henderson, David to Frances Bateman 9-18-1871 (9-20-1871)
Henderson, J. W. to Frances Poff 2-20-1867 (2-21-1867)
Henderson, James to Jane Willson 4-21-1870 (4-23-1870)
Henderson, Jorden to Susan Wilson 11-9-1866
Henly, Zackary A.? to Nancy Hays 10-13-1855 (10-14-1855)
Henry, James O. to Martha E. Hendron 9-26-1855
Henry, Wade to Mary Margaret Giles 10-30-1849 (11-1-1849)
Hering, Daniel W. to Mahalah Lamb 12-6-1847 (12-22-1847)
Herring, Marshal to Shelley Robertson 15-18-1858
Herring, William S. to Cordelia Gehan 10-23-1849 (10-24-1848?)
Herron, Needham H. to Nellie Carolton 12-27-1870 (12-28-1870)
Hertsfield, Franklin to M. E. Davis 2-12-1872 (2-13-1872)
Hetawer, William to O. Smith 4-29-1867 (4-13?-1867)
Hickerson, Thomas to Eliza Jane Green 12-29-1869
Hickine, Hughey to Mary Hill 6-23-1860
Hicks, A. R. to Peggy Wade 12-25-1873

Hicks, Michael to Betsy Claiburne 3-6-1869
Hicks, Peter Juchoore? to Temperance Lucintha Clark 6-20-1850 (7-3-1850)
Hicks, William to Harriet Whitten 12-29-1873
Hifield, F. to Mollie McNilly 6-17-1874
Hightower, John H. to Malissa J. Glass 1-30-1869 (2-4-1869)
Hill, A. B. to Harriet Thompson 1-23-1865 (1-24-1865)
Hill, Bryant to Ann Galaway 9-24-1869 (9-25-1869)
Hill, Charles H. to Sarah Y. Cockrill 10-28-1840 (10-29-1840)
Hill, Daniel to Sallie Cotton 6-8-1872 (6-9-1872)
Hill, Dorstal to Ellen Billings 9-10-1869
Hill, E. W. to Martha Steveson 9-5-1870 (9-7-1870)
Hill, F. W. to L. S. Hall 12-12-1872
Hill, Gilbert to Eliza Dyson 10-5-1871 (10-6-1871)
Hill, Henry to Mattie Whitworth 12-14-1870 (12-15-1870)
Hill, Isaac S. to Mary Wright 6-10-1867 (6-11-1867)
Hill, J. H. to Margaret J. Wood 3-12-1866
Hill, J. W. to Sarah C. Baskins 1-12-1869
Hill, James A. to Eliza J. Lauderdale 7-31-1867 (9-1-1867)
Hill, James C. to Z. T. Farrington 2-6-1867
Hill, James M. to Martha J. Nelson 11-13-1866 (11-16-1866)
Hill, James M> to Salina M. Davis 12-27-1859 (12-28-1859)
Hill, James to Ella Richardson 2-3-1870
Hill, Jessee to Rachael Hartsfield 12-5-1860
Hill, John N. to Julia A. Holmes 2-19-1866 (2-20-1866)
Hill, John to Lusina Alston 11-9-1866 (11-10-1866)
Hill, LaFayette to Elizabeth Catharine Haynie 10-13-1847
Hill, LaFayette to Seraphina C. Tipton 11-15-1855
Hill, Mike to Silvia Adkins 10-13-1874 (10-14-1874)
Hill, Pelly to Mary Winn 12-24-1873 (12-25-1873)
Hill, Peter to Hanna Bledsoe 2-7-1867
Hill, Rufus to Elizabeth Shepard 12-16-1870 (12-17-1870)
Hill, Thomas J. to Amanda J. Johnson 3-21-1870
Hill, Thomas J. to Lucretia Jane Smith 4-16-1869 (4-18-1869)
Hill, W. E. H. to M. J. Simmons 12-12-1870 (12-15-1870)
Hill, W. to Emaline Smith 10-16-1873 B
Hill, Wm. Henry to Martha Burton McGrogan 2-8-1859
Himey, Elijah Robert to Margaret Ann Smith 8-20-1857
Hindman, Alexander to Elizabeth McClerkin 3-26-1860 (3-29-1860)
Hindman, David to Lousella Wolen 2-26-1870
Hindman, James G. to Sarah J. Linn 2-1-1858 (2-2-1858)
Hindman, Jos. C. to Emeline S. Townsend 2-2-1870
Hine?, William to Jane Band 12-1-1852
Hint?, James Osburn to Ann Eliza Pilkington 12-9-1851 (12-10-1851)
Hise, W. H. to Elizabeth Ladd 9-4-1874 (9-6-1874)
Hobbs, John M. to Susan L. McCullough 8-18-1874 (8-20-1874)
Hoffler, Charles Webster to Martha Agnes Walker 8-7-1849
Hoffler, Nathaniel C. to Elizabeth Jane Tinnen 12-12-1853 (12-13-1853)
Hogan, Calumbus to Eliza Polk 12-1-1869 (12-2-1869)
Hogan, Columbus to Joanah Howard 9-11-1871
Hogue, Jeptha to Martha Maria Hunt 2-24-1847 (2-25-1847)
Hoke, Michael Wesley to Mary Ann Roton 10-21-1851
Holland, Caleb to Nancy Bird 3-25-1867 (4-6-1867)
Holland, George to Mary Dunn 2-24-1874
Holland, John to Emily Jane Locke 6-11-1844
Holland, Robert to Mary Turner 11-6-1867
Hollaway, Wm. to Sallie Ann Moore 9-9-1857 (9-21-1857)
Holloway, David T. to Adaline L. Sharp 7-24-1855
Holloway, Frank to Hanna Mason 1-10-1872 (1-15-1872)
Holmes, Geo. D. to Sallie E. Munford 1-18-1866
Holmes, George to Ann Eliza Rice 7-27-1847 (7-?-1847)
Holmes, Saml. A. to Frances Ann Bragg 12-17-1851
Holms, David to Mary Jackson 9-8-1874
Holoway, Henry to A. E. Twisdale 12-26-1859 (12-28-1859)
Holton, James to Mary Wilson 5-7-1841 (5-8-1841)
Homan, A. to N. J. Bringle 12-11-1869 (12-12-1869)
Homan, George to Adaline Walker 8-1-1867 (8-9-1867)
Home, James to Susanah Stevens 9-25-1857
Home, Josiah to Susan M. Thomas 10-16-1848 (10-18-1848)
Hooks, A. D. to Octavia Branch 10-19-1865 (10-24-1865)
Hooper, Joseph to Tempe Bonds 12-10-1873 (12-16-1873)
Hopkins, John D. to Annie Culbreath 10-2-1871 (10-5-1871)
Horne, Simeon to Ann M. Cowan 4-27-1841
Horne, Thos. C. to Eliza Miller 10-5-1870 (10-10-1870)
Horning?, Samuel K. to Nancy C. Wright 9-21-1842
Horton, John to Cy McLister 4-25-1866
Houlsouser, Howard to Sarah Walk 12-29-1858 (12-28?-1858)
House?, Hugh to George Perry 6-1-1869 (6-2-1869)
Houston, H. M. to Emma L. Wilson 7-9-1868
Howard, Geo. C. to Eliz. J. Crenshaw 10-28-1851 (10-29-1851)
Howard, Hiram to Sarah Boswell 9-28-1872 (9-29-1872)
Howard, J. H. to S. E. Myers 5-10-1871 (5-11-1871)
Howard, Peola? to Mary Butler 12-22-1842 (12-?-1842)
Howard, Rufus to Harriet Gillun 5-25-1867
Howard, Solaman to Kate Valley 3-20-1867 (3-21-1867)
Howard, Thomas C. to Mary J. Vaughan 4-28-1852
Howell, G. G. to Caroline Isom 8-8-1863 (8-9-1863)
Howell, J. I. to Sallie Bond 11-26-1872
Howell, W. H. to S. C. Duncan 5-28-1873 (5-29-1873)
Howerd, George to Malinda Smith 8-17-1872
Howsar, Lippman jr. to Caroline Yarbro 8-27-1867 (8-29-1867)
Hudleston, Samuel W. to Mary A. Morrison 9-3-1872
Hudson, Henry H. to Mary E. Hudson 1-25-1866 (1-30-1866)
Hudson, John W. to Ann Branch Perkinson 9-27-1841 (9-28-1841)
Huffman, Flranklin to Eve Ann Bungle 1-29-1846
Huffman, Franklin to Hester Ann Dacus 10-3-1859 (10-4-1859)
Huffman, G. A. to Catharine F. Morrisett 1-8-1872 (1-9-1872)
Huffman, G. L. to Ellen Shankle 11-20-1871 (11-21-1871)
Huffman, James to Nancy Thompson 11-12-1857
Huffman, W. C. to Amanda Guinn 11-30-1873 (12-2-1874?)
Huffman, Wm. A. to Julia A. C. Banks 11-29-1854 (12-1-1854)
Hughes, Harvey to Evalina Pantillie? Couch 5-15-1843
Hughes, Hiram to Hannah Bledsoe 9-29-1874
Hughes, Sam to Paula? McBride 5-20-1874
Hughes, Saml. Henry to Henrietta Stewart 7-15-1850 (7-16-1850)
Hughes, Wm. to Frances Tilman 10-23-1873
Hughlett, Fed to Rebecca Brown 3-5-1873 (3-6-1873)
Hughlette, Adkin to Marth Hill 12-28-1866 (12-29-1865)
Humphreys, Absolum T. J. to Mary E. Smith 10-7-1844 (10-24-1844)
Hunley, James H. to Laura Pinson 10-25-1872
Hunt, Anderson to Mary Cooper 11-21-1860 (11-22-1868)
Hunt, Christofer to Catharine Burrel 2-22-1868
Hunt, Dempsy to Patience Whitly 11-18-1865 (12-10-1865)
Hunt, James B. to Frances J. Burton 12-7-1872 (12-12-1872)
Hunt, James to Henritta Hall 6-17-1871
Hunt, Jessee to Sallie Foreman 12-29-1866
Hunt, Milton to Neadis Isis Phelps 9-27-1847 (9-30-1847)
Hunt, Wm. R. to Mary L. Marsh 2-7-1871 (2-9-1871)
Hunter, A. D.? to Elizabeth A. Alexander 1-4-1866
Hunter, Ag? D. to Clarinda A. Weaver? 10-19-1841 (10-21-1841)
Hunter, John to Nancy Futhey 2-13-1850
Hurley, John to Sarah Forsythe 1-4-1869
Hurley, W. M. to Mattie J. Salliers 8-15-1874 (8-16-1874)
Hurt, Jacob to Emma Somervell 12-8-1866 (12-9-1866)
Hurt, John Z. to Caroline Craig 12-4-1865 (12-6-1865)
Hurt, Samuel B. to Julia M. L. Desmond? 7-2-1842 (7-16-1842)
Hurt, Samuel S. to Margaret A. Jones 12-22-1863 (12-21?-1863)
Huston, Calvin to Millley R. Richerson 7-2-1873
Hutcherson, Saml. W. to Nancy Ray 12-27-1873 (12-31-1873)
Hutcheson, Aaron to Mary Richardson 8-31-1869
Hutchinson, John P. to Ellen Thacker 8-5-1867 (8-6-1867)
Hutchinson, William Walker to Sarah Goss 4-12-1844 (4-15-1844)
Hutchison, Cyrus W. to Harriet Smith 12-16-1849
Hutchison, John Leroy to Mary Frances Ray 2-24-1853
Ikard, A. T. to Mary E. Lindsay 1-1-1869 (1-5-1869)
Ingram, James to Adaline Reece 4-4-1873 (4-5-1873)
Ingram, John to Louisa Logan 9-18-1873
Ings?, James to L. B. Epps 12-12-1874
Irbey, W. L. to Bettie Rodgers 9-26-1866
Irvin?, A. H. to M. J. Irvin 2-11-1860
Jackson, Andrew to Fannie Burnes 8-3-1871 (8-4-1871)
Jackson, Andrew to Mary Ann Alexander 12-23-1867 (12-25-1867)
Jackson, Bedford to Lukky Williams 12-27-1869
Jackson, Daniel to Mary Alexander 12-26-1872
Jackson, J. to Mary Taylor 5-16-1872 (7-24-1872)
Jackson, James C. to Tommy Colmer 12-11-1869 (12-14-1869)
Jackson, John W. to Julia C. Young 1-12-1867 (1-13-1867)
Jackson, Peter Simpson to Mary Eliz. McBride 12-3-1855 (12-6-1855)
Jackson, Ruffin to Hanna Johnson 12-?-1866

Jackson, Ruffin to Laura Taylor 11-11-1871
Jackson, Thomas to Harriet Polk 10-17-1874 (10-28-1874)
Jackson, William B. to Rachel E. Horne 12-18-1849 (12-20-1849)
Jackson, William to Margaret Somervill 12-29-1866 (12-31-1867?)
Jacobs, Caleb to Charlotte Taylor 12-24-1866 (12-25-1866)
Jacobs, John C. to Mary S. Sherrod 5-9-1859 (5-10-1859)
James, Jim to Margaret Taylor 7-4-1868
James, Joseph B. to Massey Lavinia Pennell 5-18-1849 (not executed)
James, Perley to Lucinda Parish 5-11-1846
James, Perley? to Sarah Eliz. Roberts 10-25-1852 (10-31-1852)
James, Robert R. to C. S. Thomas 10-19-1874 (10-21-1874)
Jameson, James Harris to Mary Caroline Black 6-30-1846
Jamison, J. L. to Sallie Dillahunty 12-15-1874
Jamison, James H. to Martha E. Farmer 4-23-1857
Jamison, Jordan to Gabella Ann Roberts 1-13-1870
Jamison, Robert G. to Elizabet Ellen Smith 10-21-1869
Jamison?, George to Pamelia Trayler 10-20-1855 (10-25-1855)
Jeanes, Bassel to Jane C. Griffith 3-6-1870 (5-9-1870)
Jenkins, Columbus to Harriet Smith 11-11-1873 (11-12-1873)
Jenkins, John W. to Mary E. Lindsey 9-17-1872 (9-19-1872)
Jett, Milton to Henrietta Taylor 5-26-1866 (6-2-1871?)
Jimmerson, James M. to Susan A. Dean 11-26-1873 (12-3-1873)
Johnes, Nathan to Martha Bernard 7-20-1867
Johnson, Alex to Lizzie Sherrill 6-19-1869 (6-20-1869)
Johnson, Beverly to Lily Maclin 7-26-1867 (7-27-1867)
Johnson, Beverly to Sophia Maclin 12-24-1869 (12-27-1869)
Johnson, C. A. to C. V. Gray 12-1-1874
Johnson, C. A. to M. W. Caskey 12-31-1870 (1-5-1871)
Johnson, Frank to Salina Marshall 12-30-1874
Johnson, George Anderson to Jane Hall 5-5-1873
Johnson, George to Ernesta? Bledsoe 4-6-1867 (4-7-1867)
Johnson, J. A. to Mary Williams 1-13-1873 (1-16-1873)
Johnson, John to Rose Claibun? 1-28-1867 (1-30-1867)
Johnson, John to Winnie Smith 3-1-1871 (3-2-1871)
Johnson, Joseph to Martha Jones 7-8-1872
Johnson, Martin T. to Susan E. Adams 8-14-1865 (8-15-1865)
Johnson, Mingo to Mariah Tucker Moore 1-19-1872 (1-20-1872)
Johnson, Moses to Jone? Reaves 1-4-1871
Johnson, P. B. to Eliza Elin Pinson 11-7-1874 (11-8-1874)
Johnson, Peter to Mary Wells 1-12-1874
Johnson, R. Fenner to Lizzie W. Flowers 5-20-1868 (5-21-1868)
Johnson, S. E. to Ann E. Green 5-30-1859
Johnson, Saml. P. C. to Lucy Ellen Smith 2-5-1844
Johnson, Silas to Ellen Timms 12-21-1864 (12-22-1864)
Johnson, Stephen B. to Nancy Jane Jones 4-27-1847 (4-30-1847)
Johnson, Thomas to Churney Caruthers 9-11-1873
Johnson, William to Bettie Taylor 5-20-1869
Johnson, Willis to Georga Harris 12-17-1873
Johnston, Washington to Christina Nelson 1-12-1869 (1-19-1869)
Johnston, Wm. to Nancy Williams 6-9-1866 (6-12-1866)
Joiner, John G. to ____ E. Horn 3-1-1864 (3-2-1864)
Jones, Alexander to Jane Whitman 11-30-1843
Jones, Allen to Malissa Jackson 5-10-1873 B
Jones, Anthony to Amelia Rose 7-29-1873 (8-14-1873)
Jones, Ben to Margaret White 1-11-1871
Jones, Booker to Susan J. Green 3-12-1860
Jones, Brother M. to Susan A. Green 3-12-1860 (3-20-1860)
Jones, Charles to Callie Turner 10-21-1874
Jones, D. L. to Mary J. Carter 12-28-1859 (12-29-1859)
Jones, G. W. to Mary Jane Smith 6-10-1861 (6-11-1861)
Jones, G.? J. to Amanda J. Billings 1-1-1863
Jones, George to Leer Moore 4-17-1871
Jones, Green to Mary Harris 1-1-1874
Jones, Henry to Adaline Upchurch 7-14-1872 (7-15-1872)
Jones, Henry to Emeline Smith 11-26-1869
Jones, J. H. to Florrence Cole 6-25-1867 (6-30-1867)
Jones, J. J. to A. C. Cullum 1-4-1871 (1-5-1871)
Jones, Jacob to Margaret Compton 12-17-1872 (12-22-1872)
Jones, James C. to Christena Feezor 12-24-1849
Jones, James M. to Lettie Hays 9-24-1872 (11-24-1872)
Jones, James to Florence Harris 5-13-1874
Jones, James to Gracey Maclin 12-7-1874
Jones, Leroy to Marier Green 12-28-1865
Jones, Lewis to Ally Gooddin 1-27-1868 (1-30-1868)
Jones, Nicholas to Mary Coleman 11-13-1871
Jones, Richard James to Ellen Conway Rose 1-7-1850 (1-10-1850)
Jones, Robert B. to Mary Jeans 3-11-1861
Jones, Sam to Mary Kilpatrick 9-14-1872
Jones, Saml. to Mary Parsons 9-8-1857
Jones, Spencer to Dafney Coleman 8-23-1866 (8-26-1866)
Jones, Thomas to Chainey Howard 10-3-1874
Jones, W. F. to D. E. Davis 12-17-1868 (1-7-1869)
Jones, W. F. to V. C. David 12-17-1868 (12-3-1869?)
Jones, Wesley to Elizabeth Wells 12-31-1873
Jones, Wesley to Frances Maclin 12-21-1869
Jones, William to Mary Elkin 9-7-1868 (9-10-1868)
Joodard, James A. to Martha M. Walker 3-13-1861
Jordan, Albert to Alabama Faulk 12-21-1867 (12-22-1867)
Jordan, James to Rachel McQuiston 6-1-1866 (6-3-1866)
Jorden, Joseph to Harriet Young 10-29-1867 (10-30-1867)
Joseph, Henry to Nellie Robison 5-29-1867
Joyner, H. H. to Ann H. Drummons 11-5-1866 (11-6-1866)
Joyner, Robert to Sarah Price 12-28-1868 (12-3-1869?)
Joyner, Washington to Sarah Ann Forbess 7-21-1868 (7-23-1868)
Joyner, Wm. Henry to Mary E. Forbess 2-27-1866 (3-1-1866)
Justice, William to Mary Margaret Kimey 12-20-1856 (12-23-1856)
Keathley, Johnathan to Sarah Houston 12-28-1859 (12-29-1859)
Keaton, J. P. to Amanda Larimore 2-25-1868
Keene, M. L. to M. E. Hult? 12-16-1874
Kelley, A. A. to C. A. Kelley 1-1-1874
Kelley, A. J. to M. F. Baker 9-14-1859
Kelley, Albert Ambrose to Martha Jane Roberts 10-27-1855 (10-29-1855)
Kelley, Isaac N. to Paulina Jordan 12-18-1848 (12-24-1848)
Kelley, Munro to Nancy Shankle 8-12-1873
Kelley, Oliver P. to Julia Ann Hartsfield 7-14-1847
Kelley, P. G. to D. A. Kelley 12-14-1870 (12-15-1870)
Kelley, Tho. Jefferson to Mary Jane McMinns 7-20-1850
Kelley, Vincent P. to S. J. Upchurch 12-30-1858
Kelley, Vincent P. to Sarah J. Upchurch 12-30-1858
Kelly, Aaron to Phebe Trigg 11-27-1872 (12-16-1873?)
Kelly, J. B. to Maggie Locke 2-16-1874
Kelly, J. M. to Malinda J. Baskins 1-21-1861 (1-23-1861)
Kelly, John to Lousanna Phillips 3-11-1854 (3-12-1854)
Kelly, John to T. Glass 10-24-1874 (10-29-1874)
Kennedy, John to A. B. Dunn 12-4-1872
Kennedy, Louis to Martha Hughlett 12-27-1865
Kent, J. B. to Fannie Morgan 9-23-1865
Kent, Thos. B. to Sarah McGregor 1-13-1866
Kent, Wm. Alexr. to Rachel Gray 11-29-1851 (12-3-1851)
Kents, Wm. J. to Margaret E. Cotton 12-18-1852 (12-21-1852)
Kerkpatrick, J. S. to C. D. Gray 12-6-1873
Kern, Thomas to Elizabeth Jenkins 5-24-1841 (5-26-1841)
Kerr, Miles Wade to Elisabeth Nancy Wilbanks 4-22-1865
Kidd, William to Jennet Wilson 1-2-1866 (1-10-1866)
Killingsworth, Morris to Elizabeth Clark 1-31-1844 (1-?-1844)
Kilpatrick, Chas. to Emalin Hanna 2-22-1872
Kilpatrick, John W. to Frances S. Buster 11-17-1869
Kilpatrick, Needham to Laura Morrison 6-3-1869 (6-4-1869)
Kilpatrick, Needhan to Martha Hughlett 9-28-1872
Kimbro, William R. to Rachael E. Reed 7-16-1858 (7-17-1858)
Kimbrough, Nat M. to Fannie S. Hunt 5-20-1867 (5-22-1867)
Kincaid, James P. to Lizzie West 3-3-1874 (3-4-1874)
Kincaid, Sidney to Sallie Murphy 10-1-1874
Kindrick, Saml. to Elizabeth Anderson 5-18-1872 (5-19-1872)
Kiney, William A. to Mary S. Wiseman 2-29-1860
King, Newton W. to Cynthia C. Roe 10-15-1868 (10-18-1868)
Kingkade, Asa to Riller Ray 10-12-1867 (10-30-1867)
Kinney, G. L. to Mary E. Smith 12-16-1873 (12-17-1873)
Kinney, J. C. to Sarah E. Walton 2-20-1873
Kinney, James K. to Sophronia Yarbro 1-24-1861
Kinney, Jesse to Frances J. Goren 11-23-1859 (11-24-1859)
Kinney, Thomas to Albertine Smith 5-25-1846
Kinney, Thomas to Emeline Smith 9-26-1855
Kinney, Wm. A. to M. E. Wiseman 2-29-1860
Kinney, Wm. A. to Mary E. Wiseman 2-29-1860
Kinny, George T. to Msaggie W. Kerr 12-23-1873 (12-24-1873)
Kinny, Jessee to Perlina Best 12-30-1873 (12-31-1873)
Kirk, William Addison to Mary Strawn 10-24-1848 (11-1-1848)
Kirkland, S. P. to Martha Butler 1-2-1860 (1-4-1860)

Kirkman, Jesse to Sophia Gray 10-27-1871 (10-28-1871)
Kirkpatrick, John to Jane Walker 7-30-1849 (8-14-1849)
Kirtland, S. P. to Martha J. Butler no dates (with 1860)
Kirts, James to Margaret Adkins 3-20-1865
Kitchen, Wallace to George A. Strong 3-27-1869 (3-30-1869)
Knight, F. M. to Rebeca A. Dacus 11-22-1860
Knight, JSames A. to Margaret Elam 11-13-1866
Knight, Joseph to Elizabeth Barwell 1-12-1869 (1-13-1869)
Knight, Woodson to Fannie Ellison 5-16-1870
Knox, John B. to Jennetta L. McFarland 3-7-1848 (3-?-1848)
Knox, John Bray to Amanda Williams 8-8-1851 (8-17-1851)
Knox, R. M. to Dicy Culbreath 7-1-1868 (7-2-1868)
Koonce, J. W. to M. E. J. McMullin 4-8-1874 (4-9-1874)
Koonce, John W. to Matilda J. McMullins 12-23-1867
Kurts, John to L. A. Lock 12-21-1858
Kurts?, Martin Harvey to Ellen Ann White 9-24-1853 (9-28-1853)
Kyle, Dr. T. A. to Mattie G. Adams 7-2-1860 (7-3-1860)
Lainn?, Isaac to Mary Ann Orwell 1-19-1847
Laird, James to Catheran Conner 12-19-1866
Lake, Allen Debow to Indiana Crenshaw 11-15-1848 (11-16-1848)
Lake, Armistead to Mary Green 7-1-1867?
Lake, Daniel T. to Elizabeth A. Ivey 4-4-1861
Lake, Daniel T. to Virginia Culbreath 1-11-1855
Lake, James C. to Mary Ann Siler 11-25-1857 (11-26-1857)
Lamar, Andrew to Sarah Easley 8-1-1867 (8-2-1867)
Lamar, Frank to Mary Harrison 8-1-1867 (8-2-1867)
Lamb, Enos to Frances Parish 2-5-1849
Lambkins, J. to Susan Ann Davis 8-8-1873 (8-9-1873)
Lamkin, Robert to Louisa Chapman 4-14-1874
Lamkin, Thomas H. to Bettie McCraw 4-1-1869
Lampkin, Archer to Mary Vaughan 6-4-1870
Landadal, Wm.H. to Mary Susan Ausbon 3-21-1872
Landen, James to Emma H. Fairfax 12-17-1869
Landerstedet, John to Anna Ereka Norquist 9-6-1873
Lane, Albert to Rosetta Boyd 11-21-1872
Lane, Lawson to Margaret Wright 1-26-1870
Lane, T. D. to Mrs. L. J. Herrell 12-17-1873
Langstaff, Alfred A. to Sallie A. McCall 11-13-1871 (11-15-1871)
Lanier, James C. to Jane Ann Cosby 5-16-1854 (5-17-1854)
Lanier, John to Delia Ann Nelson 12-6-1873
Lanier, Kenneth B. to Janie Frances Farmer? 1-13-1856 (1-31-1856)
Lanton, Albert Gallatin to Mary Amanda Turnage 12-16-1843 (12-22-1843)
Laremore, A. to Sina McBride 8-1-1872 (8-4-1872)
Laremore, Aderson to Mary Hutton 2-27-1869 (3-4-1869)
Larimore, Hana? Miller to Catharine Howard 5-31-1853
Larimore, Pleasant K. to Sarah George 5-18-1847 (5-20-1847)
Lark, Peter to Rosetta Harris 1-18-1872 (1-20-1872)
Lassater, Loyd to Jane Hall 3-14-1867 (3-17-1867)
Lassiter, M. A. to Lenord Clements 12-17-1872 (12-19-1872)
Lauderdale, Henry to Parelee Johnson 11-12-1874
Lauderdale, James H. to Roasina Hatch 6-2-1841
Lauderdale, Josiah H. to Clara H. Lauderdale 4-4-1866 (4-4-1865?)
Lauderdale, Lymas to Susan Yarbro 12-18-1872
Lauderdale, Thos. S. to L. J. Tipton 1-30-1861
Lauderdale, Wesley H. to Agnes Truitt 3-26-1869 (4-4-1869)
Lauderdale, William to Alcy Walk 5-24-1867 (5-26-1867)
Lavell, Isaac to Alvin A. Pace 8-21-1874 (9-8-1874)
Lavell, Patrick to Manerva Ann Williams 12-12-1859 (12-13-1859)
Lavell, Thomas to Sarah Ann Baskins 11-27-1869 (12-2-1869)
Lawrence?, Wm. Alen to Amanda Minerva McBride 3-12-1856 (3-13-1856)
Lawson, Tom to Aggie Alston 11-20-1871 (11-23-1871)
Lawton?, Mathew M. to M. E. Penson 1?-30-1868
Laxton, J. J. to Nancy J. McBride 2-2-1870 (2-3-1870)
Leach, Asa to Emily Matilda Brown 11-28-1854
Leach, J. N. to Maggie Dewease 12-18-1874 (12-22-1874)
Leach, James Madison to Louisa Rutherford 7-17-1849
Leach, James to Eliza Cannon 6-24-1854 (6-26-1854)
Leach, John to Armenta Brown 4-8-1855 (4-14-1855)
Leach, Wm. H. to Catharine E. Scott 12-10-1860
Lebdor, Henry to Elizabeth Gibbons 4-8-1850
Lee, C. E. to Lydia A. Timms 8-27-1874
Lee, Francis Marion to Mary A. Henry 10-9-1848 (10-12-1848)
Lee, John to Nancy Hay 4-19-1873
Lee, Thomas to Easter Turner 12-30-1873 (12-3?-1873)
Leech, Charles H. to Mary G. A. Allen 11-28-1867
Leftwich, Isaac to Frances Dunn 12-24-1870
Lemes?, Charles to Cylvia Gibbs 5-26-1866 (5-27-1866)
Lemmon, Jas. W. to Miss M. B. Jones 2-5-1866 (2-8-1866)
Lemons, Saml. O. to Mollie M. Williams 9-18-1871 (9-21-1871)
Lenek?, Asa? to Elizabeth Jane Brown 2-19-1853
Levto?, Authen J. to Lavinia Orr 2-9-1869
Lewellen, George to Mahala J. Roberts 8-1-1861
Lewis, Frank to Fannie Taylor 3-15-1873
Lewis, James to L. Stevens 11-16-1864 (11-17-1864)
Lewis, Thomas to Manda Dentenac 8-15-1867
Ligon, Benj. Haskins to Elizabeth E. Weller 12-30-1846 (12-31-1846)
Ligon, Benjamin H. to Louisa Adaline Owen 11-22-1841 (11-26-1841)
Ligon, Henry B. to Mary Jane Wood 1-4-1848 (1-5-1848)
Ligon, Washington to Mary Smith 1-17-1874 (1-4?-1874)
Ligon, William H. to Martha Wood 9-12-1842 (9-20-1842)
Limbarger, David Henry to Sarah Adeline Green 3-1-1865
Linden, Robt to Bettie Greenfield 12-28-1874
Lindsay, Jesse B. to Delilah Harris 8-3-1843
Lindsey, N. M. to Mary E. Trobough 2-28-1862
Litten, Isham to Sindy Foster 4-23-1874 (4-25-1874)
Llewelling, Adam T. to Rachel Cronk? 1-13-1856
Lock, B. F. to Sarah Smith 3-1-1860
Locke, Ben F. to Sarah Smith 3-1-1860 (3-3-1860)
Locke, Jas. Monroe to Lorina Kurts 1-2-1856
Lockett, Jessee to Rebecca A. Sloss 3-4-1861 (3-17-1861)
Logan, W. R. M. to Georgia Ann Reatherford 12-28-1859
Long, H. J. to Sallie McIlwaine 5-22-1871 (5-23-1871)
Long, Peter to Lucy Darr 12-9-1840
Long, Pleasant M. to Rachel Ann Erwood 9-20-1873 (9-21-1873)
Long, Sam to Sarah C. White 8-21-1861
Long, Virgil to Laura L. Beavers 9-1-1866 (9-6-1866)
Loovell, David to Martha Sulfrick 3-3-1859 (3-9-1859)
Louisen, Allen to Mariah English 9-7-1866 (9-9-1866)
Loveene?, Henry M. to Irena R. Pickard 7-2-1872 (7-4-1872)
Lovell, Pat? to Frances Baskin 12-23-1867 (12-24-1867)
Lowe, Samuel to Ellen Herrin 5-10?-1868
Lowe, Willis to Cle. Hill 12-22-1870
Lowry, J. J. to Sarah A. Poor 7-17-1860 (7-19-1860)
Lowry, Robert to Orlina Jane Petty 12-29-1855 (1-5-1856)
Loyd, Andrew J. to Adaline G. Delashmet 1-16-1872 (1-17-1872)
Loyd, John to Amanda Walk 10-19-1869
Loyd, W. A. to M. J.? Hannah 12-12-1866 (12-13-1866)
Lucado, E. P. to Margret Simonton 6-28-1856 (7-11-1856)
Ludwick, John to Lavina Cox 7-17-1865
Lundy, Balam to Zilpha Giffrey 3-9-1867 (3-12-1867)
Luster, Barton to Caralin Pearce 3-3-1868 (3-4-1868)
Luttrell, Silas to Rachel M. Hartfield 9-25-1867 (9-26-1867)
Lyles, N.L. to Josephine Jones 4-7-1873 (4-10-1873)
Lynn, Henry to Susanna Morrison 7-3-1869
Lynn, Hugh M. to Martha S. Simpson 4-9-1862
Lynn, J. W. to M. E. McCain 6-2-1869 (6-3-1869)
Lynn, James O. to Margaret W. Caskey 12-31-1870 (1-2-1871)
Lynn, IJ. P. to R. Shaw 1-9-1871 (1-10-1871)
Lynn?, J. A. to Bettie Heffman 12-31-1870
Lyons, Ben to Lessie? Johnson 11-27-1867
Maburn, George to Bammer Pool 9-7-1871 (9-9-1871)
Mackado, Calvin to Nancy Stallins 5-16-1871
Macklin, Andrew to Amanda Jett? 10-23-1865 (10-29-1865)
Macklin, Bob to Ann Smith 5-13-1869
Macklin, Paul to Eudora Taylor 6-21-1867
Macklin, Robert to Fathy Williamson 1-29-1866
Maclin, Albert to Vergun Taylor 12-24-1869
Maclin, George to Louisa Maclin 4-8-1870
Maclin, Harvey to 'Bettie Taylor 1-14-1868
Maclin, Lackfield to Sallie D. Alston 12-30-1871 (1-3-1875?)
Maclin, Samuel to A. Marshall 9-30-1871 (10-6-1871)
Maclin, Smith to Mattie Lacey 1-25-1871
Maclin, Washington to Mary Rhodes 1-19-1868 (1-20-1868)
Maclin, William to Easter Maclin 2-27-1874
Maclin, Willie to Nellie Jackson 11-11-1874
Maclin, Wm. to Looky Plummer 12-20-1871
Macon, Willia to Eleanor H. Somerville 12-25-1843
Magee, Henry to Lily Green 10-23-1873 (12-16-1873)

Mailey, Anderson to Lavicey Ann Wood 3-16-1848
Mailey, Henry J. to Nancy Jane Tucker 1-23-1851
Mailey, Henry James to Sarah Ann Eliz. Richardson 5-16-1843 (5-18-1843)
Mailey, James O. to Julia Ann L. Wiseman 3-27-1853
Mailey?, John to Angeline Jane Morents? 4-5-1843 (4-6-1843)
Maley, James S. to Fannie C. Turner 12-31-1866 (1-1-1867)
Malone, Alex to Phebe Ann Brodway 10-13-1865
Malone, C. to Fannie Twisdale 1-3-1870
Malone, Harrison to Martha Smith 11-8-1872
Malone, W. P. to Mary A. Jacobs 5-21-1870 (5-22-1870)
Manasco, Charles to Jane Macafee 1-10-1866
Manasco, J. R. to Mary Payne 9-24-1861 (9-27-1861)
Manasco, James to Emily Webb 6-21-1859 (6-23-1859)
Manasco, James to Mary M. Kitchen 6-30-1860 (7-7-1860)
Manasco, Jeremiah to Mary Jane Flanakin 7-6-1857
Manasco, Jerry to Eugenie P. Moore 2-27-1871 (3-1-1871)
Manasco, Joel R. to Mary M. Boothe 12-20-1859 (12-21-1859)
Manasco, John to Senith Elizabeth Maston 4-22-1874 (4-23-1874)
Manasco, Pleasant to Lucy C. Kitchen 6-30-1860 (7-5-1860)
Manasco, Plesant to Josephin Crofford 6-19-1867 (6-18?-1867)
Manasco, Plesant to S. A. Crofford 5-6-1870 (5-8-1870)
Manasco, Plesant to V. T. Slass 11-2-1868 (11-4-1868)
Manasker, George Washington to Mary Jane Walker 12-19-1848 (12-7?-1848)
Mann, George to Elizabeth Angus 1-4-1869 (1-10-1869)
Manual, George to Margaret Wood 10-18-1872 (10-19-1872)
Marbury, W. C. to Mary S. Barnett 5-11-1872
Margan, Asa to Ellen Smith 10-28-1865
Mariner, Edward Joseph to Mary Frances Lamb 3-8-1850 (3-11-1850)
Markham, Thomas W. to Indianna P. Booker 5-28-1846
Markham, Thos. to Louisa Claiburne 2-1-1866 (2-7-1866)
Markham?, J.? W.? to Sophia? Moss? 11-26-1862
Marsh, Saml. J. to Martha V. Acock 12-22-1874 (12-23-1874)
Marsh, Saml. J. to Permelia Long 6-20-1859 (6-21-1859)
Marsh, William C. to Sarah J. Bass 1-19-1860 (6?-19-1860)
Marsh, Wm. Carroll to Mary Valentia Davidson 12-21-1853 (12-22-1853)
Marshall, Archibald to Ellen Moore 10-13-1854 (11-1-1854)
Marshall, John T. Z. to L. R. McClannohan 11-26-1867 (11-28-1867)
Marshall, Joseph to Bettie Smith 10-12-1867
Marshall, L. P. to T. C. Culbreth 9-28-1870
Marshall, William J. to Sarah Thompson 5-31-1847 (4?-?-1847)
Marshall, Wm. to Carnea Culbeath? 11-15-1865 (11-16-1865)
Martain, Albert to Mary Janice Dickerson 7-12-1871 (7-21?-1872?)
Martain, Allen to Ellen Owen 2-25-1869
Martain, Nathan to Mariah Jones 1-25-1873 (1-28-1873)
Martin, Allen to Matilda Elizabeth Owens 9-15-1868
Martin, Buckham to Adeline Claiburn 1-6-1868 (1-11-1868)
Martin, James Norfleet to Parthenia Ann Melisa Cox 7-8-1844
Martin, John J. to Eliza Jane Cox 4-1-1844
Martin, John W. to M. J. Hill 11-25-1873 (11-15-1873?)
Martin, Michael B. to Malinda Cooper 10-20-1849 (10-21-1849)
Martin, O. E. to K. F. McGregor 2-10-1874
Martin, Peter to Jane Haynie 10-20-1866 (10-21-1866)
Martin, Richard to Nancy Trentham 10-30-1872 (10-31-1872)
Martin, Sidney to E. F. Hill 8-24-1872 (8-25-1872)
Martin, T. P. to Maggie Mitchell 10-9-1874 (10-10-1874)
Martin, W. A. to Mary C. Lamb 9-5-1859 (9-6-1859)
Martin, William to Rebecca Dunn 12-27-1873 (12-28-1873)
Martin, Wm. to Martha R. Breedmon 6-3-1868
Martin, _____ to JSane Dosson 5-26-1863 (5-28-1863)
Maser, Wm. M. to Mary Ann Parker 9-27-1855
Mason, Daniel to Lucy Buttner? 11-20-1872
Mason, John to Adaline L. Britt 12-9-1843 (12-?-1843)
Mason, W. H. to Elizabeth Stevens 2-25-1870 (2-27-1870)
Mason?, J. A. to Laura Harris 10-26-1871 (10-27-1871)
Massey, A. J. to Lilly Ann Prince 2-3-1871
Mathews, Ben to Emeline Mathews 12-17-1874
Mathews, Bird L. to Ellen M. Pennel 6-3-1861 (6-5-1861)
Mathews, John G. to Sarah J. Strong 12-23-1850
Mathews, Mussintyre? Sloane to Mary Frances Houston? 11-10-1842
Mathis, James W. to Tennie E. Mitchell 9-5-1867
Matthews, Amos Jay to Mary Tipton 10-29-1846 (11-?-1846)
Matthews, James to Sarah Titus 10-8-1866
Matthews, John G. to B. M. Hill 12-18-1872
Matthis, B. L. to V.? F. Byrd 2-21-1866 (2-22-1866)
Mattice, W. H. to E. G. Malone 7-19-1873
Mauzy, John to Mary Ladd 8-21-1872 (8-25-1872)
Max, Ed. Jeruiza? to Mary Harris 9-11-1869 (9-15-1869)
Max, Francis M. to Elizabeth Billing 11-26-1866 (11-27-1866)
Max, W. A. to M. J. Yarbro 8-19-1868 (8-26-1868)
Maxwell, E. D. to Harriet E. Beaty 1-3-1856
Maxwell, E. J. to Mary Elam? Archer 2-11-1856 (2-14-1856)
Maxwell, James J. to Mary Eliza Maxwell 9-26-1867 (9-27-1867)
Maxwell, Joseph to Amanda Wood 11-28-1861
Maxwell, Thomas A. to Margaret Feezor 8-27-1866 (8-29-1866)
Mayberry, John to Elizabeth Wallace 11-15-1866 (11-18-1866)
Maye, Lucian to Nancy J. Partlow 5-31-1866
Mayes, J. S. to L. J. Elam 4-1-1867 (4-2-1867)
Mayo, Henry J.W. to Maggie E. Templeton 2-24-1868 (2-26-1868)
Mayo, Lucien to Mary Ann Partlow 12-21-1859 (12-22-1859)
Mays, James to K. T. Calhoun 11-27-1871 (11-28-1871)
McAdams, Tom to Nancy Williams 2-19-1867 (2-10-1867)
McAfee, J. A. T. to Rosana Smith 9-14-1864 (9-15-1864)
McAlilly, F. M. to Sarah Jane Lodgings 7-27-1858
McBride, Barzilla C. to Crarisa C. Bringle 2-3-1853
McBride, D. L. to D. W. Trobough 6-16-1866 (6-20-1866)
McBride, George J. to Emma F. Fisher 1-20-1869 (1-21-1869)
McBride, J. C. to A. S. George 11-4-1865 (11-7-1865)
McBride, J. G. to D. R. Trobough 2-22-1869 (2-27-1869)
McBride, Solomon to Juley Ann Orshin? 5-20-1864 (3?-21-1864)
McBride, W. W. to Mary E. Jamison 1-27-1857 (1-28-1857)
McBride, William to Margaret Rice 2-7-1847
McCain, J. G. to O. C. Davis 1-26-1862 (1-29-1862)
McCain, Jefferson to Ann Elam 8-9-1867 (8-10-1867)
McCain, L. to Elizabeth Strong 9-23-1865
McCain, Wm. Ross? to Leticia Simonton 2-13-1856
McCall, Alfred to Caroline Stevens 10-16-1869
McCall, James R> to Mary A. Hooks 4-23-1846 (5-25-1846)
McCall, M. S. to Elizabeth Driver 9-21-1871
McCall, W. J. to W. S. Whitley 11-1-1873 (11-7-1873)
McCalla, John L. to Mollie E. Gooch 1-3-1870 (1-4-1870)
McCallie, R. M. to N. E. Lynn 10-5-1868 (10-6-1868)
McCam, George to Nancy Stevenson 10-1-1870
McCan, John to Fannie Ann Field 4-8-1870
McCan, John to Farrie Ann Field 4-8-1870
McCann, Jefferson to Mary Randolph 4-5-1873 (4-11-1873)
McCauley, John C. to Eliza J. Hall 11-8-1855 (11-16-1855)
McCauley, Nelson to Margaret Foster 4-23-1874
McCetcham, Joseph W. to Martha H. Culbreath 1-12-1869 (1-13-1869)
McCheshire, James M. to Roxanne W. Hindman 9-18-1850
McClain, J. H. to Mary A. Golden 1-31-1870 (2-1-1870)
McClanahan, Henry to Nancy Rhodes 3-31-1871 (4-1-1871)
McClanahan, John D. to Margaret Ann Robertson 10-17-1840 (10-22-1840)
McClellan, Wm. Green to Nancy E. Bryant 11-14-1849
McClelland, James to Frances Smith 9-22-1859
McClelland, Williamson to Amanda Hamilton 7-12-1859
McClelland, Williamson to Mary Hamilton 11-28-1854
McClenny?, R. P. to Lucey A. Hill 3-21-1868 (3-24-1868)
McClerkin, J. K. to I. J. Smith 3-28-1871 (3-29-1871)
McClerkin, James to Elizabeth E. Kelley 11-8-1856 (11-11-1856)
McCluney, S. G. to J. M. Cooper 9-5-1870 (9-13-1870)
McCool, Martin to Martha E. Stanley 2-5-1844 (2-7-1844)
McCorkle, John J.? to Jane Moore 4-27-1840 (5-5-1840)
McCormack, James to Margaret English 3-20-1865
McCormick, G. N. to Sarah S. Hindman 1-22-1861 (1-23-1861)
McCormick, N. R. to Julia A. Huffman 8-29-1855
McCoy, Chas. David to Frances Malvina Hartsfield 12-22-1853 (SB 1852?)
McCoy, W. B. to M. J. Draffin 5-5-1873
McCraw, Frank to Sallie Williams 1-17-1874 (1-18-1874)
McCraw, Gabriel to Nancy Sullivan 6-29-1841
McCraw, J. A. to F. A. E. Sanders 12-7-1870 (12-8-1870)
McCraw, Thomas C. to Harriet Childers 1-28-1860
McCraw, Thomas C. to Mary E. Freeman 2-22-1865 (2-23-1865)
McCraw, Thomas C. to Mary Freeman 3-14-1868
McCraw, Thos. C. to Elizabeth McCraw 10-26-1861

McCrory, Cyrus G. to Sarah C. Bateman 10-20-1851
McCrutchen, Abe W. to Louisa Hill 2-2-1869 (2-3-1869)
McCuin, Albert Gallatin to Martha Jane Simonton 7-25-1850
McCullough, Hally? to Tucy Still 12-28-1871
McCullough, John to Mary Tennant 4-8-1851 (4-9-1851)
McCullough, Robert to Elizabeth Moore 10-29-1851 (10-30-1851)
McCullough, Robert to Nancy Bird 7-25-1853 (7-26-1853)
McCullough, Silas to Emily Smith 8-19-1871
McDaniel, E. to Minnie E. Smith 2-26-1874
McDaniel, J. B. to S. E. Mattice? 7-19-1873 (7-23-1873)
McDaniel, J. L. to Elizabeth Baird 6-6-1861
McDaniel, John Ready to Martha McQuiston 5-5-1851
McDanniel, E. to Lusetta Bernard 4-22-1868
McDaw, John to Sarah Smith 9-1-1867 (9-12-1867)
McDonald, David to Jane M. Banks 12-3-1851 (12-4-1851)
McDonald, James to Catharine McDouggle 11-23-1869 (11-25-1869)
McDow, J. J. to Mary A. Pullin 10-30-1865 (11-1-1865)
McElmore, Mat to Sallie Densford 12-12-1872
McEwin, Robt. McComb to Elvira Moore 11-15-1850
McFadden, N. C. to Miss Mollie McFadden 1-29-1862
McFadden, N. H. to J. D. Watts 11-27-1873
McFadden, Robert L. to Margaret L. Hill 7-24-1866
McFarland, Reuben Fletcher to Helen Goheen 9-30-1850 (10-2-1850)
McFarland, Tho. D. to Mary Bass 10-7-1850 (10-9-1850)
McFarlane, Doctor Wesley to Costinza Missouri Harris 12-18-1844 (12-19-1844)
McGee, Gideon G. to Julia Ann Maley 8-23-1857
McGee, James A. to Mrs. Nancy M. Keenan 5-16-1860
McGee, John to Kitsy Elam 9-27-1872 (10-16-1872)
McGee, Tilman to Patienc Maley 1-17-1868
McGowan, Andrew to Elizabeth Williams 8-4-1866 (8-7-1866)
McGowan, Joseph to Cordelia Joyce 11-7-1854
McGrath, J. D. to Annie F. Byram 11-23-1874 (11-25-1874)
McGregor, Frank to Sallie Bledsoe 2-19-1873 (2-20-1873)
McGuire, Alfred to Louisa J. Hartsfield 2-12-1842 (2-15-1842)
McGuire, Obediah to Eliza Whitson 88-7-1846 (8-13-1846)
McGuire, William F. to Sarah M. Stephens 4-7-1858
McGuiver, John to Del Cash 3-15-1870
McGuiver, Wm. M. to Nealy Barnet 5-21-1866 (5-22-1866)
McGuiver?, Harry to Sarah A. Steele 10-29-1869 (11-13-1869)
McHale, James to Salvina? M. Davis 12-27-1859
McIntosh, James S. to Miss Lucy Walk 4-9-1862
McIntosh, James S. to Susan Smith 9-14-1867 (9-15-1867)
McIntosh, Jas. S. to Lucy A. Walk 7-21-1866
McIntosh, William to Minnoy? Smith 7-29-1865
McIntyre, James to Mary Cooper 3-20-1843 (3-23-1843)
McIntyre, Thos. to Matilda Clay 7-3-1872 (7-4-1872)
McKenzie, John to Arelia David 5-10-1861 (7-8-1861)
McKeown, James to W. Drummond 2-8-1869 (2-10-1869)
McKinny, W. W. to Mary J. Delaney 8-3-1872 (8-4-1872)
McKinstry, Wm. to Eliza Ann Davis 12-16-1858
McKnight, John D. to Victoria A. Williams 3-9-1867 (3-14-1867)
McLain, Francis to Jane Sexton 7-25-1866 (8-20-1866)
McLain, William to Parthena A. M. Butler 8-9-1861 (8-10-1861)
McLaughlin, John to Nancy White 10-11-1854 (10-12-1854)
McLaughlin, R. W. to H. E. McDill 5-25-1871 (5-30-1871)
McLaughlin, W. R. to Mary E. McClerkin 3-7-1874 (3-18?-1874)
McLeary, Saml. D. to Sarah A. Weller 10-11-1841 (10-?-1841)
McLeary?, James Allen to Mary S. Weller 7-17-1855 (7-18-1855)
McLemore, Frank to Darcus Smith 12-12-1870 (12-15-1870)
McLennen, Daniel to Emer H. Adkins 12-23-1865 (12-26-1865)
McLennon, John to Susanna M. C. Adkins 1-24-1850
McLewain, R. G. to Laura L. Pullen 11-18-1858 (11-23-1858)
McLillie, James to Martha Jane C. Richardson 8-7-1871 (8-8-1871)
McLintock, Jas. L. to R. B. McCormick 5-6-1867
McLister, John C. to Mary Adaline Allen 11-21-1855 (11-22-1855)
McLoughland, John to Mary A. Strong 12-8-1860 (12-12-1860)
McLuster, J. C. to E. C. Faussette 7-10-1873 (7-11-1873)
McMallen, Thomas to Sarah E. Laxton? 1-26-1870 (1-27-1870)]
McMicken, John to Mary Bledsoe 12-26-1867
McMillan, Edward A. to Drucilla White 7-28-1841
McNair, Evander to Mary J. McBride 11-23-1860 (11-27-1860)
McNair, Hector to Eliza Parker 2-14-1852 (2-15-1852)
McNair, W. H. to Martha Carter 2-25-1860
McNaire?, Saml. to Martha A. Paten 5-3-1867
McNar, Z. H. to Martha Carter 2-25-1860
McNary, Willis to Frances Carothers 6-13-1866 (6-15-1866)
McNeal, Andrew to Mattie McGill 11-1-1873
McNeal, Isham G. to Jacinda? Gamewell 9-6-1867 (9-14-1869?)
McNeal, John S. to Lucy A. Townsend 11-23-1857 (11-26-1857)
McQuerter, David Hemphill to Nancy Jane Wham? 5-6-1853
McQuistian, Louis to Nancy McLain 9-16-1865
McQuistin, David H. to Margaret Wright 4-8-1843 (4-11-1843)
McQuiston, Alexander J. to Margaret G. McCain 12-16-1845
McQuiston, D. H. to Mary Ann Mcquiston 8-31-1870
McQuiston, H. W. to M. A. McDier? 2-26-1870 (3-1-1870)
McQuiston, Thomas to Sallie Robinson 12-19-1870 (12-24-1871?)
McQuiston, William H. to Sarah Wilson 9-26-1855
McQuiston, William sr. to Eliza Ann Baird 7-23-1844 (7-25-1844)
McWilliams, P. B. to Joanna Caskey 1-20-1869 (1-21-1869)
Mears, John G. to Eliza McGuise 12-24-1856 (1-1-1857)
Mears, John G. to Frances M. Tucker 6-18-1860 (6-29-1860)
Mears, William P. to Amy Bowles 1-17-1848 (1-?-1848)
Mears, William to Elzabeth Delashmet 11-21-1848 (11-22-1848)
Menasco?, John to Permelia Jane McClellan 3-8-1852
Menefee, W. O. to Martha E. Calhoun 11-14-1860 (11-15-1860)
Menes, Jacob C. to Rachael A. Hartsfield 7-3-1858
Menken, Peter to Bettie McFadden 7-23-1874 (7-24-1874)
Merrill, Burgis to Sallie Shaw 1-20-1864 (1-7?-1864)
Merrill, D. A. to Mary Miller 12-29-1856
Mill, Fred Augustus to Easter Jane Taylor 7-24-1867 (7-25-1867)
Millen, Henry to Ann Yarbro 11-19-1868
Miller (see Weller), to
Miller, Fred Marion to Nancy S. Smith 11-4-1850 (11-6-1850)
Miller, George W. to Elizabeth Monroe? 3-9-1841 (3-10-1841)
Miller, Isaac M. to Martha P. Wright 7-25-1855 (7-26-1855)
Miller, Jacob Hillman to Amanda Malvina Clark 12-21-1853 (12-22-1853)
Miller, James R. to A. Jackson 1-11-1865 (1-12-1865)
Miller, John F. to Eliza M. Miller 10-26-1869
Miller, John F. to Laura A. Payne 4-11-1871 (4-12-1871)
Miller, Joshua M. to Elizabeth Ann Mailey 7-28-1845 (8-1-1845)
Miller, Joshua M. to Nancy Ann Murphy 7-8-1847
Miller, Lee to Fannie Rhodes 1-9-1873
Miller, Lewis W. to ary Robinson 5-13-1844 (5-17-1844)
Miller, Robert to Harriet R. McCreight 9-5-1848 (9-7-1848)
Miller, Samuel B. to Eliza Ann Foster 2-19-1842 (2-27-1842)
Miller, W. G. to Eliza Huffman 12-9-1856 (12-11-1856)
Miller, William P. to Mary M. Forest 10-5-1858 (10-6-1858)
Miller, Wm. T. to Adaline Clark 1-13-1859
Mills, J. C. to Mary E. Solomon 9-2-1872 (9-6-1872)
Mills, J. C. to Mary J. McKenny 5-6-1868 (5-7-1868)
Mills, James to Anny Johnson 8-30-1866
Mills, Saml. J. to Mary E. Mills 8-28-1865
Milton, Frank to Ann L. Smith 12-27-1865
Mitchel, B. F. to Mary D. Searcy 5-19-1866 (5-25-1866)
Mitchel, Ben to Eliza Jane Elder 3-31-1873 (4-3-1873)
Mitchel, P. R. to L. Harris 1-30-1872 (1-31-1872)
Mitchell, George to Rosa Williams 8-9-1871 (8-10-1871)
Mitchell, Joshua Thomas to Mary Evans 8-16-1847 (8-17-1847)
Mitchell, Maurice to Mary Miller 9-5-1849 (9-9-1849)
Mitchell, Moses to Caroline Hawkins 12-19-1873
Mitchell, P. R. to Margaret Vanderver 1-4-1873 (1-5-1873)
Mitchell, Saml. D. to Malina Tinnan 9-5-1855 (9-8-1855)
Mitchell, William to Jane Stockley 5-27-1872 (6-14-1872)
Moffatt, Augustus P. to Nancy Jane McClurkin 2-6-1850
Moffatt, Wm. S. to Martha Jane Wilson 4-16-1856 (4-17-1856)
Moffet, J. C. to M. E. Simonton 9-20-1870
Moffett, Chas. Christopher to Margaret Jane Bonner 10-27-1855 (10-30-1855)
Moffett, David to Martha L. Strong 10-23-1867 (10-24-1867)
Monroe, George F. to Elizabet M. Williams 12-24-1873 (1-5-1874)
Monroe, Josiah A. to Indiana Deakins 3-23-1852 (3-25-1852)
Montgoery, Ross to Charlotte Coleman 8-23-1866 (8-26-1866)
Montgomery, A. J. to J. F. Flanakin 5-7-1868
Montgomery, A. J. to Mary Joyce 2-5-1866 (2-8-1866)
Montgomery, Alexander A. to Margaret Hamilton 12-29-1856 (12-30-1856)
Montgomery, Andrew to Lucinda Mears 5-19-1849 (5-20-1849)
Montgomery, Wm. to Mailsey Jane Trousdale no date (with 11-1874)

Moore, Covey to Amanda Dixon 12-1-1873 (12-3-1873)
Moore, David Fletcher to Susan Ann Sullivan 9-17-1844 (9-19-1844)
Moore, Henry to Lucinda Pile 6-25-1869
Moore, Henry to Martha J. Hannah 5-15-1855 (5-16-1855)
Moore, J. A. to M. J. McCain 12-3-1866 (12-4-1866)
Moore, J. W. to S. F. Adams 12-1-1874 (12-2-1874)
Moore, James A. to Margaret E. Wilson 5-14-1864 (5-16-1864)
Moore, James Chalmers to Sarah Ann Cousar? 11-5-1842 (11-8-1842)
Moore, James V. to Mary Campbell 9-18-1865 (9-19-1865)
Moore, Jasper to Catheran Phillips 3-1-1867 (3-16-1867)
Moore, John A. to Mary C. Easley 10-4-1842
Moore, John A. to Mary Jane McCluhen 11-31-1857 (12-1-1857)
Moore, John B. to Isabella Shelton 11-18-1847
Moore, John D. to S. E. Davidson 8-2-1872 (8-6-1872)
Moore, John to Catherine Wright 11-12-1869
Moore, Lum? Tho. to Octavia Shepherd 12-19-1855 (12-20-1855)
Moore, Melvil A. to Mary L. Moore 11-17-1869 (11-18-1869)
Moore, N. to M. Calhoun 12-22-1874 (12-24-1874)
Moore, R. R. to Mary Elizabeth Forrest 12-5-1874 (12-8-1874)
Moore, Russell to Mary Walker 3-20-1854 (3-21-1854)
Morehead, John Walter to Harriet Anderson Rice? 7-12-1843 (7-18-1843)
Morgan, Albert to Sallie Tipton 7-26-1866
Morgan, Arch to Mary Hill 3-15-1867 (7-4-1867)
Morgan, Ben to Sallie Robbs? 7-17-1871
Morgan, Edwin James to Martha Hill Stone 8-10-1852 (8-11-1852)
Morgan, Ephraim to Indy Tipton 1-11-1866
Morgan, J. T. to C. P. Patterson 10-30-1869 (11-3-1869)
Morgan, James to C. C. Dobson 12-20-1870 (12-22-1870)
Morgan, Jerie to Martha Bledsoe 12-30-1865
Morgan, Jerre to Martha Bledsoe 12-30-1865
Morgan, Jerry to Martha Bledsoe 12-30-1867 (12-30-1866?)
Morgan, John P. to Frances R. Allen 4-24-1866
Morgan, Robt. to Harriet Givens 8-20-1870
Morgan, W. T. to Nannie E. Morrison 12-11-1874
Morison?, John to Lucisa N. Phelps 8-12-1856 (8-14-1856)
Morrasett, J. R. to Martha Ann Huffman 1-8-1872 (1-9-1872)
Morris, Moses to Harriet Gilhan 1-1-1871? (1-1-1872)
Morris, Robert J. to Susanna L. Osborne 9-29-1849 (10-1-1849)
Morris, Thomas J. to Sallie E. Shepard 4-?-1871 (5-1-1871)
Morris, Wm. Wilson to Sarah Jane Clark 1-31-1866
Morrison, Alexander to Adaline Lynn 3-16-1869 (3-6?-1869)
Morrison, Archie to Sarah Jane Barnes 12-23-1872 (12-25-1873)
Morrison, Geo. to Mary Hall 12-2-1865
Morrison, Heb. C. to Miss M. E. Hill 3-28-1861
Morrison, Hugh to Lucinda Arnett 12-22-1869 (12-23-1869)
Morrison, Isaac to Adeline B. Mitchell 1-8-1849
Morrison, T. M. to Mary E. Mears 6-18-1861 (6-19-1861)
Morrison, Thomas to Sarah Clementine Monroe 3-6-1844 (3-7-1844)
Morrow, Josiah A. to Mildred N. Champion 9-3-1849 (9-6-1849)
Morrow, Josiah A. to Sarah E. Wilson 7-8-1847
Morrow?, Willis to Nancy Trobough 10-8-1873
Morse, Elihu to Sarah E. Weatherford 12-13-1865 (12-14-1865)
Morterson?, James H. to Rebecca J. Massey 2-20-1843 (3-15-1843)
Morton, John W. to R. V. Yarbroh 3-21-1865 (3-22-1865)
Mosley, Benj. A. to Mildred A. Parrish 10-7-1867 (10-16-1867)
Moss, Mason to Sophia C. Webb 7-3-1858 (7-4-1858)
Moten, Jerry to Bettie Angus 5-6-1867 (5-7-1867)
Moten, W. H. to M. A. Fleming 7-16-1867 (7-18-1867)
Motin, F. G. N. to Ann Archer 5-31-1858
Moton, John W. to R. V. Yarbroh 3-21-1865
Muehler, Frederick N. to Sarah H. Taylor 1-20-1844
Mullens, James M. to Delpha Jones 5-28-1873
Mullins, Jesse V. to America W. Oaks 8-29-1860 (8-31-1860)
Murchison, J. A. to L. C. Benson 1-27-1873 (1-29-1873)
Murchison, Micado to Jane E. Hood 2-4-1841 (3-15-1841)
Murphey, A. W. to Julia Ann Ewell 12-20-1869 (12-21-1869)
Murphey, Alexander to Mary Yount 1-12-1874 (1-13-1874)
Murphey, John E. to Rosa Ann Coats 2-7-1872 (2-8-1872)
Murphey, R. H. to Martha L. Marshall 9-30-1865
Murphey, W. H. to M. B. Malone 1-17-1870
Murphy, Alex to Frances E. Hartsfield 2-7-1859 (2-10-1857)
Murphy, Alexr. W. to Mary Jane Campbell 2-5-1851
Murphy, John W. to M. A. Haynie 5-11-1869
Murphy, Robt. J. to Martha Jane Seay 11-6-1852 (11-7-1852)
Murrin, James to L. P. Weathington 2-11-1860
Myers, Alfred A. to Sarah E. Maley 9-13-1855
Myers, J. W. to Hellen Smith 4-2-1874
Myers, John Carr to Frances Jane Wiseman? 2-25-1858
Myers, Rufus Wsh. to Evaline Grace 1-18-1853
Myers, Thomas to Louisa J. Maly 8-17-1869
Myers, W. N. to W. P. Larimore 2-18-1873 (2-20-1873)
Myers, sDaniel M. to Martha C. Hartsfield 12-28-1843
Myres, A. A. to Martha Goforth 2-22-1860
Napier, Walter to Virginia Maley 11-23-1872 (11-24-1872)
Neal, Samuel to Elizabeth Richards 4-13-1841
Nealey, Allen to Mary Jane Roark 12-2-1844
Nealey, Wm. to A. Hall 12-18-1874 (12-19-1874)
Needham, John to Margaret Donohoo 10-24-1867
Neeley, Jas. to Lizzie Hill 3-14-1874
Neeley, Taylor to Amanda Koonce 11-26-1874
Nelms, H. F. to Mary E. Pinkston 3-5-1870 (3-6-1870)
Nelson, Alex to Pamiel? Taylor 4-28-1866
Nelson, James C. to M. J. K. ____ 3-20-1860 (3-22-1860)
Nelson, James C. to Marth J. Kilpatrick 3-22-1860
Nelson, James C. to Martha Helperin? 3-20-1860
Nelson, Jonathan A. to Margaret Moore 8-17-1846 (8-18-1846)
Nelson, R. M. to Georga Carter 5-7-1872 (5-8-1872)
Neron?, Rainy to Matilda Gann 11-21-1871
Nevils, George M. to Ive Ann Deming 2-11-1871 (2-12-1871)
Newman, Pomp to Eliza Stafford 5-6-1867 (5-30-1867)
Newsom, J. T. to Shelley Knox 12-26-1872
Newton, Charles F. to C. D. Brinkley 9-5-1872 (9-8-1872)
Nichols, James to Eliza Ann Deason 7-19-1846
Nichols, W. M. to M. A. Miller 1-11-1865 (2-6-1865)
Nicholson, James E.? to Mrs. Mary A. Petty 10-21-1874
Nickleson, W. D. to Martha A. Goodman 11-15-1865
Nobles, George to Mary E. Wiseman 7-18-1866 (7-19-1866)
Noell, Chas. P. to Fannie S. Green 9-23-1873 (9-24-1873)
Northern, P. E. to Mary F. Maclin 3-4-1874 (3-5-1874)
Norton, Wm. Campbell to Estella Ann Pinson 9-7-1852
Nowel, W. C. to Mary E. Tate 1-15-1866 (1-17-1866)
O'Conor, Mulucky? to Mary O'Bryan 6-7-1871 (6-8-1871)
O'Mahony, John to Mary Barnett 5-21-1868 (5-23-1868)
Oates, Thomas J. to Eliza Stevens 6-8-1846
Obrien, William to Martha Loyd 1-29-1867 (1-31-1867)
Odam, William H. to Martha Jane Williams 12-16-1848 (12-20-1848)
Oglesby, John to Annie Wilson 11-4-1867 (11-5-1867)
Old, William A. to Cecilia Beverly Darby 1-30-1847 (2-?-1847)
Oldham, Chas. Thos. to E. J. Walker 3-18-1842
Olive, Henry to Anne Brown 12-19-1874 (12-20-1874)
Omara, Jerry to Ofilia Davis 1-8-1867
Orr, James to Sarah Glass 2-24-1869 (2-25-1869)
Oumage?, James W. to Mary Manaslk? no date (with 1868)
Overall, A. M. to Amanda Jane Williams 11-15-1869 (11-16-1869)
Overall, Albert L. to Ellen V. Bowers 4-27-1868 (4-28-1868)
Overall, Ed to Sallie Hemphill 1-31-1871 (2-1-1871)
Overall, George W. to Aggie J. Bowers 9-24-1867
Overall, James P. to Mary Owen 1-22-1867 (1-23-1867)
Owen, A. M. to L. A. Upchurch 1-15-1862
Owen, Alfred B. to Margaret Jane Billings 5-22-1844
Owen, Alfred B. to Matilda Elizabeth Wiseman 3-15-1849
Owen, Alfred W. to Mary A. Rice 10-30-1865 (11-2-1865)
Owen, David to Margaret English 3-9-1866
Owen, Isaac W. to S. Evolin Fortner 3-24-1862
Owen, J. A. to Namie Smith 12-4-1866
Owen, James H. to Jetty F. Ralph 4-16-1857
Owen, John to Malinda Sawyer? 12-26-1868 (12-27-1868)
Owen, Jos. R. to Milly Las? 1-23-1869 (1-24-1869)
Owen, Peter to Mary Sweeney 1-5-1867 (1-6-1867)
Owen, Richard B. to Sarah F. Walton 12-18-1867
Owen, Robert H. to Susanah Whitson 2-16-1859
Owen, Robert H. to Susanah Whitson 7-16-1859
Owen, S. Y. to Mary E. Brown 1-21-1869 (1-23-1869)
Owens, John to Ellen Bradshaw 12-31-1873
Pace, Benj. Franklin to Lowrana? Webb 1-26-1856 (1-29-1856)
Pace, John C. to Louisianna C. Smith 2-25-1847 (3-?-1847)
Pace, Kinchin to Mary Magdalin Hoke 5-6-1851
Pace, W. J. to Elizabeth Boswell 10-5-1857 (10-16-1857)
Paden, William to Jane H. McCanla 4-27-1840

Page, Alfred to Bettie A. Myers 7-24-1871 (7-26-1871)
Page, Lawrence to Artemisia Ann Montgomery 2-1-1851 (2-6-1851)
Page, William to Everline Myers 7-5-1866
Pain, Phil to Fanny Kent 8-25-1870
Palmer, Henry to P. A. Sadler 3-23-1867 (3-30-1867)
Palmer, Jesse to Matilda M. Parsons 4-15-1843 (4-16-1843)
Paremore, Daniel W. to Mary Thomas Stafford 8-8-1871
Parish, David M. to Sarah Ann Deakins 2-12-1853 (2-16-1853)
Parish, Joel Currin to Paulina A. Lamb 2-18-1849 (2-22-1849)
Parish, Thornton to Mary Jamison 8-12-1870 (8-13-1870)
Parker, A. P. to M. F. Howard 5-30-1871 (5-31-1871)
Parker, James P. to Eliza F. Green 1-4-1868 (1-5-1868)
Parker, James to Marth J. Carr 3-31-1843
Parker, R. A. jr. to Sarah Jane Flowers 5-24-1858 (5-25-1858)
Parker, Thos. to Harriet Daniel 8-1-1868 (8-3-1868)
Parker, William to Winnie L. Falanigan? 6-22-1871
Parrot, John H. to Sibbey Ellis 8-15-1850 (8-18-1850)
Parrot, Wm. to Elizabeth Knight 6-27-1858
Parsons, J. B. to Mary Smith 6-9-1866 (6-10-1866)
Parsons, J.B. to Margaret Scales 3-13-1872
Parsons, John B. to Mary Martin Lyles 9-30-1853 (10-2-1853)
Parsons, Thomas to Laura Ann Edwards 8-16-1850 (8-20-1850)
Pate, Geo. W. to Gyaura? Saunders 10-28-1874
Patten, Jessee to Lizzie Waggoner 10-12-1867 (10-13-1867)
Patten, John R. to Elizabeth J. Dunn 11-2-1857
Patten, John to Mariah Brown 10-17-1874
Patterson, Samuel to Mrs. Malissa Beverly 1-13-1870
Patterson, Thos. F. to Anna W. Holmes 10-25-1866
Payne, Daniel Wiley to Cora Dickson 11-12-1867 (11-14-1867)
Payne, Daniel to Elizabeth ANn Myers 9-3-1849
Payne, Friday to Cassa Harris 2-5-1870
Payne, G. W. to Sarah Fina McCoy 3-22-1860
Payne, Gilbert to Josephine Adkins 12-24-1868 (12-26-1868)
Payne, Henry to Nancy Alston 7-5-1873 (7-6-1873)
Payne, Isaac to Jennie Gant 10-9-1874
Payne, Isaac to Louisa Brooks 1-26-1867 (2-2-1867)
Payne, Isaac to Mary Yarbro 4-17-1869 (6-9-1869)
Payne, J. W. to M. J. Smith 2-20-1871 (3-7-1871)
Payne, James to Frances Jane Gorin 12-17-1850
Payne, John Booker to Sarah L. Foster 12-2-1863 (12-3-1863)
Payne, John L. to Mary Fannie McGregor 2-6-1861 (2-7-1861)
Payne, Richard T. to Elizabeth W. Rodgers 5-1-1854 (5-6-1854)
Payne, Saml. to Sallie McClelland 2-17-1866
Payne, V. L. to S. M. Barton 5-17-1873 (5-20-1873)
Payne, Wiley to Elizabeth Adkins 2-4-1841
Payne, William to M. F. Davis 9-6-1865 (9-7-1865)
Payton?, Lewis to Carusa Coffman 12-31-1873
Peebles, John Jarrett to Mary C. Haynie 2-24-1852
Peeler, W. L. to Ann E. McGuire 12-19-1865
Peeler, Willis to Anna Lee Williams 3-13-1874 (3-4?-1874)
Peete, Austin to V. Ann Miller 1-14-1873
Peete, Ed to Jennie Maclin 12-26-1870
Peete, Edwin Robert to Jane Eleanor Taylor 10-21-1851 (10-22-1851)
Peete, Ferry to Ann Peete 12-23-1865 (12-25-1865)
Peete, John S. to Ann E. Whitley 10-21-1844
Peete, Joseph to Sallie M. Whitley 10-3-1864 (10-5-1864)
Peete, Phillips to Mary Lucy Taylor 6-5-1867 (6-8-1867)
Peete, West to Bettie Clement 12-25-1873
Pennel, George W. to Sarah E. Crouch 1-14-1846 (1-15-1846)
Pennel, Thomas D. to Sarah E. Cultin 12-16-1858 (12-23-1858)
Pennel, Thos. D. to Sarah F. Farriss 8-10-1861 (8-14-1861)
Pennell, Francis Marion to Sarah Ann Timms? 1-1-1851 (1-4-1851)
Perry, Dr. A. to Miss Emma C. Day 11-12-1860 (11-13-1860)
Perry, G. W. to Elizabeth Campbell 8-8-1874 (8-17-1874)
Perry, M. to S. P. Day 2-6-1866
Person, W. E. to Mary C. Green 2-19-1862
Perwit?, James Willis to Amanda J. Bashears 9-6-1868 (9-7-1868)
Pete, Napolion to Cathran Day 3-26-1866 (3-31-1866)
Petty, Jas. H. to Mary A. Goodman 5-21-1867
Petty, Nathan to Nancy E. M. Tilley 10-22-1860
Pewett, Tom J. to Mary Ann Simmons 10-27-1861 (10-29-1861)
Pewitt, James C. to Harriet Murren 12-23-1840 (12-24-1840)
Pewitt, Wm. Pleasant to Virginia C. Locke 4-25-1852
Pews, Daniel to Charlett Trigg 7-2-1872 (7-13-1872)
Philips, John J. to Catherine Holsowser 8-16-1866 (8-17--1866)
Philips, John J. to Mary Eliza Rose 6-23-1857 (6-24-1857)
Philips, John James to Sarah Ann Rose 7-25-1849 (8-1-1849)
Phillips, A. F. to Lucy kA. Rogers 11-18-1871
Phillips, A. M. to Aubanett Green 10-7-1867 (10-10-1867)
Phillips, George to Caroline Faulk 1-1-1874 (1-2-1874)
Pierce, James to Mollie Herrin 10-25-1871 (10-26-1871)
Pierce, John to Mary L. Moore 5-8-1841
Pilkington, Saml. Woodfin to Elizabeth Ann Faris? 12-3-1851
Pinkston, G. C. to Anna J. Hunter 2-8-1871
Pinkston, George Croghan to Eliz. Ann Whitlock 3-19-1850
Pinkston, Jackson to Jane Miller 8-26-1871 (8-29-1871)
Pinner, J. W. to Margaret J. Draffin 1-3-1874 (1-15-1874)
Pinner, Sterling Harris to Margaret Forbus 12-22-1845
Pinner, Sterling to Eliza Yunt 12-31-1847 (1-7-1848)
Pinson, Archibald to Mary Culbreath 1-11-1841 (1-?-1841)
Pinson, J. W. to Mollie Clement 9-23-1872
Pippin, Benjamin to Ann Kendrick 10-30-1861
Pittman, A. W. C. to L. Jane Duncan 10-21-1872 (10-24-1872)
Poindexter, C. C. to Ella A. Shelton 11-15-1873 (11-18-1873)
Poindexter, Thos. H. to Sallie B. Hunt? 11-16-1872 (11-20-1872)
Poindexter, W. G. to Dora O. Hunt 11-16-1872 (11-20-1872)
Polk, Saml. to Eldora Cotherun 1-5-1870
Pollard, John L. to Lucy E. Weatherford 11-18-1867 (11-19-1867)
Pool, John W. to Sarah A. Morris 6-1-1872
Pool, John to Jane Miller 1-29-1868
Pool, John to Mary E. Robertson 5-12-1870
Pool, John to Mary Helen Baldock 12-26-1854 (12-28-1854)
Pool, Robert A. to Mary Hammon 2-10-1869
Pool, Wm. to Mary E. Gray 5-8-1854 (5-9-1854)
Porter, A. A. to N. M. Ivy 10-25-1865 (11-6-1865)
Porter, Alex to Harriet Boyd 1-4-1872 (1-15-1872)
Posey, Horace to R. A. McDowell 11-10-1870 (1-14-1871)
Prater, R. M. to Louisa Trim 9-12-1868 (9-15-1868)
Prehit, Fredrick to Jane Brown 1-18-1867
Prewett,, W. F. to Mollie E. Culbreath 12-15-1874
Price, John W. to Sarah E. James 5-9-1860 (5-15-1860)
Price, Wm. to Rener Calhoun 4-11-1874 (4-8?-1874) B
Prier, Bill to Rebecca Moore 2-12-1874 (2-13-1874)
Prince, John Y. to Cyntha V. Hudson 5-8-1862 (5-11-1862)
Prince, William J. to Tillie A. E. Daniel 4-6-1867 (4-9-1867)
Prince, Wm. Jasper to Ruby Elmira Gregory 9-12-1860 (9-13-1860)
Pryer, Isaac to Mariah Burchet 4-26-1870
Pryor, William Oscar to Laura Elizabeth Bernard 1-6-1850
Pugh, N. T. to Martha A. Billings 10-19-1867 (10-20-1867)
Pugh, T. M. to Nanna Cavnaugh 8-1-1872 (8-4-1872)
Pullen, William A. to Susan A. Thomas 2-20-1868
Pullin, Aaron to Mary Sadler 11-26-1865 (11-6?-1865)
Pullin, Edmond to Mollie Borum 11-19-1872
Pullin, John B. to Christina E. Roan 10-30-1865 (10-31-1865)
Pullin, Richard to N. A. Wooten 2-4-1867 (2-15-1867)
Pullin, William to Amanda Ann Johnson 3-5-1868
Quimmly, John Allen to Harriet Jane Eliz. Faris 9-26-1853 (9-27-1853)
Quin, James L. to Elizabeth L. Jones 9-23-1873 (9-25-1873)
Rachels, Nathan to Sarah Weaver 8-19-1852
Ragens, W. J. to N. E. White 10-5-1868 (10-8-1868)
Rainer, Joseph Sutton to Sarah Mainer 3-22-1842 (10-?-1842)
Ralph, Alfred H. to Orlenia McCraw 8-6-1855 (8-16-1855)
Ralph, Canter B. to Margaret J. Grant 9-12-1855
Ralph, Hiram H. to Eleanor W. Owen 12-8-1846 (12-10-1846)
Ralph, James W. to Lucinda E. Johnson 8-5-1854 (8-27-1854)
Ralph, John Ligon to Malvina Sylvester 9-24-1851
Ralph, Robert H. to Margaret F. Maley 2-17-1870 (2-20-1870)
Ralph, Robert H. to Nancy E. Delashmit 8-8-1871 (8-10-1871)
Ralph, Thoas to Mary Ann Brown? 12-2-1843
Ralph, William to Elizabeth Dagling 11-7-1866 (11-8-1867?)
Ralph, William to Grizzy Ann Branch 8-4-1841
Ramsey, John to Ellen McFerren 6-9-1869
Randolph, John to Betty Alston 7-28-1871 (7-18?-1871)
Randolph, John to Fannie Dickson 5-15-1867 (5-18-1867)
Randolph, Johnb to Mary _____ 5-20-1869
Ravenall, A. to Miss R. S. Kimbro 1-7-1861 (1-8-1861)
Ray, Elisha B. to Mary Susan Lake 1-27-1852 (1-28-1852)
Ray, Saml. to Martha J. Gray 7-16-1870 (7-17-1870)
Ray, Wm. G. to Bettie A. Malone 11-15-1852 (11-18-1852)

Raynor, Lawrence to Elizabeth Coats 9-4-1861 (9-5-1861)
Rayond, Archer to Bettie Harris 10-2-1869
Read, Evans to Mary Johnson 1-4-1873 (1-6-1873)
Read, F. T. to A. E. Pace 12-18-1871 (12-20-1871)
Read, John T. to N. J. Read 12-30-1869
Read, Peter to Jane Miller 7-7-1866
Reaves, W. B. to E. C. Carother 3-29-1866 (4-5-1866)
Redden, G. W. to Mary Trimm? 9-?-1874 (9-22-1874)
Reddick, George to Harrit Maclin 12-31-1870 (1-2-1871)
Redditt, George W. to Malinda J. Roberts 11-6-1866 (11-8-1866)
Reed, C. L. to Martha Reed 9-11-1866 (9-19-1866)
Reese, Zachariah to Malinda Starr 10-13-1841 (10-15-1841)
Reid, Booker to Hanner Jones 3-10-1874
Reid, Jno. D. to Susan L. Flemming 1-1-1866
Reynolds, Norman to Mary Elizabeth Darby 6-26-1850
Reynolds, Wm. C. to Amanda Sloss 1-13-1857 (1-22-1857)
Rhodes, Alexander to Elizabeth Smith 8-19-1869
Rhodes, Clink to Emma Mathis 12-25-1871 (12-26-1871)
Rhodes, Daniel Mordecai to Mary Jane Townsend 8-11-1846 (8-?-1846)
Rhodes, Isaac to Maria Jackson 12-16-1874
Rhodes, Isaac to Rena Lake 12-10-1868
Rhodes, J. C. to Margaret Fleming 1-23-1861 (1-24-1861)
Rhodes, James Cicero to Sarah ANn Townsend 7-23-1844 (7-?-1844)
Rhodes, James to Henrietta Howard 4-28-1868 (5-2-1868)
Rhodes, Mansfield to Martha Ann Trusdale 11-6-1869 (11-7-1869)
Rhodes, Osborn to Hannah Johnston 9-12-1867 (9-22-1867)
Rhodes, Saml. to Elizabeth Williamson 10-27-1866 (12-1-1866)
Rhodes, Saml. to Grace Somervill 9-30-1869
Rhodes, Solomon A. to Henrietta B. Bradshaw 12-21-1846 (12-23-1846)
Rhodes, Thornton to Nancy Leach 10-4-1851 (10-5-1851)
Rhodes, Willis to Mary Taylor 8-30-1870
Rice, Cyrus C. to Martha V. Feezor 1-30-1859
Rice, J. J. to Sallie A. Calhoun 12-6-1866
Rice, James C. to Sallie Wormik 1-5-1872 (1-10-1872)
Rice, Joseph to Tempe Hunt 1-3-1866? (1-5-1867)
Rice, Robert A. to Martha J. McBride 1-?-1867 (1-16-1867)
Rice, Robt. A. to Mary A. Austin 12-17-1871 (12-19-1871)
Rice, Thomas to Mary Stitt 9-26-1873 (10-6-1873)
Rice, William Daniel to Mary Ann Roberts 7-26-1847 (7-?-1847)
Rice, Wm. J. to Eliza E. Griffith 12-21-1868 (12-22-1868)
Richard, Alfred to Jane Turnage 1-14-1871
Richards, Solomon to Maria Johnson 11-21-1871
Richardson, Dick to Susan Veneer 5-9-1874
Richardson, E. to Susanna Wormick 11-29-1866
Richardson, George to Margaret C. Rogers 9-4-1873 (9-14-1873)
Richardson, Henry to Elizabeth Killy 2-20-1868 (2-25-1868)
Richardson, J. to Nancy C. Hill 1-7-1860
Richardson, John to Malina Clemmit 11-27-1874
Richardson, M. T. to S. T. Culbreath 7-16-1872 (7-20-1872)
Richardson, Ned to Sallie Gainer 5-8-1872
Richardson, Shed to Ann Tool 9-5-1871
Richardson, Simeon to Mary Wilson 5-8-1874
Richardson, Solaman to Susan Roberts 7-18-1874 (7-22-1874)
Richardson, W. H. to Eva M. Alston 8-31-1868 (9-2-1868)
Richardson, William to Melvinia Littlejohn 1-4-1873
Riche, Jessee to Elizabeth Alston 4-29-1868 (5-21-1868)
Richerson, Patrick to Polly Hunt 1-13-1866
Richmond, J. H. C. to Sarah T. Bashears 8-7-1865 (8-8-1865)
Riley, James G. to V. L. Shankle 1-1-1866
Rives, Richard H. to Eulah H. Thomas 11-15-1873 (11-18-1873)
Roane, Albert to Mrs. Salina Walker 7-19-1867 (7-21-1867)
Roane, Sterling S. to Mary Sharp 4-28-1841 (4-27?-1841)
Roane, Thos. W. to Mary Hillen Somervill 11-13-1858 (11-17-1858)
Robb, J. V. to Nancy C. Jacobbs 9-4-1869
Roberson, James D. to L. E. Corbet 11-24-1869 (11-25-1869)
Roberts, George to Mary Macklin 12-19-1867
Roberts, Isham B. to Susan E. Horne 9-18-1848 (9-19-1848)
Roberts, James W. to Elizabeth Appleberry 2-22-1869 (2-24-1869)
Roberts, Joseph L. to Mary Susan Davis 12-8-1852 (12-9-1852)
Roberts, M. to Fannie Clements 8-17-1867 (8-18-1867)
Roberts, Samuel to Lucinda Roach 3-15-1852 (3-22-1852)
Roberts, Thomas Wesley to Frances Betcy Bays 9-10-1857 (9-11-1857)
Roberts, W. J. to Mary A. Clements 11-6-1865 (12-5-1865)
Roberts, Wm. Jas. to Lucinda Webb 4-11-1855
Robertson, Bill to Eliza Somervill 12-16-1865 (12-25-1865)
Robertson, Frank to Joanah Howard 7-31-1868 (8-1-1868)
Robertson, Lafayette to Mary Crenshaw 12-28-1868
Robertson, Loyd to Lucy Jane Taylor 12-28-1868
Robinett, W. B. to Sarah Ann Hanegin 5-9-1846 (5-12-1846)
Robinson, Andrew to Ann Wood 9-7-1866 (9-16-1866)
Robinson, Jack to Hannah Somervell 12-8-1866 (12-9-1866)
Robinson, Jerry to Elizabeth Logan 1-12-1872 (1-17-1872)
Robinson, John K. to Jane? Faulk 10-28-1841
Robinson, Moses to Martha Clements 10-17-1871
Robinson, William to Virginia Taylor 12-8-1845 (12-17-1845)
Robinson, Wm. B. to Laura B. Pettie 3-8-1870 (3-10-1870)
Rode, Adam to Miss Mary Ann Townsend 5-20-1874
Rodgers, W. E.? to Ann E. Lambert 9-21-1864 (10-25-1864)
Roe, John to Fannie Page 8-29-1874 (8-30-1874)
Roe, Saml. to Amanda C. Wood 1-4-1869 (1-5-1869)
Roe, Samuel to Jane Harrison 6-24-1851 (6-26-1851)
Roe, William Joseph to Franky Jane Shankle 8-17-1867 (8-18-1867)
Rogers, George W. to Elizabeth W. Turnage 1-11-1841 (1-12-1841)
Rogers, J. V. B. to Frances A. Clevies 2-24-1869 (2-25-1869)
Rogers, Sampson to Elizabeth Stokes 11-7-1853 (11-15-1853)
Rogers, W. J. to Amanda Williams 5-11-1865 (5-12-1865)
Roland, Jacob to Sarah Elizabeth Malone 10-29-1874 (10-31-1874)
Rollins, George to Mary Harris 3-9-1871
Rollins, William H. to Manerva F. Harris 6-1-1867 (6-2-1867)
Rose, Edmond to Eliza Jones 11-24-1866
Rose, Erasmus to Mary Goforth 12-20-1853 (12-21-1853)
Rose, James to Mary Fannin Newman 10-28-1856 (10-29-1856)
Rose, John Thomas to Susan E. Phillips 2-14-1854
Rose, John W. to Mary M. Walton 4-21-1858
Rose, John W. to Urilda C. Tally 4-25-1867
Rose, Robert A. to Elizabeth Ford 7-19-1869 (7-20-1869)
Rose, Sam? P. to Mildred L. Boyd 4-12-1871
Rose, Samuel J. to Dorothy Ann Jones 5-27-1847 (5-28-1847)
Ross, Anthony to M. Miller 12-29-1869 (12-30-1869)
Ross, George to Emaline Hall 2-24-1866
Ross, John to Susan Carothers 8-8-1870
Ross, Thomas J. to Theodocia E. Farington 5-13-1858
Rowland, John to Mary E. Dickerson 8-22-1850
Rucker, Alfred C. to Mary N. Philips 11-4-1854 (11-8-1854)
Rudd, James to Bettie Reece 2-26-1873 (2-27-1873)
Runnels, Granville to Adelia Montgomery 4-29-1871 (5-2-1871)
Runnels, Wm. to Eliza Dogget 5-5-1869 (5-9-1869)
Russel, Jno. K. to Eva L. Douglas 5-19-1869
Russell, W. B. to Ellen F. Schooley 3-4-1869 (3-7-1869)
Rutherford, Charles to Millie Williams 11-13-1873
Rutherford, John C. to Sallie Hill 12-18-1873 (12-17?-1873)
Rutherford, Lewis to Ellen Hill 10-21-1869 (10-22-1869)
Rutherford, Thomas H. to Hettie L. Bernard 10-18-1869 (10-19-1869)
Ryan, John V. to Flavia Phillips 3-30-1871 (4-4-1871)
Sadden?, Phill to Lucy Bradshaw 12-24-1869 (1-9-1870)
Sadler?, Rihd. to Maria Cockrill 10-7-1867 (10-13-1867)
Sale, G. B. to Lola Wooten 11-16-1869 (11-17-1869)
Sale, Thomas to Susan Williams 12-19-1870 (12-25-1870)
Sanford, Bailey to Susan G. Hill 1-6-1865
Sanford, Ben J. to Sue M. Taylor 10-29-1873 (10-30-1873)
Sanford, James R. to Ann D. Tipton 2-9-1859
Sanford, Louis to Elizabeth Flemming 12-17-1865 (12-28-1865)
Sanford, Louis to Harriet Ligon 4-17-1868 (4-18-1868)
Sanford, Nathan to Leeva? Caruthers 10-2-1873
Sanford, Nelson to Mary Somerville 3-30-1867 (3-31-1867)
Sanford, Saml. W. to Rozelle Tipton 12-2-1874
Sanford, William to Bettie Douglas 1-17-1867
Sanford?, Saml. Crawford to Eliz. Lucretia Elmore 11-22-1855
Sargent, G. W. to J. Merrill 4-5-1871 (4-9-1871)
Saunders, Richman to Mary Taylor 1-7-1872
Sawyers, Joel to Sarah Bennett 9-20-1873 (9-21-1873)
Sawyers, John J. to Sarah Peacock 9-27-1867 (9-28-1867)
Saxton, James W. to Eliza Ann Curtis 11-21-1844
Scarbrough, John G. to Katie A. Malone 4-1-1872 (4-2-1872)
Scarbrough, L. A. to Edna E. Malone 3-21-1866 (3-22-1866)
Scarimon?, Robt. to Lou Mullin 6-3-1867 (6-1?-1867)
Schmeller, John to Caroline Zimmermann 11-19-1858
Schooley, James K. to Frances Eleanor Pendergrass 1-1-1850

Scott, G. T. to M. A. Neil 5-26-1869
Scott, James E. to Rosa Brigman 7-17-1873 (7-18-1873)
Scott, John to Fany Smith 6-19-1869
Scott, John to Mariah Cooke 2-27-1871 (3-2-1871)
Scott, Peter to Elizabeth Gardner 7-28-1858 (8-1-1858)
Scott, Samuel B. to Mary Williams 12-17-1845 (12-19-1845)
Scott, Thomas F. to Virginia L. Bragg 11-2-1870 (11-3-1870)
Scurry, Jacob to Mary Glass 11-8-1873
Scurry, Louis to Lyda Jones 1-11-1866
Searcy, Robert to Susan Ann Stevens 8-3-1851 (8-10-1851)
Sears, Alexander to Mary Stevens 7-31-1869
Selfridge, William H. to Martha Starnes 10-2-1849 (10-3-1849)
Settle, John Calvin to Martha Ann Twisdale 6-22-1850 (6-25-1850)
Sexton, Frank to Caroline Trigg 9-18-1871 (9-25-1871)
Shackleford, Wm. to Henrietta Dickens 12-16-1868 (12-25-1868)
Shaf, J. H. to T. A. Laremore 7-27-1874 (7-29-1874)
Shankle, Edward to S. C. Hartsfield 6-4-1860 (6-14-1860)
Shankle, Edward to Susan E. Ewell 9-4-1855 (9-6-1855)
Shankle, Jacob to Mary Hinds 7-20-1853
Shankle, James T. to Laura Mitchell 8-24-1869 (8-29-1869)
Shankle, Terrell to Elizabeth Evans 1-1-1842
Shantly, Jefferson to Indiana Freeman 9-17-1866 (9-19-1866)
Sharp, Christopher Col. to Ann Jane Ligon 9-6-1854
Sharp, Granderson to Mary C. Whitlock 2-4-1868 (2-5-1868)
Sharp, James R. to Mary L. Sheffield 3-12-1850
Sharp, James R. to Mary Siler 11-10-1858
Sharp, John to Viney Stevens 9-15-1866 (9-22-1866)
Sharp, Saml. to Sallie Boyd 5-11-1872 (5-12-1872)
Shaw, A. W. to S. E. Hunter 1-29-1869 (1-30-1869)
Shaw, Daniel E. to Martha Shaw 11-24-1865 (11-?-1865)
Shaw, Elizah C. to Pearl F. Russell 8-23-1873 (8-24-1873)
Shaw, Isaac to K. Whitley 12-22-1870
Shaw, Phillip to Pennie Burl 12-5-1874
Shaw, William to Mary Williams 5-8-1871 (5-11-1871)
Shelton, Elijah to Mary Grimes 9-10-1866 (9-16-1866)
Shelton, George W. to M. J. Sawyers 10-13-1873
Shelton, James B. to Lue Thompson 10-30-1867 (10-31-1867)
Shelton, Jno. M. to F. M. Walk 11-27-1873
Shelton, John W. to Bettie J. Reatherford 1-30-1861
Shelton, Lemuel to Milly Dyson 8-18-1866
Shelton, Richard to Luiza Ward 12-27-1871 (12-28-1871)
Shelton, Saml. R. to Sallie B. Rutherford 5-4-1857 (5-5-1857)
Shepard, Jas. R. to Susan Steviss? 9-13-1871
Shepard, Robt. to Amy Wood 11-4-1865 (11-6-1865)
Sherill, J. G. to Mary B. Dacus 8-8-1860
Sherrell, Nelson to Annie Williams 12-11-1871 (12-14-1871)
Sherrill, Amus to Ellen Alston 9-23-1869 (9-26-1869)
Sherrill, Enos Alexander to Ceelin Ethalinda Hall 4-7-1845 (4-16-1845)
Sherrill, F. J. to Lenny Fleming 11-4-1868
Sherrill, Francis J. to Mary E. Forsythe 11-15-1871
Sherrill, George Washington to Caroline Thomas 12-26-1866 (12-27-1866)
Sherrill, George to Emma Johnson 12-25-1873
Sherrill, Hosea W. to Catharine M. Bledsoe 4-1-1850 (4-3-1850)
Sherrill, Jerry to Nancy Holland 3-2-1874
Sherrill, Jessee to Henrietta Alston 10-14-1874
Sherrill, Wm. E. to E. E. Hall 2-8-1866
Sherrod, Jno. G. to Nia Sherrod 12-26-1865 (12--29-1865)
Sherrod, John J. to Lucinda C. Smith 5-13-1857
Sherrod, Joshua to Elizabeth Morgan 12-24-1866 (12-29-1866)
Sherrod, Lumon to Emily Clements 1-5-1867 (1-6-1867)
Sherrod, Soloman to Florence Bond 12-25-1866
Sherrod, Vernas? to Susan McCall 12-29-1866
Siler, John M. to Ann M. Hooks 2-2-1848
Silvers, John S. to Martha J. Lewellen 5-11-1858
Silvertooth, Jacob to Callie H. McFadden 2-14-1871
Simmons, Benj. K. to Sarah A. Dennis 2-17-1868 (2-18-1868)
Simmons, E. Z. to Maggie D. McClamick 11-23-1870
Simmons, James to Emerline Morrison 11-28-1868 (11-30-1868)
Simmons, Tom to Polly Bragg 12-26-1868 (1-1-1869)
Simmons, Wm. to Elizabeth Prewitt 12-23-1852
Simmonton, Charles B. to Mary A. McDill 10-15-1866 (10-16-1866)
Simons, Samuel Darby to Nancy Emaline Harrison 7-22-1845 (7-?-1845)
Simonton, Alex to Hanna Ellis 10-7-1873 (10-9-1873)
Simonton, C. J. to N. E. Thompson 7-24-1865 (7-25-1865)
Simonton, Christopher A. to Margaret C. Thompson 2-5-1848 (2-10-1848)
Simonton, Christopher to artha Baird 8-31-1853
Simonton, Henry to Nancy McQuiston 7-3-1871 (7-4-1871)
Simonton, John to Martha A. Miller 5-18-1847 (5-21-1847)
Simonton, R. C. to Martha E. Wilson 9-5-1859
Simonton, R. R. to Mary Huffman 2-8-1870
Simonton, Robert to Margaret McQuiston 9-4-1855
Simonton, William B. to Eliza A. Miller 12-18-1866 (12-19-1866)
Simonton?, Archibald M. to Lotty Strong 2-19-1842 (3-3-1842)
Simpson, George to Mary Ann Dalton 1-9-1854 (1-12-1854)
Simpson, Jesse to Martha Ann Simpson 7-31-1872 (8-1-1872)
Simpson, William P. to Mary Ann White 12-11-1858 (12-13-1858)
Singleton, Washington to Margaret Pickard 2-28-1872 (3-9-1872)
Sink, Jacob H. to Tobitha A. Gaither 12-2-1848 (12-6-1848)
Sitton, Isham to Sindey Foster 4-24-1874
Skiles, Thomas W. to Jane Richardson 12-20-1858
Slack, C. F. to Frances F. Flemming 9-8-1866
Slate, W. R. to Caroline c. Hainie 12-7-1858 (12-9-1858)
Slate, W. R. to S. A. Elam 11-13-1866 (11-14-1866)
Slaughter, Bill to C. Boston 12-28-1874
Slaughter, David Cannon to Susan America Ovnall? 7-15-1850 (7-?-1850)
Slaughter, Dennis to Elvira Kinney 9-23-1851 (9-25-1851)
Slaughter, Gabriel J. to Elizabeth Glover Fisher 3-6-1849
Slone, M. A. to Elizabeth Trobaugh 12-22-1874 (12-23-1874)
Small, Henry to Vicey Lorimore 2-8-1872
Small, Joshua to Allace Smith 5-12-1873
Small, Peter to Rody Alexander 8-13-1867
Smith, A. P. to Annie Maurring? 12-1-1869
Smith, Albert to Jane Rose 1-18-1869 (1-19-1869)
Smith, Albert to Susan Miller 2-21-1873 (2-22-1873)
Smith, Alexander to Hannah Smith 5-10-1852
Smith, Alford to Cathrine Moran 5-27-1854 (5-28-1854)
Smith, Andrew to Louisa Winford 4-27-1870
Smith, Augustus W. to Mary E. Yarbrough 9-29-1845 (10-2-1845)
Smith, Benjamin Franklin to Delitha Coats 12-22-1873 (12-23-1873)
Smith, Bradford to Cynthia Couts? 3-24-1842
Smith, Burton L. to Fannie Farrar 12-19-1868
Smith, Casper M. to Sarah Smith 2-27-1844
Smith, Charles E. to Mildred E. Malone 9-20-1853 (9-22-1853)
Smith, Charles to Katie Burrel 12-17-1873
Smith, Chas. G. to Catherine E. Smith 1-13-1870
Smith, D. H. to Mary J. Rhodes 2-6-1869 (2-7-1869)
Smith, D. H. to Sallie O. Goodman 5-2-1871 (5-3-1871)
Smith, D. to Rachel Paden 9-23-1871 (9-26-1871)
Smith, Dabney to Tennessee Lunford 1-14-1873 (1-16-1873)
Smith, Dan to Nancy Lowe 12-7-1871 (12-9-1871)
Smith, Daniel? to Hannah Clark 11-24-1869 (11-25-1869)
Smith, David H. to Polly Smith 2-4-1841
Smith, Elias to Mary Jane Farrow 6-5-1868
Smith, Ephm. to Allice Smith 1-2-1868
Smith, Ephraim Hall to Susan Elizabeth Collier 10-16-1851
Smith, F. L. to M. J. Cheek 9-5-1871 (9-6-1871)
Smith, Fenton to Livia? Alston 10-5-1874
Smith, Frank to Ann Cotherin 12-2-1869 (12-3-1869)
Smith, G. T. to M. B. Yarbro 11-19-1872 (11-20-1872)
Smith, George W. to Parale Linder 2-14-1872
Smith, George W. to Virginia E. Smith 10-30-1867
Smith, George to Delia Ann Smith 7-1-1868 (7-19-1868)
Smith, George to Lucy Bernard 1-4-1868
Smith, Giles to Everline Pullim 10-27-1866 (10-28-1866)
Smith, Giles to Margaret Chambers 4-25-1873 (4-26-1873)
Smith, Green to Ann Eliza Pewitt 2-15-1865
Smith, Harrison to Florence Gilland 9-5-1872
Smith, Hemphill to Margaret Jane Thompson 11-13-1867
Smith, Henry to Ann Douglass 12-30-1865
Smith, Henry to Margaret Miller 1-12-1846 (1-15-1846)
Smith, Henry to Maud Hunter Jacob 4-18-1873
Smith, Isaac to Martha Clark 3-1-1870 (3-2-1870)
Smith, J. D. to N. W. Turnage 1-7-1861 (1-10-1861)
Smith, J. E. to Amanda F. Fleming 10-24-1874 (10-25-1874)
Smith, J. F. to M. J. Atkins 11-20-1872

Smith, Jack to Eliza T. Smith 1-4-1869
Smith, Jackson to Susan Jones 10-17-1874 (10-20-1874)
Smith, Jacob F. to Samuella McIntosh 10-24-1867
Smith, Jacob to Elanor Wiseman 8-17-1841
Smith, James A. to Jessie E. Curry 12-31-1870 (1-2-1871)
Smith, James G. to Sarah Eliza Allen 1-2-1854
Smith, James N. to Julia Catharine Turnage 4-17-1850
Smith, James S. to Jane W. Tennant 8-5-1858
Smith, James Spencer to Susan McClelland 2-9-1853 (2-15-1853)
Smith, Jas. M> to Harriet E. Yarbroh 2-7-1864
Smith, John A. to Jerusah D. Walker 10-25-1859 (10-28-1859)
Smith, John Douglas to Sadie (Sallie?) Cage 7-21-1874
Smith, John E. to Malinda Harris 4-10-1848 (4-15-1848)
Smith, John H. to Susan Smith 12-22-1858 (12-23-1858)
Smith, John W. to Elizabeth E. Searcey 12-4-1866 (12-5-1866)
Smith, John to Ann Pool 9-26-1870
Smith, John to Margaret Bringle 1-1-1873 (1-2-1873)
Smith, John to Mildred Smith 12-29-1868 (12-31-1868)
Smith, John to Sarah Ann Clark 1-26-1843 (1-?-1843)
Smith, John to Sina Wagner 1-15-1874
Smith, Joseph to Sinora Fields 5-24-1871
Smith, L. B. to Catharine R. Bowers 1-23-1861 (1-24-1861)
Smith, L. B. to Nancy Dickey 5-11-1874 (5-13-1874)
Smith, Leonard Brantlin to Caroline Bowers 10-2-1848 (10-4-1848)
Smith, Leroy to Flora Sherrill 10-6-1870
Smith, Manuel to Milley Archer 8-30-1866 (8-31-1866)
Smith, Moses to Celia Sherrid 8-4-1866
Smith, Moses to Frances M. Campbell 3-10-1845 (3-17-1845)
Smith, Needham to Becka Walton 4-14-1874 (4-15-1874)
Smith, Oliver to Sarah Billing 12-13-1867
Smith, Peter Perkins to Elizabeth Moore 6-6-1845 (6-15-1845)
Smith, Phill to Claricy Trigg 7-2-1872 (9-30-1872)
Smith, R. C. to Hattie Cocke 6-12-1867
Smith, R. P. to Mary Jane Bragg 8-7-1857
Smith, Robert W. to Minerva Jane McGuire 1-24-1852 (1-28-1852)
Smith, Robert to Ann Rlayner 3-8-1867 (3-9-1867)
Smith, Robert to Louisa Brooks 1-6-1868
Smith, Robert to Martha Jane Dobson 12-11-1867
Smith, S. R. to Hariet L. Rice 2-27-1866 (2-28-1866)
Smith, S. R. to Jane Maley 6-20-1872
Smith, Saml. Robert to Nancy Smith 1-13-1844 (1-14-1844)
Smith, Saml. to Annie? Archer 4-5-1871
Smith, Sandy to Sylva Smith 9-6-1869 (9-7-1869)
Smith, Scott to Rebecca Payne 12-3-1872 (12-4-1872)
Smith, Solomon to Susan Bledsoe 1-28-1870
Smith, Stephen to Mary Ann Cole 2-3-1844 (2-8-1844)
Smith, Thos. J. to Sarah F. Hatchell 2-19-1870 (2-20-1870)
Smith, W. E. to F. M. Kinney 12-10-1872 (12-11-1872)
Smith, Washington to Maggie Bunton 3-15-1871
Smith, Watkin? to Fannie Dyson 11-9-1872 (11-15-1872)
Smith, William D. to Caroline A. Palmer 7-25-1868 (7-26-1868)
Smith, William to Angelin Winston? 7-9-1869
Smith, William to Susan Smith 1-15-1868
Smith, Wm. Henry to Jane Mildred Black 11-13-1852 (11-16-1852)
Smith, Wm. to Elizabeth Coats 3-30-1872 (4-14-1872)
Smitheal, Green W. to Florence S. Menefee 10-27-1870
Smithin, Wilkins to Ann Taylor 12-22-1868
Smithson, John M. to Anne Hassler 11-7-1872
Snelling, Rubin to Rachal Green 12-10-1870
Snider, Jonathan to Missouri A. Marsh 1-15-1849 (12-24-1848?)
Sodden?, Phill to Lucy Bradshaw 12-24-1869
Somervill, A. C. to M. B. Somervill 10-10-1859 (10-11-1859)
Somervill, Charles to Tinah Sumervill 12-27-1867
Somervill, Richard B. to Virginia Triplett Taylor 3-13-1847 (3-16-1847)
Somerville, John M. to Ellin G. Somerville 8-3-1868 (8-4-1868)
Somerville, John to Catherin Luster 3-22-1869 (3-24-1869)
Somerville, John to Nerva Locket 2-16-1874 (2-25-1874)
Sommerville, Ben to Ellen Simmons 10-18-1870
Sommerville, R. B. to Elizabeth T. Hunt 1-9-1853 (1-12-1853)
Sommerville, W. F. to Mary Sommervill 12-28-1865 (12-30-1865)
Spencer, Dabna to Sallie Bowers 11-9-1874
Spencer, Jonathan to Nancy A. Moore 9-3-1860 (9-5-1860)
Spencer, Jonathan to Nancy A. Moore 9-5-1860
Spesard, Charles M. to Elizabeth Archer 12-29-1866 (12-30-1866)
Stanford, William to Isabel Tinnen 5-18-1867 (5-19-1867)
Stanup?, Hamilton to Canna? Cage 5-8-1869 (2-19-1871?)
Stanus, John Wesley to Mary E. Manasco 9-6-1860 (9-13-1860)
Staret, William to Mary M. Farmer 1-10-1867
Staritt, John to Frances D. Rhodes 5-16-1865
Starling, William Shadrach to Mary Quimmly? 7-20-1846 (7-30-1846)
Starnes, A. Pinckney to Ann Boothe 3-23-1844
Starnes, H. C. to Mary M. Manasco 3-7-1865 (3-8-1865)
Starnes, Harvey C. to Delila M. Shultz 6-1-1867 (6-2-1867)
Starnes, J. R. to Josephine Stokes 7-20-1853 (7-21-1853)
Starnes, James to D. Ann Davidson 3-13-1866 (3-14-1866)
Starnes, John W. to Sarah Johnson 12-2-1867 (12-4-1867)
Starnes, Wm. to Nancy Timms 7-9-1860 (7-12-1860)
Staton, Wm. F. to Martha S. H. Gray 6-3-1867 (6-6-1867)
Stearns, John to Martha Massey no date (with 1862)
Steele, John to Margaret L. Wilson 1-6-1845 (1-9-1845)
Stegall, W. L. to Mary M. McIlwaine 4-16-1872
Stephens, J. M. to Jane Joyner 11-26-1874 (11-27-1874)
Stephens, Lawrence to Margaret Siser? 12-4-1854 (12-15-1854)
Steven, W. A. to Mary Shelton 9-18-1869 (9-19-1869)
Stevens, Andrew to Rebecca Ann Gendren 8-20-1845 (8-21-1845)
Stevens, Edmond to Amand Winn? 1-27-1873 (1-28-1873)
Stevens, G. H. to Elizabeth Joyner 10-24-1856
Stevens, Haywood to Nancy J. Rose 12-17-1851 (12-18-1851)
Stevens, Henry to Winny Hall 12-28-1870 (12-29-1870)
Stevens, J. H. to Mary A. Feezor 1-3-1865
Stevens, J. M. to M. E. Stokes 2-26-1872
Stevens, James to Marth E. McBride 4-3-1867
Stevens, Joel to Martha Ann Stevens 8-18-1852 (8-19-1852)
Stevens, John B. to Mary Williams 3-22-1850
Stevens, John to Anna? Beavers 5-10-1869 (5-13-1869)
Stevens, John to Mary Rice 11-6-1866
Stevens, John to Winnie Smith 9-17-1866
Stevens, Lewis to Mary Jane Menafee 5-5-1871 (5-7-1871)
Stevens, Lovod to Nancy Eleanor Fortner 1-20-1858
Stevens, Moore to Catharine McDonald 12-24-1849
Stevens, Needham to Laura E. Smith 12-15-1874 (12-16-1874)
Stevens, S. to Polly Ann Simpson 9-29-1856
Stevens, W. A. to Mary Shelton 9-18-1869
Stevens, Wiley to Sarah Wiseman 3-18-1865 (3-21-1865)
Stevens, William to Fannie Balis 11-25-1871
Stevens, Willis to Clarisa Field 1-14-1874
Stevens, Wylie to Nancy Jane Searcey 6-3-1855
Stevenson, Noah to Julia Pullims 12-16-1865 (12-26-1865)
Stevenson, Noah to July Pullim 12-16-1865
Stevenson, Saml. E. to Rebecca Owen 4-24-1866 (4-29-1866)
Stewart, James to Sarah J. Hendren 11-7-1866
Still, Alexander to Ann Ellis 12-26-1873 (12-29-1873)
Still, Dick to Rebecca Calhoun 6-20-1872
Stillwell, Coleman to Ann Banks 12-28-1868 (12-29-1868)
Stitt, Alex to Siller Sherrill 7-20-1872
Stitt, James Leander to Elizabeth R. Hall 8-9-1854
Stitt, Jas. L. to Addie Sraynie? 9-12-1860 (9-13-1860)
Stitt, Samuel W. to Mollie J. Calhoun 1-10-1860 (1-11-1860)
Stokes, John A. to Nancy P. Hill 11-28-1861
Stokes, John Adams to Sarah Sopornia? Freeman 8-6-1851 (8-7-1851)
Stone, James to A. C. Farrington 1-2-1866 (1-3-1866)
Strain, Joseph Hagans to Jane Forsyth 1-26-1854
Strain, Peter to Martha Walker 12-25-1866
Strain, William D. to Jennette McQuiston 12-17-1847
Strain, Wm. Druffin to Eliz. Agnes Faulkner 4-8-1851
Straing, R. P. to Margaret E. McQuiston 11-22-1870
Strange, Jessee to Susan Giles Smith 11-17-1842
Strange, Sam to Mollie Cothran 6-18-1874
Strange, Wm. H. to Sallie E. Boyd 10-10-1866 (10-11-1866)
Strayhorn, Jesse D. to Martha Ann Shepherd 3-10-1873
Street, A. G. to E. C. Kinney 5-7-1870 (5-9-1870)
Street, J. C. to M. J. Kinney 8-2?-1871 (8-3-1871)
Stricklun, Wm. to Joanna Howard 11-10-1866
Strong, Alfred to Caroline McCain 12-2-1865 (12-7-1865)
Strong, Andrew to Laura Wood? 10-26-1869
Strong, Belfast to Amanda McCain 1-19-1869 (1-21-1869)
Strong, C. F. to Sallie Simonton 9-25-1860 (9-26-1860)
Strong, Charles to Martha Ann Dickson 1-21-1857 (1-22-1857)
Strong, Henry to Matilda Reed 12-19-1866

Strong, K.? to Martha Moffit 11-15-1871
Strong, R. S. to Isabella Jackson 4-12-1870 (4-13-1870)
Strong, Saml. to Charletta Yarbro 12-11-1867
Strong, William James to Lauretta L. Bernard 11-16-1847
Strong, Wm. James to Mary Ann McCreight 9-25-1850 (9-26-1850)
Stroud, J. M. to Susan J. Jones 7-24-1871 (7-26-1871)
Stuart, Johnson to Eliza Anderson 10-30-1871 (11-4-1871)
Stubbs, Berry to Susan Weaver 3-9-1866
Stubbs, Julius to Susan Clements 12-27-1866
Sturgis, Joshua L. to Mary D. Hays 3-14-1861
Stutham, William to Martha Russell 5-30-1849 (5-31-1845)
Sulfrige, W. to Margaret Johnson 12-31-1872 (1-2-1873)
Sullinger, John E. to Patsey A. Clanton 9-5-1868
Sullinger, John E. to Patsey Clanton 9-5-1868 (9-7-1868)
Sullivan, H. to Mary Jane Pennel 10-23-1856 (11-3-1856)
Sullivan, Jacob A. to Mary F. Wooten 9-7-1869 (9-8-1869)
Sullivan, Jacob to Elizabeth J. Trobough 12-21-1842 (12-23-1842)
Sullivan, John E. to Sally Galbreath 9-23-1867
Sullivan, John to Elizabeth Wilson 1-9-1855 (1-11-1855)
Sullivan, N. A. to N. W. Mears 11-25-1871 (11-30-1871)
Sullivan, Robt. P. to Clara Rousan 5-29-1867 (5-30-1867)
Swain, Edmond to Amanda Smith 8-28-1868 (8-29-1868)
T____, James to Martha Ann Frances Smith 12-10-1842 (12-15-1842)
Talley, Dock to Martha Chamber 2-25-1873 (2-26-1873)
Talley, Henry to Rose Allen 1-19-1871
Talley, John to Emma Waller 11-21-1874
Talley, Joseph J.? to Caroline L. Wissen 4-22-1840 (4-23-1840)
Tanner, Elyer? to Amanda Calhoun 1-4-1867 (1-14-1867)
Tarbrok, Elias D. to Eliza Clark 2-11-1857
Tarrey, Edward to Holland Dots 12-25-1874 (12-27-1874)
Tarry, Allen to Bell Blackwell 12-31-1872
Tarry, Jim to Rosa Alexander 12-21-1873
Tarry, Wm. Little to Sallie Anderson Hunt 4-4-1850 (4-10-1850)
Tarvoaler, W. M. to Gussie M. Somervill 10-27-1859 (11-17-1859)
Tate, Edmond to Mary Clark 3-4-1869
Tate, Wm. R. to Mary H. Weatherford 11-18-1867 (12-19-1867)
Taylor, Albert to Philis Taylor 5-6-1867
Taylor, Alexander to Patsey Williamson 2-27-1867
Taylor, Alexander to Veria Mason 12-23-1874
Taylor, Andrew to Nancy Kimbro 9-6-1869
Taylor, Caldwell to Sallie Taylor 2-20-1866
Taylor, Cambridge to Mary Burrel 12-28-1869
Taylor, Charles to Annie Eliza Parker 12-23-1873 (12-26-1873)
Taylor, Charles to Beckey Johnson 12-28-1869
Taylor, Chas. to R. Goodman 1-1-1872
Taylor, Daniel to Mary Lane 11-27-1870
Taylor, Geo. Ardmore? to Ann F. Sommervill 11-16-1852
Taylor, Ike to Hettie Elcan 3-10-1873
Taylor, J. to Caroline Thompson 12-3-1874
Taylor, James Allan to Frances A. Taylor 2-6-1843 (2-8-1843)
Taylor, James Carroll to Mary Hood McCauley 1-8-1845 (1-9-1845)
Taylor, James to Fanny Taylor 2-11-1869
Taylor, John P. to Mary L. Smith 6-2-1858
Taylor, John to Margaret Johnson 1-5-1870
Taylor, John to Mrs. Gary 12-1-1863
Taylor, Lawson to Sarah Reeves 8-13-1870
Taylor, Louis to Polly Montgomery 12-24-1867
Taylor, M.W. to America J. Ralph 4-16-1857
Taylor, Nathaniel to Nancy Taylor 1-2-1866
Taylor, Nowell to Lutish Taylor 1-9-1869
Taylor, Profeit to Sallie Elkin 3-3-1869
Taylor, Rasmus to C. Gammelle 10-13-1871
Taylor, Robert to D. Baptist 12-23-1872
Taylor, Sam to Levinia Taylor 1-25-1868
Taylor, Samuel L. to Sarah M. Mitchell 10-31-1860
Taylor, Shelton D. to Parthenia H. M. Martin 10-11-1846
Taylor, Weddle to Maria Claibourne 3-6-1871
Taylor, Wedly to Sallie Macklin 9-6-1866
Taylor, William to R. Clement 3-23-1866 (4-1-1866)
Taylor, Wm. O. to Susan Green no date (with 1868)
Taylor, Wm. to Florenc Jackson 9-17-1868 (9-18-1868)
Taylor, Wm. to Frankie Maclin 1-28-1870
Taylor, Wm. to L. Jane Cumins 1-10-1870
Tayne?, Banyan to Nancy M. Wright 7-22-1841
Tedwell, James to Nancy Ann Manasco 7-3-1867 (7-4-1867)
Templeton, Augustus A. to C. E. Brooks 12-3-1872 (12-5-1872)
Templeton, John J. to Margaret E. Stevenson 3-12-1866 (3-14-1866)
Templeton, Richard S. to Eliza K. Cherry 12-18-1860 (12-20-1860)
Tennant, William to Elizabeth McGowan 10-25-1850 (10-27-1850)
Tenny, J. R. to Rosa Futhery? 1-27-1868 (1-29-1868)
Terrell, Benjamin H. to G.? A. Clark 12-19-1868 (12-22-1868)
Terrell, Isaac to Artemisia Glass 1-25-1856
Terry, J. M. to Susan Kinney 7-2-1874
Terry, James M. to Sarah Elenor Kelley 9-20-1858 (9-21-1858)
Terry, Ras.? to Hester Ann Taylor 4-7-1866 (4-29-1866)
Terry, Steven to Rebeca Kelly 1-3-1853 (1-25-1853)
Thomas, Alfred to Martha Hall 3-12-1873 (4-5-1873)
Thomas, Edward to Ann Craighead 9-10-1872
Thomas, Edward to Susan Smith 3-31-1870
Thomas, Elam F. to Alice A. Rhodes 9-3-1844
Thomas, Francis to Nannie McClenahan 1-14-1869 (1-20-1869)
Thomas, Henry to S. Turnage 12-24-1873 (12-27-1873)
Thomas, J. A. to Nancy Pinson 1-10-1870
Thomas, J. A. to Nancy Pinson 1-10-1870 (1-13-1870)
Thomas, Lewis to Malinda Ashburn 11-27-1843
Thomas, Owen to Jenny Clements 11-23-1866 (11-24-1866)
Thomas, Peter to Dina Brown 10-1-1874 (10-3-1874)
Thomas, Saml. to Sarah Porter Carter 12-19-1873 (12-20-1873)
Thompson, Albert to Nancy Fagan 1-26-1870
Thompson, Allen to Edith Mathews 12-28-1872
Thompson, Henry to Polly Whitley 8-31-1866
Thompson, Jas. P. to Nancy Eckford 11-10-1865 (11-12-1865)
Thompson, John B. to Martha Ann Reid 12-24-1861
Thompson, John B. to Susan Orr 5-25-1870 (5-26-1870)
Thompson, John D. to Annie A. Miller 2-21-1865 (2-22-1865)
Thompson, P. C. to Bettie Ray 11-2-1863
Thompson, Peter to Penny Williamson 2-13-1867 (2-15-1867)
Thompson, R. C. to Mollie Dickson 12-28-1869 (12-30-1869)
Thompson, S. R. to M. R. Kirk 12-10-1873
Thompson, Saml. Alexr. to Jane Campbell 2-13-1843 (2-16-1843)
Thompson, Talbert to Eliza Wood 3-6-1871 (3-8-1871)
Thompson, Thoas to Emily Ford 1-24-1849
Thompson, Tobe to Eveline Glisson 12-10-1867 (12-12-1867)
Thompson, W. J. to Martha Jane Cole 12-17-1860 (12-19-1860)
Thompson, William to Dona Osborn 5-3-1871
Thompson, Wm. H. to Sarah Ann McClerkin 12-1-1873
Thorton?, Edward to Easter Berry? no date (with 1874)
Ticer, William H. to Susan Cooper 11-4-1858 (1-28-1859)
Tillman, Bryan to Mary Ann Murrin 6-17-1865
Tillman, Geo. to Margaret Wiseman 2-27-1871 (2-28-1871)
Tillman, Jas. Henry to America J. Wood 1-8-1872 (1-11-1872)
Tillman, Thos. H. to Frances Wiseman 1-1-1862
Tillman, W. Thos. to Jane Bealtin? 1-30-1869 (2-4-1869)
Tilman, William F. to Susan Ann Bryant 6-15-1866 (6-17-1866)
Tilmon, John to Martha Windham 10-13-1842 (10-17-1842)
Tilson?, Elijah to America Williams 6-23-1863
Timberlick, Saml. R. to Marth J. Delashmet 5-6-1867 (5-14-1867)
Timbs, James to Elizabeth Wade Davidson 12-21-1853 (12-22-1853)
Timmon, J. F. to Mrs. E. A. Byrd 12-19-1867 (12-22-1867)
Timms, Alexander to Margaret J. P. Wade 12-17-1873 (12-23-1873)
Timms, Benjam. to Sarah Walker 8-31-1869 (9-1-1869)
Timms, H. M. to A. V. Bird 1-4-1871 (1-12-1871)
Timms, Jabus to Ellen C. Davidson 12-28-1859 (12-29-1859)
Timms, John N. to Sarah C. Hannis? 4-9-1867 (4-10-1867)
Timms, M. C. to Mary T. Timms 12-28-1871 (12-29-1870?)
Timms, Sidney R. to Marteller Ann Hammond 10-16-1867 (10-19-1867)
Tims, Alexander to Sarah Narcissa Bayse 3-1-1854 (3-2-1854)
Tims, Benj. to Sarah Booth 12-17-1871 (12-19-1871)
Tims, John to Martha C. Helms 12-13-1871 (12-14-1871)
Tims, Nathaniel to Irena E. L. Tims 2-15-1871
Tims, Samuel to Nancy C. Moore 2-18-1845 (2-19-1845)
Tims, Thomas to Martha Ann Scheen 9-11-1858 (9-12-1858)
Tinnen, J. F. to Sarah E. Hurt 8-10-1861 (8-14-1861)
Tinnen, John to Nancy Jane Davis 2-7-1859
Tinnen, W. H. to Susan Billings 2-4-1869 (1?-31-1869)
Tinnen, William M. to Julia L. Mitchell 12-11-1858 (12-12-1858)
Tinsly, Aubner to Tempe Fields 2-21-1871
Tipton, Dallas to Sallie Jackson 8-13-1868
Tipton, Dick to Rosina Morgan 11-16-1865

Tipton, Jack to Minerva Miller 6-22-1867 (6-23-1867)
Tipton, John to Candis Clements 3-12-1870
Tipton, John to Matilda Bell 12-26-1873 (12-27-1873)
Tipton, Nat to Laura A. Stone 11-21-1850
Tipton, Wm. to Harriet Morgan 8-11-1866
Tisdale, Lewelyn T. to Susannah W. Bell 12-16-1854 (12-17-1854)
Tisdale, P. E. to Lucetta P. Townsend 10-10-1857 (10-15-1857)
Toliver, Frank to Meter Mayo 12-28-1869 (1-1-1870)
Tolliver, James to Sarah Adams 11-22-1871 (11-23-1871)
Tool, Jas. to Susan Hamilton 7-26-1874 (7-29-1874)
Torbiss?, Arthur to Eliza Hutcherson 12-10-1842 (12-15-1842)
Tornton, Henry to Nancy Walk 8-18-1870 (8-19-1870)
Towns, Henry to Chatherine Taylor 3-6-1871
Townsend, George Goodram to Priscilla Sanford 11-10-1842
Townsend, George W. W. to Nancy E. Townsend 8-2-1865
Townsend, James to Isabell Richard 2-9-1867
Townsend, John P. to Sarah Elizabeth Hill 3-16-1852 (3-17-1852)
Townsend, John R. to Dicy M. Byars 12-17-1872 (12-18-1872)
Townsend, John to Judith Moore 5-2-1868
Townsend, Peter to Maria Ketuna Townsend 2-6-1850 (2-7-1850)
Townsend, R. M. to Sarah A. Anderson 11-23-1869
Townsend, Wm. Hunley to Permelia Foster 2-10-1855 (2-14-1855)
Trantham, William to Margaret Goforth 1-11-1845 (1-13-1845)
Trass?, Allen to Louisa Nelson 1-26-1867 (2-18-1867)
Travis, Henry to Mary Ann Parker 9-14-1848 (9-?-1848)
Tredway, Richard to L. J. Scott 9-21-1869 (1-1-1870)
Trice, Francis to Jane E. Wenstram? 10-22-1855 (10-23-1855)
Trigg, Isaac to Maria _____ 7-2-1872
Trigg, Jas. W. to Katy Williams 2-20-1869 (3-1-1869)
Trigg, Moses to Elsie Manna Sims 12-31-1873
Trim, Samuel H. to Martha E. McKnatt 9-10-1872
Trobough, Daniel Adams to Mary Ann Burton 6-24-1846 (6-25-1846)
Trobough, J. W. to Jane D. Bambridge 6-4-1872 (6-5-1872)
Trobough, Jas. W. to Mary Louisa Tyree? 10-24-1856 (10-25-1855?)
Trobough, L. W. to M. E. Pool 5-21-1862?
Trobough, Littleton W. to Patsey W. McCraw 5-29-1844
Trobough, R. H. to Jane Boyd 12-14-1865
Trobough, Tho. B. to Eliza Jane Jackson 3-16-1850 (3-19-1850)
Trobough, _____ to Mary? A. Williams 4-18-1863 (4-21-1863)
Trotter, Richard to Mary Carolin Hutchinson 9-3-1867
Trout, Wm. to Delia Smith no date (c. Sep 1866)
Tucker, Calvin to Martha Ramsey 2-17-1845 (2-20-1845)
Tucker, George to Minnie Scott 7-1-1867 (7-6-1867)
Tucker, James to Laura A. Correthers 12-5-1857 (12-8-1857)
Tucker, Joseph S. to Frances E. Tucker 8-23-1869 (8-24-1869)
Tucker, William A. to Hulen H. Tucker 12-20-1867 (12-23-1867)
Tuikler, John to May J. McCamack 12-17-1856
Tumer, Sipio to Susan A. Taylor 12-20-1872 (12-26-1872)
Turnage, E. J. to A. F. Beaver 7-10-1872 (7-11-1872)
Turnage, Henry M. to Eliz. Murphy Tucker 10-14-1850 (10-16-1850)
Turnage, Henry Martin to Rebecka Frances Manly 12-30-1857 (12-31-1857)
Turnage, Ily D. to Susan M. Phelps 10-26-1847 (11-10-1847)
Turnage, J. B. to M. A. Hatton 1-12-1874 (1-14-1874)
Turnage, James B. to Eliza F. Robinson 12-3-1866 (12-4-1866)
Turnage, James W. to Mary Manasco 12-16-1868 (12-17-1868)
Turnage, John L. to Mariah W. Delashmeit 7-1-1865
Turnage, Owen to V. Carolin Cocke 10-30-1867 (10-31-1867)
Turnage, Walker to Martha A. Simpson 3-27-1844 (3-28-1844)
Turnage, William B. to Elizabeth Caroline Hughes 6-5-1843 (6-6-1843)
Turnage, Wm. A. jr. to Mildred Beaver 2-14-1865
Turner, Chas. to Frances Williamson 4-17-1866
Turner, George W. to Susan A. Miller 10-31-1854 (11-2-1854)
Turner, Robert B. to Lucy M. Bragg 9-27-1869 (9-28-1869)
Turner, S. B. to B. L. Goodman 12-21-1869
Turner, Walter to Ann Cotten 12-30-1874
Turner, William E. to Maggie E. Wade 1-3-1866
Turner, William to Josephine H. Goodman 3-23-1871
Turner, Wm. to Adaline Huston 7-15-1871
Turner, Y. B. to Mary E. Tucker 11-19-1866 (11-20-1866)
Twisdale, D. M. to Miss Jane Huison? 12-12-1865 (12-13-1865)
Tycen, George W. to Msary Barnes no date (with 1862)
Tycen, Robert E. to Martha Flanakin 10-3-1857
Tycer, _____ to Anne? McCraw 5-18-1863
Tyre, Zachariah to Mary Elizabeth McCraw 2-9-1842
Upchurch, Calvin to Adaline Jackson 2-24-1873 (2-26-1873)
Upchurch, James W. to Sallie J. Yarbroh 2-18-1861
Upchurch, John to Ellen Taylor 1-20-1866 (1-21-1866)
Upchurch, John to Jane Hill 7-20-1867 (7-21-1867)
Upchurch, P. Green to Ann Elmore 10-16-1873
Upchurch, W. G. to Julia Clark ?-21-1861 (1-20-1861)
Upton, Edward to Susan Malugin 1-17-1872
Valentine, W. T. to Nancy Jane Gross 7-21-1865
Van Buren, Martin to Marie White 8-12?-1868
Van Davelt?, M. to Caroline Field 1-18-1871 (1-19-1871)
VanLien, Henry Clay to Hannah Jane Foster 6-15-1848 (6-24-1848)
Vanderbilt, Mark to Amanda Jane Smith 10-23-1845
Vaughan, Craddock to Mary Margaret McCoy 1-20-1846 (1-21-1846)
Vaughan, Gilbert to Renetta Somervill 3-24-1869
Vaughan, James D. to Martha Carter 12-4-1869 (12-5-1869)
Vaughan, Moses to Martha S. Smith 11-20-1865 (11-22-1865)
Vaughan, Richd. to Sarah L. Downing 8-4-1868
Vaughan, T. S. to Nancy M. Montgomery 9-7-1870
Vaughan, T. W. to Sarah Sanders 4-15-1865 (5-24-1865)
Vaughn, Henry to Mariah Jackson 12-26-1867
Vaughn, John to Lethia Jamison 11-12-1870
Vaughn, Melvill to Fannie Hall 3-9-1869 (3-11-1869)
Vaughn, Peter to Silusla? H. Hill 4-4-1867
Vaughn, Richmond to Leutitia Jiles 10-4-1873
Vincent, Abner to Abby McCall 12-7-1868 (12-20-1869?)
Vincent, John A. to Mary M. Shelton? 2-14-1843
Vincent, Peter to Nancy Maburn 1-3-1871 (1-14-1871)
Vincent, Solimon to Lemess? Phillips 12-25-1867
Vincent, William to Martha Kennedy 1-1-1871
Vinston, Eli to Agness Cyle 8-23-1866 (8-26-1866)
Voss, John to Elizabeth M. McCauley 12-12-1849
WWhitten, Kent H. to Estell Curry 9-25-1871
Wade, Washington H. to Mary C. Murry 5-9-1841 (5-18-1841)
Waggener, William to Caroline Angus 3-24-1866
Wakefield, August to Sallie Sawyers 4-17-1869 (4-18-1869)
Walk, Augustus W. to Mary L. White 8-?-1866 (8-30-1866)
Walk, Thos. B. to Mrs. Sarah Upchurch 1-5-1865
Walker, Andrew to Mooney Patterson 9-9-1869 (9-11-1869)
Walker, Charles D. to Elizabeth Trotman Hoffler 2-11-1850
Walker, Charles D. to Emily R. Walker 3-3-1847 (3-4-1847)
Walker, E. A. to Elizabeth Edwards 8-18-1857 (8-20-1857)
Walker, E. F. to Mary C. Doldon? 9-14-1859
Walker, E. P. to Emma C. Bratton 10-25-1870 (10-30-1870)
Walker, Ebenezer T. to Lucy Culbreath 1-3-1842 (1-4-1842)
Walker, Frank to Eady Harris 12-16-1867
Walker, Frank to Eady Harris 8-12-1867
Walker, George A. to Nannie M. Cavenor 12-26-1870 (12-29-1870)
Walker, H. H. to Mima Twyman 2-11-1873
Walker, James S. to Martha George 12-10-1868 (12-15-1868)
Walker, John B. to Elizabet J. Walker 3-4-1852
Walker, John W. to Lydia Frances Marshall 12-13-1847 (12-?-1847)
Walker, Jordan to Adaline Harte? 3-15-1872
Walker, Joseph H. to Mary Tenant 1-12-1850
Walker, Milton to Lucy Hill 9-12-1873
Walker, Robert A. to Mary A. Daniel 5-8-1873 (5-3?-18730
Walker, Robert L. to Martha McNair 4-24-1865
Wall, F. F. to Ann Ashford 4-23-1857
Wall, J. P. to Axie McDaniel 12-22-1873
Wall, Wm. H. to Miss Fannie Steele 11-28-1864 (11-29-1864)
Wallace, George to Mary Adams 6-12-1874
Wallace, Jacob to Nancy Caroline Morrison 1-19-1854
Wallace, _____ to Mary Gillum 5-25-1867
Waller, J. S. to M. E. White 8-1-1870 (8-5-1870)
Waller, Joseph S. to Mary Frances Culbreth 11-14-1857 (3-20-1858)
Wallis, Robt. Mathews to Mahala Jane Kelley 3-11-1856
Walt, James L. to Mary R. Bateman 12-5-1859 (12-8-1859)
Walt, Mathew to Martha McCarrol 1-12-1869 (1-28-1869)
Walton, Anthony to Martha Green 4-17-1872
Walton, Geo. Washington to Minerva Jane Myers 3-21-1849
Walton, George W. to Elizabeth A. Brown 12-25-1867 (12-29-1867)
Walton, George W. to Mary Yarbro 6-8-1870 (6-9-1870)
Walton, George to Emaly Acock 8-19-1872 (8-20-1872)
Walton, Jackson to Isau? Taylor 12-15-1874
Walton, William D. to Sarah Frances Cox 2-12-1844 (2-13-1844)

Walton, William H. to Mariah J. McIntosh 11-25-1869
Walton, Wm. D. to Martha A. A. Rice 4-16-1856
Ward, James M. to Martha Ann Kelly 12-8-1841
Ward, Josiah to Louisa Henley 6-8-1843
Ward, Lee to Margaret Bert 3-21-1874
Ward, W. T. to N. C. Walker 11-26-1873
Warf, Burrell to Athey Wooten 1-3-1850
Warmack, Jno. D. to Addie L. Calhoun 12-15-1873 (12-16-1873)
Warmouth, Robert W. to Catharine Yarbrok 2-3-1858 (2-4-1858)
Warr, L. L. to Sallie Wiseman 9-9-1868
Warren, Charles H. to Mattie E. Linsey 12-22-1874
Warren, Lane to Liller Williams 8-4-1870 (8-7-1870)
Washington, George to Jack Ann Rhodes 8-6-1870 (8-7-1870)
Washington, George to Sallie Dison 8-21-1873
Wass?, James to Elisabeth Jones 8-22-1868 (8-23-1868)
Watson, J. A. to Susan A. Ellison 10-27-1874 (10-28-1874)
Watson, James M. to L. L. Wade 11-24-1868 (11-26-1868)
Wayman, John to Frances McKinney 8-18-1841
Weatherford, E. A. to Sarah E. Tate 12-11-1866
Weatherford, James to Sarah Moss 7-21-1865 (7-26-1865)
Weatherington, Joshua to Mary Billings 1-8-1857
Weatherington, Robert to Martha Collier 9-11-1869 (9-12-1869)
Weatherly, George to Jane Stephens 9-22-1866 (9-30-1866)
Weatherred, William D. to Lavina Adams 12-20-1870 (12-22-1870)
Weathers, Jordan to Lucinda Wright 2-23-1874
Weathers, Moses to Sina Ann Trusdale 12-30-1873 (12-3?-1873)
Weaver, Charles A. to Mary Coward 12-28-1869
Weaver, Governor to Amanda Wilson 10-14-1874
Weaver, J. J. to M. C. Elmore 11-7-1867 (11-8-1867)
Weaver, Tip to Patra Brown 10-14-1874
Webb, Chas. Wm. to Rosanna Kulbreath 12-19-1850
Webb, John W. to J. A. David 6-17-1871 (6-19-1871)
Webb, John to Rachel Baty 12-28-1867 (12-29-1867)
Webb, Joseph B. to Jennie M. Bunch 12-5-1872
Webster, Joseph H. to Narcissus Woods 1-17-1851 (1-19-1851)
Webster, L. L. to Mattie J. T. Linn 7-13-1874 (7-15-1874)
Weever, E. J. to M. E. C. Hobs 12-17-1874
Weisheiver, John C. to Nanny Freeman 8-15-1870 (8-16-1870)
Welb, James R. to Sarah Ballard 8-26-1857 (8-31-1857)
Welch, Charles H. to Cordelia T. Lyle 12-22-1868 (12-24-1868)
Weller (Miller?), Cyrus W. to Elizabeth E. McLeary 9-1-1840 (9-2-1840)
Wellingham, Anderson to Nancy Stitt 3-19-1869 (4-11-1869)
Wells, John to Josey White 4-19-1873 (4-20-1873)
Wellsman, J. C. to Eliza Buff 10-10-1868
Wesson, Bolivar C. to Ann Rebecca Ford 11-22-1848 (11-23-1848)
Wesson?, James D. to Rebecca McFarlane 1-14-1844 (1-16-1844)
Westbrooks, Fagan to Mary Shelton 3-6-1867
Wethington, Allen to Mary Elkins 6-21-1853 (6-23-1853)
Wharton, James C. to Amanda Jane Lunsford 6-7-1842 (6-9-1842)
Wheelock, John Ambrose to Ellen Rose Newman 9-19-1850
White, David Ewing to Welthy Ann Hopper 5-26-1855 (5-27-1855)
White, George W. to Sarah Hood 1-16-1844 (1-18-1844)
White, James to Marilyn Freeman 7-5-1851 (7-?-1851)
White, Robert H. to Willie Helen Dalle? 3-23-1871
White, Thomas to Julia Bevins 9-5-1872
White, Thomas to Martha Squiers 9-5-1872
White, Thomas to Martha Squires 9-5-1872 (9-13-1872)
White, Tom to Amanda McCain 8-1-1874
White, W. H. to M. J. H. Hill 10-15-1863
Whiteman, John to Deffilue? Jones 12-23-1870
Whitfield, H. C. to Amanda Boswell 1-22-1862
Whitis, Lafayett to Mollie Stitt 12-22-1869 (12-23-1869)
Whitley, Andrew J. to Henrietta Roane 8-25-1851
Whitley, Claiburn to Jenny Maclin 7-18-1868
Whitley, David to Rhode Maclin 6-16-1866 (6-17-1866)
Whitley, E.B. to Sarah E. Peeler 12-31-1866 (1-1-1867)
Whitley, Frank J. to Mary T. Somerville 4-5-1874 (4-13-1874)
Whitley, John to Frances Baptist 2-12-1872
Whitley, Joseph D. to Eliza Rufina Sherrod 12-16-1854
Whitley, Robert E. to Amanda Rose 1-6-1869
Whitley, Wm. S. to Emily Ann Banks 12-21-1854
Whitlock, George W. to Rosa V. Maten 6-29-1869 (7-1-1869)
Whitlock, Wm. Ray to Evaline Smith 2-5-1849 (2-8-1849)
Whitmore, James A. to Jane Snider 7-24-1856
Whitson, John G. to Sallie M. Gregg 3-30-1872
Whitson, T. J. to E. J. Lamb 9-17-1861 (9-18-1861)
Wiley, John W. to Jennie Jones 9-30-1871 (10-1-1871)
Wiley, John to Anna Erwin 11-16-1867 (11-20-1867)
Wiley, Thomas? James to Sarah Jane Davis 8-10-1854
Wilie, John W. to Nancy E. Miller 7-31-1855 (8-2-1855)
Wilie, Nelson to Caroline Brown 1-7-1872 (1-9-1872)
Wilkerson, Lamb to Easter Williamson 3-12-1870
Wilkins, George to Nancy Shaw 4-28-1857 (4-29-1857)
Wilkins, J. C. to Mary J. Stephenson 2-22-1871 (2-25-1871)
Wilkins, James to Ann H. Owen 7-19-1855
Wilkins, James to Josephine Timms 4-21-1868 (4-23-1869?)
Wilkins, W. to America F. McGuin 5-4-1859
Wilkins, West to Melissa Trantham 5-19-1840
Wilkins, William to Catharine H. Smith 7-14-1852 (7-15-1852)
William, Napolian to Lucy Thomas 8-1-1867 (8-2-1867)
Williams, Albert to Marget Dinwoody 9-19-1859
Williams, Alexander to Emmer Williams 12-27-1870 (12-28-1870)
Williams, Alexander to Galaney Rigsby 10-18-1847 (10-19-1847)
Williams, Allen to Sarah Scot 3-13-1858 (3-14-1858)
Williams, Anderson to Phillis Harper 12-28-1868 (12-30-1868)
Williams, Buck to Percilla West 6-8-1867 (6-11-1867)
Williams, Butler to Chainey Smith 9-12-1871 (9-16-1871)
Williams, Charles to Clarinda Crenshaw 1-21-1874
Williams, Charles to Louisa Fink 5-7-1873
Williams, Daniel to Martha Harris 2-25-1846 (2-26-1846)
Williams, David to Emaline Stockley 11-10-1870 (12-14-1870)
Williams, Essex to Ruth Wilson 10-20-1871
Williams, Ezekiel Smith to Mary A. H. Wright 1-29-1855 (1-31-1855)
Williams, Francis to Livina Harris 7-30-1870
Williams, Henry to Harriet Richardson 12-28-1868 (12-30-1868)
Williams, James A. to Ellen L. Weatherford 9-20-1859
Williams, James J. to Missouri A. B. Williams 6-22-1857
Williams, James to Maattie Jones 1-1-1873 (1-2-1873)
Williams, James to Uminie Partlow 9-11-1873
Williams, John C. to Sarah O. Williams 11-5-1868
Williams, John F. to Indiana Hill 9-19-1865 (9-20-1865)
Williams, John F. to Indianna Hill 9-19-1865
Williams, John W. to Lavina E. Clemant 6-6-1854 (6-7-1854)
Williams, Johnathan (Norman?) to Sarah A. F. Gilleland 10-7-1873 (10-9-1873)
Williams, Jones J. to Amanda L. Powell? 12-21-1841 (12-27-1842?)
Williams, Lemuel to Rachel Jackson 10-9-1852 (10-12-1852)
Williams, Lemuel to Sarah C. Kelly 8-31-1867 (9-3-1867)
Williams, Lewis to Susan Holmes 9-30-1871
Williams, Pleasant B. to Mary Flinn 2-5-1847
Williams, R. F. to S. J. Roane 1-1-1872 (1-4-1872)
Williams, Robert Sevier to Tebitha Emaline Smith 2-13-1854 (2-15-1854)
Williams, Robt. Alex to Mary Catharine Wilkins 2-18-1861 (2-19-1861)
Williams, Saml. M. to Manerva A. E. Davis 2-11-1857 (2-12-1857)
Williams, Thomas M. to Jane M. Smith 5-25-1861
Williams, Thomas M. to Mary A. Clements 10-9-1848 (10-11-1848)
Williams, Tias to Cary Ann Berry 7-16-1869 (7-17-1869)
Williams, William to Delilia Houston 11-13-1872 (11-27-1872)
Williams, Z. to Annis Greer 7-6-1869
Williams, Zack to Charlotte Yarbro 4-18-1873 (4-13?-1873)
Williamson, John to Leaner Malone 2-23-1867 (2-28-1867)
Williamson, Lawson to Sissee Hunt 1-31-1870
Williamson, Lewis to Lutia Tarry 3-21-1866
Wils?, Wash to Maria Bowers 9-12-1873 (9-15-1873)
Wilson, A. J. to Eliza H. McCain 12-15-1857
Wilson, Bob to Amey Edwards 11-14-1874
Wilson, David to Elizabeth Boothe 7-21-1851 (7-22-1851)
Wilson, E. T. to Bettie Calhoun 8-21-1860 (8-22-1860)
Wilson, Fred Wm. to Famia Haywood 11-9-1871
Wilson, Geo. to Emma Hughlett 1-18-1868 (1-19-1868)
Wilson, Gobe to Amanda Yarbro 8-11-1874 (8-12-1874)
Wilson, Isaac to ________ 12-20-1869
Wilson, J. E. to S. P. Williamson 9-14-1874 (9-17-1874)
Wilson, J. H. to Mary D. Mitchell 9-29-1872
Wilson, Jacob to Celia Cotten 3-13-1866 (8-27-1866)
Wilson, James to Ceralda Keeth 12-13-1872
Wilson, Jim to Hettie Burnet 11-7-1874 (11-9-1874)

Wilson, John to Catharine Smith 12-28-1868 (12-31-1868)
Wilson, Lewis to Maggie Johnson 12-24-1875 (12-24-1874?)
Wilson, P. H. to N. E. Wiley 12-17-1872
Wilson, Peter M. to Viney Dacus 1-12-1869
Wilson, R. T. to Margaret A. Simeton? 2-24-1866
Wilson, Spencer to Mary Wallis 10-1-1866 (10-5-1866)
Wilson, Thos. H. to Martha Solomon 2-13-1861 (2-14-1861)
Wilson, William Henry to Margaret L.? Harris 4-16-1840
Wilson, William to Lydia Beard 4-30-1873
Wilson, William to Sallie Fields 8-4-1873 (8-9-1873)
Wilson, William to Sarah McCulough 12-31-1857
Wilson, Willis A. to Martha C. Kelly 3-21-1868
Wilson, Wm. L. to Nancy McCarroll 9-8-1854 (9-14-1854)
Winburn, Jas. T. to Nancy Maxwell 9-22-1855
Windiss, Henry to Nancy Jane Ralph 4-21-1847 (4-22-1847)
Winfield, Isaac to Mary E. Smith 10-9-1872
Winford, Andrew to S. V. Winford 7-25-1865? (7-26-1866)
Winford, Isaac T. to Margaret A. Brimley 6-9-1870 (6-12-1870)
Winford, J. S.? to Viola S. Crenshaw 4-13-1857
Winford, John S. to Viola S. Crenshaw 4-13-1857 (4-16-1857)
Winford, Mat to Sarah Claiburn 10-17-1869 (1-3-1869?)
Winford, Thomas B. to America Jane Gardner 10-13-1841
Winford, William W. to Mary Read 12-30-1868
Winfree, Saml. to Mary E. Culbreath 2-26-1868
Winfrow?, Mat. to Sarah Claiburn 10-17-1868
Winkler, Richmond to Eleanor Goss 1-13-1841 (1-14-1841)
Winn, Charles to Maria Smith 2-23-1866 (2-24-1866)
Winn, John to Adeline Jackson 2-2-1871
Winn, Philip S. to Martha Jane Punch? 1-11-1843
Winn, Robt to Fannie Hall 11-1-1873 (11-2-1873)
Winn, T. W. to Susan A. Malone 10-23-1856
Winn, William H. to Mary Pitt 3-1-1865 (3-3-1865)
Winn, William to Emma Hunt 4-13-1874
Winn, Wm. to Emma Hunt 4-13-1874
Winn, Wm. to Jennie Taylor 1-17-1866 (1-20-1866)
Winn?, G. W. to Rebecca J. Howard 6-10-1863
Winters, James Carroll to Jane Ballard 7-28-1855 (7-29-1855)
Wiseman, Franklin to Bettie Coats 2-18-1871 (2-19-1871)
Wiseman, H. H. to Miss M. E. Winn 12-27-1860
Wiseman, Isaac to Emeline Spencer 9-25-1866
Wiseman, John Bowen? to Elizabeth Lamb 12-12-1846 (12-24-1846)
Wiseman, Joseph F. to Martha F. Feezor 11-16-1865
Wiseman, L. W. to Martha Coats 12-1-1874 (12-2-1874)
Wiseman, O. O. to J. E. Kinny 12-22-1873 (1-7-1874)
Wiseman, William to Nancy J. Harrison 12-17-1860
Wiseman, Wm. O. to Mary A. Ralph 8-14-1852
Wiseman, ____ to Jane Martin 1-26-1874 (1-28-1874)
Wisener?, HGenry to Mary Elizabeth Goodnoe 2-13-1844 (2-16-1844)
Witherington, J. M. to Harriet J. Smith 1-27-1866 (1-28-1866)
Wood, Alexander Carroll to Camdis D. Taylor 4-10-1854 (4-12-1854)
Wood, Alexander to Catharine Bringle 6-4-1846
Wood, David H. to Mary E. Deakins 12-17-1850 (12-19-1850)
Wood, David to Martha A. Gracy 4-19-1855
Wood, George to Matilda Butler 10-7-1869
Wood, Henry to Juda Williamson 1-20-1874
Wood, John E. to S. E. Walker 8-3-1874 (8-6-1874)
Wood, John H. to Frances M. McCoy 6-18-1856 (6-19-1856)
Wood, John to Indiania Shelton 7-27-1868
Wood, Jordan C. to Mary F. Wood 12-16-1868
Wood, O. H. P. to Rebecca J. H. Durham 5-7-1840
Wood, Peter P. to Eliza Ralph 4-12-1849
Wood, Peter P. to Sarah Elizabeth Hartsfield 7-7-1869 (7-8-1869)
Wood, Richard to Candis Furnandez 9-19-1867 (9-21-1867)
Wood, Thomas A. to Sarah F. Smith 1-3-1874 (1-4-1874)
Wood, Thomas D. to Louisa Jane Witherington 7-1-1842
Wood, Thos. to Sarah M. Roe 12-11-1865 (12-13-1865)
Wood, William to Margaret Wilson 12-23-1870
Woodard, David to Judith Taylor 8-8-1864 (8-10-1864)
Woodard, H. L. to Jane Angus 1-13-1857 (1-14-1857)
Woods, Bill to Ella? Smith 10-4-1873
Woods, David H. to Ann Eliza Deakins 12-8-1847 (12-?-1847)
Woods, John H. to Martha J. Blous? 7-25-1860
Woods, John to Frances Jones 3-25-1874 (3-26-1874)
Woods?, Saml. M. to Narcissa Robinson 1-13-1844 (1-18-1844)
Woodson, W. A. to Mary Jane George 9-17-1856 (9-18-1856)
Woolfirk, Wesley to Catherine Rose 4-4-1873 (4-8-1873)
Wooten, Arthur F. to Ann Eliza Joice 5-14-1842 (5-15-1842)
Wooten, Ben to Aanda Miller 1-20-1869
Wooten, John to Phillis Clements 1-13-1866 (1-14-1866)
Wooten, W. H. to Mahala Pickard 9-24-1861
Wooten, William Henry to Caroline Winiford Howerton 12-14-1841
Wooton, Cannon Smith to Helen Tucker 9-28-1843
Worley, W. C. to N. J. Hightower 12-12-1874 (12-27-1874)
Wormath, John R. to Mary Elizabeth Prewitt 10-23-1874 (10-24-1874)
Wormley, Nathaniel Green to Mary Hardy Alston 6-22-1850 (6-23-1850)
Wortham, Nathaniel to Henrietta Smith 4-29-1852
Wortham, Pinkney to Julia Ann Hise 3-26-1868
Wright, Andrew J. to Eliza A. McQuiston 1-29-1868 (1-30-1868)
Wright, Austem to Eliza Hill 2-27-1871 (2-28-1871)
Wright, Cirus to Nancy Siler 3-1-1867 (3-2-1867)
Wright, George S. to Rebecca D. Pettey 2-26-1861
Wright, Isham A. to Mary Bernard 1-3-1848 (1-6-1848)
Wright, J. A. to Mary J. Barville 11-2-1874 (11-6-1874)
Wright, J. S. to Margaret N. Shaw 1-29-1869 (1-30-1869)
Wright, James L. to Mary McCrare? 9-1-1853
Wright, James M. to Elizabeth McQuisten 3-20-1841 (3-23-1841)
Wright, James to Mary McGregor 1-?-1871) (1-19-1871)
Wright, Jesse to Willie Ross 11-21-1872 (11-22-1872)
Wright, Jessee to Virgina C. Hurt 10-11-1873 (10-13-1873)
Wright, John S. to Mary S. Hunter 2-1-1865 (2-2-1865)
Wright, John to Mary G. Simpson 7-31-1872 (8-1-1872)
Wright, Joshua to Rose Boyce 12-27-1867 (12-28-1867)
Wright, L. to Ann Elam 3-17-1866 (3-18-1866)
Wright, Richard Turner to Penelope McCraw 11-18-1848 (11-20-1848)
Wright, Willia G. to Elizabeth Mitchell 2-8-1844 (2-27-1844)
Wright, William to Mary J. Sullivan 6-28-1871 (7-2-1871)
Wright, William to Matilda Brown 6-10-1867
Wright, William to Mollie Saunders 12-18-1872
Wright, Wm. to Anna Yarbro 5-7-1873
Wylie, A. R. to Martha Dillahunty 9-12-1870 (9-13-1870)
Wylie, Francis to Julia M. Thompson 12-12-1854 (12-13-1854)
Wylie, Gilbert to Lucinda Miller 2-13-1873
Wynne, Geo. W. to Ophelia P. Howard 6-21-1871 (6-22-1871)
Yager, William H. to Elizabeth F. Ore 3-18-1867
Yancey, John B. to Georgia Ann Newton 12-18-1868 (12-20-1868)
Yancy, John Thos. to Eliza Holley 12-23-1867 (12-25-1867)
Yancy, William H. to Elizath. A. Wright 12-21-1867 (12-22-1867)
Yarbre?, Elias O. to Sarah Jane Winn 10-25-1855
Yarbro, A. A. to Charlotte M. Street 3-20-1872 (3-21-1872)
Yarbro, Andrew to Hester M. L. Newton 1-17-1868 (2-6-1868)
Yarbro, Charles A. to Samuella Smith 3-10-1869
Yarbro, Clay to Emerline Smith 12-25-1866
Yarbro, Erwin? to Emmer Hughlette 6-8-1867
Yarbro, James H. to Mary A. Epperson 1-20-1870
Yarbro, John A. to Rosetta J. Hanna 10-13-1866 (10-16-1866)
Yarbro, Joseph M. to Alice Walk 1-2-1867
Yarbro, Saml. M. to Mary R. Sullivan 12-26-1870 (12-29-1870)
Yarbro, Thomas to Maria Calhoun 6-2-1870
Yarbro, Uriah Pinckney to Sarah Jane Marshall 1-15-1853 (1-20-1853)
Yarbro, Wm. Granville to Ariadna Angus 6-23-1851 (6-24-1851)
Yarbroh, William to Frances Cook 12-8-1857 (12-9-1857)
Yarbrok, Edward to Aggy Austin 2-17-1858 (2-18-1858)
Yarbrough, Edmond Tho. to Mary Ann Butler 7-14-1853
Yarbrough, Landon B. to Susan McGuin 3-31-1846 (4-3-1846)
Yarbrough, Landon Bradford to Safroney Smith 6-2-1853
Yarbrough, Wm. A. to Mary A. Glass 11-12-1851 (11-13-1851)
Yates, Cornelius to Ann Willis Lyn 5-3-1870
Yates, Vaulentine to Anne Nichols 6-21-1841
Yates, William to Nancy Bynum 8-4-1866 (8-5-1866)
Yewell, James to Sallie A. Hartsfield 1-15-1862 (1-16-1862)
Young, Alfred to Jane Pinner? 12-7-1852
Young, Green B. to Elizabeth Leach 11-14-1849
Young, J. G. to Annie Hall 1-15-1873
Young, James Franklin to Erena Lamb 9-2-1844 (9-4-1844)
Young, James to Claricy J. Vaughan 1-13-1857
Young, Jno. W. to Martha Roe 8-4-1874 (8-12-1874)
Young, R. C. to Lucinda Dillahunty 3-19-1874
Young, Robert to Mary Ferguson 3-12-1856 (3-13-1856)
Yount, Henry to Ann Batewright 7-24-1868

Yount, Hiram Malachi to Mary Catharine Starnes 3-12-1851 (3-13-1851)

____, Milson? D. to Adaline M. Goforth 9-29-1842

Acock, Emaly to George Walton 8-19-1872 (8-20-1872)
Acock, Martha V. to Saml. J. Marsh 12-22-1874 (12-23-1874)
Acock, Sarah E. to J. B. Fletcher 8-4-1873 (8-7-1873)
Adams, Easter to Hugh Gerred? 3-15-1853
Adams, Eliza Ann to William Cup 10-21-1869 (10-22-1869)
Adams, Emma P. to James B. Bright 10-29-1873 (10-30-1873)
Adams, Frances W. to James G. Hanley 5-24-1842 (5-25-1842)
Adams, Jane to John Becksterling 8-18-1863 (8-20-1863)
Adams, Lavina to William D. Weatherred 12-20-1870 (12-22-1870)
Adams, Lucinda to Archer Allen 2?-17-1867 (3-26-1867)
Adams, M. J. to B. J. Blescot(Hescot?) 12-2-1874
Adams, Mary A. to Thos. C. Anthony 4-11-1866
Adams, Mary L. to Jas. O. Harris 1-3-1853
Adams, Mary to George Wallace 6-12-1874
Adams, Mattie G. to Dr. T. A. Kyle 7-2-1860 (7-3-1860)
Adams, S. F. to J. W. Moore 12-1-1874 (12-2-1874)
Adams, Sarah E. to James M. Black 12-29-1858 (12-30-1858)
Adams, Sarah P. to C. M. Brown 2-12-1872 (2-13-1872)
Adams, Sarah to James Tolliver 11-22-1871 (11-23-1871)
Adams, Susan E. to Martin T. Johnson 8-14-1865 (8-15-1865)
Adkins, Bettie J. to W. D. Hawze 6-18-1874 (6-25-1874)
Adkins, Charlott to James Faulk 1-2-1872
Adkins, Charlotte to Adam Calaway 6-15-1873
Adkins, Elizabeth to Wiley Payne 2-4-1841
Adkins, Emer H. to Daniel McLennen 12-23-1865 (12-26-1865)
Adkins, Georgetter to Granderson Downing 5-14-1874 (4?-15-1874)
Adkins, Josephine to Gilbert Payne 12-24-1868 (12-26-1868)
Adkins, Margaret to James Kirts 3-20-1865
Adkins, Silvia to Mike Hill 10-13-1874 (10-14-1874)
Adkins, Susanna M. C. to John McLennon 1-24-1850
Adkisson, Louisa to David J. Bushins? 8-5-1846 (8-6-1846)
Aikin, Aceneth E. to W. S. Bays 4-10-1861 (4-17-1861)
Akin, Ellen to James Thos. Burton 11-5-1867 (11-6-1867)
Akin, Mary Catharine to Tho. J. Barnes 3-12-1856 (3-13-1856)
Aldridge, Clarisa to John Fell Fowler 9-14-1868
Aldridge, L. C. to G. W. Daniel 12-26-1864 (1-2-1864?)
Alexander, Bettie to Guss Chambers 12-13-1873 (12-15-1873)
Alexander, Elizabeth A. to A. D.? Hunter 1-4-1866
Alexander, Elizabeth to Jack Alexander 10-8-1873 (10-20-18730
Alexander, Hanna to Parriss? Harper 3-13-1869 (3-14-1869)
Alexander, Mary Ann to Andrew Jackson 12-23-1867 (12-25-1867)
Alexander, Mary to Daniel Jackson 12-26-1872
Alexander, Rody to Peter Small 8-13-1867
Alexander, Rosa to Jim Tarry 12-21-1873
Alfred, Margaret? to Jonathan Budgett? 12-29-1862
Allen, Amanda to Edward Glenn 9-28-1867 (9-29-1867)
Allen, Frances R. to John P. Morgan 4-24-1866
Allen, Louisa to William Fletcher 1-19-1871 (1-22-1871)
Allen, Mary Adaline to John C. McLister 11-21-1855 (11-22-1855)
Allen, Mary G. A. to Charles H. Leech 11-28-1867
Allen, Rebeca to William Gillespie 8-7-1845 (8-8-1845)
Allen, Rose to Henry Talley 1-19-1871
Allen, Sarah Eliza to James G. Smith 1-2-1854
Allen, Setta to James Allen 10-29-1870 (11-2-1870)
Alston, Aggie to Tom Lawson 11-20-1871 (11-23-1871)
Alston, Agnes to Thos. Alston 12-30-1867 (12-2-1868?)
Alston, Betty to John Randolph 7-28-1871 (7-18?-1871)
Alston, Elizabeth to Jessee Riche 4-29-1868 (5-21-1868)
Alston, Ellen to Amus Sherrill 9-23-1869 (9-26-1869)
Alston, Eva M. to W. H. Richardson 8-31-1868 (9-2-1868)
Alston, Fanny to Abe Armstrong 11-20-1871 911-23-1871
Alston, Henrietta to Jessee Sherrill 10-14-1874
Alston, Katie to Wylie Alston 9-28-1872 (9-29-1872)
Alston, Livia? to Fenton Smith 10-5-1874
Alston, Lucy to Tob? Brooks 7-10-1868 (7-11-1868)
Alston, Lusina to John Hill 11-9-1866 (11-10-1866)
Alston, Mary Hardy to Nathaniel Green Wormley 6-22-1850 (6-23-1850)
Alston, Mary to Richard Alston 12-27-1867 (12-2-1868?)
Alston, Matilda to James Barnell 1-28-1870
Alston, Missouri to Geo. Dickens 12-23-1872 (12-25-1872)
Alston, Nancy to Henry Payne 7-5-1873 (7-6-1873)
Alston, Sallie D. to Lackfield Maclin 12-30-1871 (1-3-1875?)
Alston, Sarah to William Bell 4-25-1872 (4-27-1872)
Anderson, Catharine to Wash Hall 3-2-1874
Anderson, Cylvia to Charly Ales 10-13-1871
Anderson, Eliza to Johnson Stuart 10-30-1871 (11-4-1871)
Anderson, Elizabeth to Saml. Kindrick 5-18-1872 (5-19-1872)
Anderson, Julia M. to Wm. P. Grant 11-7-1871 (11-8-1871)
Anderson, Sarah A. to R. M. Townsend 11-23-1869
Angus, Ariadna to Wm. Granville Yarbro 6-23-1851 (6-24-1851)
Angus, Bettie to Jerry Moten 5-6-1867 (5-7-1867)
Angus, Caroline to William Waggener 3-24-1866
Angus, Eliza J. P. to Hesekiah Cobb 11-2-1857 (11-3-1857)
Angus, Elizabeth to George Mann 1-4-1869 (1-10-1869)
Angus, Jane to H. L. Woodard 1-13-1857 (1-14-1857)
Angus, Maria to Phil Alston 3-8-1867 (3-10-1867)
Appleberry, Elizabeth to James W. Roberts 2-22-1869 (2-24-1869)
Archer, Ann to F. G. N. Motin 5-31-1858
Archer, Annie? to Saml. Smith 4-5-1871
Archer, Eliz. Mary Isabella to Thomas C. Campbell 12-5-1849 (12-6-1849)
Archer, Elizabeth to Charles M. Spesard 12-29-1866 (12-30-1866)
Archer, Mary Elam? to E. J. Maxwell 2-11-1856 (2-14-1856)
Archer, Milley to Manuel Smith 8-30-1866 (8-31-1866)
Armstrong, Mary A. to William L. Coppedge 9-21-1844 (9-?-1844)
Arnett, Lucinda to Hugh Morrison 12-22-1869 (12-23-1869)
Ashburn, Malinda to Lewis Thomas 11-27-1843
Ashford, Ann to F. F. Wall 4-23-1857
Atkins, M. J. to J. F. Smith 11-20-1872
Ausbon, Mary Susan to Wm.H. Landadal 3-21-1872
Austin, Aggy to Edward Yarbrok 2-17-1858 (2-18-1858)
Austin, Mary A. to Robt. A. Rice 12-17-1871 (12-19-1871)
Avery, Alace to Armstead Gray 6-28-1872
Avery, Jannie to Aaron Alston 7-10-1869 (7-13-1869)
Avery, Mollie to Shade Bass 3-14-1874
Bacyas?, Eliza to William S. Calhoon 4-2-1867
Badwell, Bell to William Burks 12-24-1866 (12-25-1866)
Bailey, Lucy to Chas. Gist 9-28-1869 (9-29-1869)
Bain?, Mary R. to Joseph S. Harris 11-11-1850 (11-12-1850)
Baird, Eliza Ann to William sr. McQuiston 7-23-1844 (7-25-1844)
Baird, Elizabeth to J. L. McDaniel 6-6-1861
Baird, artha to Christopher Simonton 8-31-1853
Baker, Ann E. to Mosel C. Danniel 12-13-1867 (12-15-1867)
Baker, Charlotte to Edwin Brooks 9-2-1840
Baker, M. F. to A. J. Kelley 9-14-1859
Baker, Martha M. to James A. Danniel 12-13-1867 (12-15-1867)
Bakers, Mary Jane to Hezekiah Burton 11-15-1843 (11-16-1843)
Baldock, Mary Helen to John Pool 12-26-1854 (12-28-1854)
Balis, Fannie to William Stevens 11-25-1871
Ballard, Carolin to John Ballard 9-18-1865 (9-19-1865)
Ballard, Jane to James Carroll Winters 7-28-1855 (7-29-1855)
Ballard, Jennie to J. H. Burlison 12-21-1873
Ballard, Martha E. A. to John D. Ballard 7-26-1858 (7-18-1858)
Ballard, Mary to John Elliett 3-5-1866 (3-8-1866)
Ballard, Sarah to James R. Welb 8-26-1857 (8-31-1857)
Bambridge, Eleanor Valentin to Jno. Boyd Campbell 2-1-1843 (2-7-1843)
Bambridge, Jane D. to J. W. Trobough 6-4-1872 (6-5-1872)
Band, Jane to William Hine? 12-1-1852
Bandy, Mary H. to William Bull 11-16-1869
Bandy, Sue A. to Thomas T. Gaines 2-27-1873
Banks, Ann to Coleman Stillwell 12-28-1868 (12-29-1868)
Banks, Ellen to David L. Fite 10-14-1857 (10-15-1857)
Banks, Emily Ann to Wm. S. Whitley 12-21-1854
Banks, Jane M. to David McDonald 12-3-1851 (12-4-1851)
Banks, Julia A. C. to Wm. A. Huffman 11-29-1854 (12-1-1854)
Baptist, Caladonia to Mack Dugget 1-21-1871
Baptist, D. to Robert Taylor 12-23-1872
Baptist, Frances to John Whitley 2-12-1872
Barker, Rachel Talbot to Gabriel M. Anderson 1-2-1855 (1-3-1855)
Barnes, Keziah to George Billings 5-26-1873 (5-27-1873)
Barnes, Msary to George W. Tycen no date (with 1862)
Barnes, Sarah Jane to Archie Morrison 12-23-1872 (12-25-1873)
Barnet, Nealy to Wm. M. McGuiver 5-21-1866 (5-22-1866)
Barnett, Mary S. to W. C. Marbury 5-11-1872
Barnett, Mary to John O'Mahony 5-21-1868 (5-23-1868)
Barret, Margret V. to Henry Fields 8-9-1865
Barret, Matilda to Wallace Clark 2-4-1870
Barret, Sallie A. to John W. Calhoun 1-19-1870

Barrett, Henrietta S. to Christopher W. Dickson 12-7-1846
Bartlett, Mary to William F. Campbell 12-31-1849 (1-2-1850)
Barton, S. M. to V. L. Payne 5-17-1873 (5-20-1873)
Barville, Mary J. to J. A. Wright 11-2-1874 (11-6-1874)
Barwell, Elizabeth to Joseph Knight 1-12-1869 (1-13-1869)
Bashears, Amanda J. to James Willis Perwit? 9-6-1868 (9-7-1868)
Bashears, Sarah T. to J. H. C. Richmond 8-7-1865 (8-8-1865)
Baskin, Eliza J. to Turby Baskin 2-26-1867 (2-28-1867)
Baskin, Frances to Pat? Lovell 12-23-1867 (12-24-1867)
Baskins, Eliza Jane to Nicholas H. Boswell 6-9-1842
Baskins, Malinda J. to J. M. Kelly 1-21-1861 (1-23-1861)
Baskins, Sarah Ann to Thomas Lavell 11-27-1869 (12-2-1869)
Baskins, Sarah C. to J. W. Hill 1-12-1869
Baskins, Tennessee to George Evans 1-4-1870 (1-6-1870)
Bass, Mary to Tho. D. McFarland 10-7-1850 (10-9-1850)
Bass, Sarah J. to William C. Marsh 1-19-1860 (6?-19-1860)
Bateman, Frances to David Henderson 9-18-1871 (9-20-1871)
Bateman, Mary R. to James L. Walt 12-5-1859 (12-8-1859)
Bateman, Sarah C. to Cyrus G. McCrory 10-20-1851
Batewright, Ann to Henry Yount 7-24-1868
Baty, Rachel to John Webb 12-28-1867 (12-29-1867)
Baugh, Fannie to John R. Baugh 4-6-1858
Bays, Frances Betcy to Thomas Wesley Roberts 9-10-1857 (9-11-1857)
Bayse, Sarah Narcissa to Alexander Tims 3-1-1854 (3-2-1854)
Bealtin?, Jane to W. Thos. Tillman 1-30-1869 (2-4-1869)
Beard, Lydia to William Wilson 4-30-1873
Beasley, Matilda to Logan T. Cole 6-14-1873 (6-17-1873)
Beaty, Harriet E. to E. D. Maxwell 1-3-1856
Beaver, A. F. to E. J. Turnage 7-10-1872 (7-11-1872)
Beaver, J. V. to A. A. Bambridge 8-6-1870 (8-9-1870)
Beaver, Mildred to Wm. A. jr. Turnage 2-14-1865
Beavers, Anna? to John Stevens 5-10-1869 (5-13-1869)
Beavers, Laura L. to Virgil Long 9-1-1866 (9-6-1866)
Belford, Rena to Dan Calhoun 5-16-1870 (5-18-1870)
Bell, F. J. to Joseph Corder 6-29-1872 (6-30-1872)
Bell, Luticia to Robt. J. Bragg 11-19-1845
Bell, Matilda to John Tipton 12-26-1873 (12-27-1873)
Bell, Rebecca to John Cobb 9-4-1866 (9-15-1866)
Bell, Susannah W. to Lewelyn T. Tisdale 12-16-1854 (12-17-1854)
Bennet?, May to Preston Elcan 11-11-1871
Bennett, Sarah to Joel Sawyers 9-20-1873 (9-21-1873)
Benson, L. C. to J. A. Murchison 1-27-1873 (1-29-1873)
Benson, Mollie A. to D. B. Elam 1-25-1873 (1-29-1873)
Bently, Louisa B. to Josiah Goforth 1-1-1873 (1-2-1873)
Bergman, Sallie E. to Phinias G. Baker 6-13-1874 (6-14-1874)
Bernard, Hettie L. to Thomas H. Rutherford 10-18-1869 (10-19-1869)
Bernard, Laura Elizabeth to William Oscar Pryor 1-6-1850
Bernard, Lauretta L. to William James Strong 11-16-1847
Bernard, Lucetta to Charles S. Dickson 9-1-1846 (9-2-1846)
Bernard, Lucy to George Smith 1-4-1868
Bernard, Lusetta to E. McDanniel 4-22-1868
Bernard, Martha to Nathan Johnes 7-20-1867
Bernard, Mary to Isham A. Wright 1-3-1848 (1-6-1848)
Bernard, Mary to William Booker 12-27-1870
Bernard, Sarah to Thos. Calhoun 6-5-1869 (6-6-1869)
Berry, Cary Ann to Tias Williams 7-16-1869 (7-17-1869)
Berry, Julia to David Brown 12-24-1874
Berry?, Easter to Edward Thorton? no date (with 1874)
Bert, Margaret to Lee Ward 3-21-1874
Best, Perlina to Jessee Kinny 12-30-1873 (12-31-1873)
Betten, Ellen to George Allen 9-16-1871 (9-21-1871)
Beverly, Mrs. Malissa to Samuel Patterson 1-13-1870
Bevins, Julia to Thomas White 9-5-1872
Bibb, Charlotte Frances to Henry Coats 2-23-1847
Bibb, Mary E. to Benj. F. Forrest 11-11-1871 (11-12-1871)
Biggs, Mary Ann to Francis M. Chapman 11-12-1842 (11-13-1842)
Bigham, Sarah C. to Samuel H. Bell 9-28-1865 (10-22-1865)
Billing, Elizabeth to Francis M. Max 11-26-1866 (11-27-1866)
Billing, Sarah to Oliver Smith 12-13-1867
Billings, Amanda J. to G.? J. Jones 1-1-1863
Billings, Barbara Luticia to James Knox Polk Glass 12-8-1859
Billings, Ellen to Dorstal Hill 9-10-1869
Billings, Margaret Jane to Alfred B. Owen 5-22-1844
Billings, Margaret to John Nicholas Bringle 7-14-1846
Billings, Martha A. to N. T. Pugh 10-19-1867 (10-20-1867)
Billings, Mary to Joshua Weatherington 1-8-1857
Billings, Susan to W. H. Tinnen 2-4-1869 (1?-31-1869)
Binam, Fannie to Anderson Bumpas 11-11-1871 (11-24-1871)
Bird, A. V. to H. M. Timms 1-4-1871 (1-12-1871)
Bird, H. J. to J. R. Hamilton 2-23-1869 (2-25-1869)
Bird, Nancy to Caleb Holland 3-25-1867 (4-6-1867)
Bird, Nancy to Robert McCullough 7-25-1853 (7-26-1853)
Black, Jane Mildred to Wm. Henry Smith 11-13-1852 (11-16-1852)
Black, Mary Caroline to James Harris Jameson 6-30-1846
Blackwell, A. L. to M. J. Green 10-1-1872 (10-2-1872)
Blackwell, Ann to Henry Dunlap 10-25-1871
Blackwell, Bell to Allen Tarry 12-31-1872
Blackwood, S. M. P. to J. D. Craig 10-21-1871 (10-25-1871)
Blasingame, Nancy J. to Calvin Davis 1-17-1872 (1-18-1872)
Bledsoe, Ann to William Allen 1-25-1871 (1-26-1871)
Bledsoe, Annie to John Adkins 8-18-1874 (8-8?-1874)
Bledsoe, Catharine M. to Hosea W. Sherrill 4-1-1850 (4-3-1850)
Bledsoe, Cynthia M. to Napolian Fleming 12-11-1868
Bledsoe, Dora to William Henry Feezor 10-17-1867
Bledsoe, Ernesta? to George Johnson 4-6-1867 (4-7-1867)
Bledsoe, Hanna to Peter Hill 2-7-1867
Bledsoe, Hannah to Hiram Hughes 9-29-1874
Bledsoe, M. J. to David A. Gardener 1-11-1866
Bledsoe, Martha to Dick Beadls? 1-12-1868
Bledsoe, Martha to Jerie Morgan 12-30-1865
Bledsoe, Martha to Jerre Morgan 12-30-1865
Bledsoe, Martha to Jerry Morgan 12-30-1867 (12-30-1866?)
Bledsoe, Mary to John McMicken 12-26-1867
Bledsoe, Sallie to Frank McGregor 2-19-1873 (2-20-1873)
Bledsoe, Susan to Solomon Smith 1-28-1870
Blous?, Martha J. to John H. Woods 7-25-1860
Bolton, Winnie to Claiborn Clements 10-4-1870 (10-8-1870)
Bond, Florence to Soloman Sherrod 12-25-1866
Bond, Mary to William Hargrove 3-14-1868
Bond, Sallie to J. I. Howell 11-26-1872
Bonds, Tempe to Joseph Hooper 12-10-1873 (12-16-1873)
Boner, Julia to John Dalin 5-17-1867
Bonigle?, Mary Ellin to Thomas P. Bowden 12-26-1866 (12-27-1866)
Bonner, Margaret Jane to Chas. Christopher Moffett 10-27-1855 (10-30-1855)
Booker, Indianna P. to Thomas W. Markham 5-28-1846
Booker, Rachel to Wm. Bernard 12-24-1867
Booth, Sarah to Benj. Tims 12-17-1871 (12-19-1871)
Boothe, Ann to A. Pinckney Starnes 3-23-1844
Boothe, Elizabeth to David Wilson 7-21-1851 (7-22-1851)
Boothe, Lucretia Ann to Elijah Gibson 9-11-1848 (9-14-1848)
Boothe, Mary M. to Joel R. Manasco 12-20-1859 (12-21-1859)
Borum, Mollie to Edmond Pullin 11-19-1872
Boston, C. to Bill Slaughter 12-28-1874
Boswell, Amanda to H. C. Whitfield 1-22-1862
Boswell, Elizabeth to Alan Coats 12-24-1843 (12-26-1843)
Boswell, Elizabeth to W. J. Pace 10-5-1857 (10-16-1857)
Boswell, Frances Jane to Felty Coats 9-18-1845
Boswell, Lucy to Hughlut Harris 2-16-1870 (2-22-1870)
Boswell, Sarah to Hiram Howard 9-28-1872 (9-29-1872)
Boswell, Virginia M. to P. A. Bonne 8-6-1857
Bowden, Mildred C. to Robert P. Erwin 9-2-1867 (9-5-1867)
Bowden, R. T. to R. P. Erwin 6-8-1874
Bowers, Aggie J. to George W. Overall 9-24-1867
Bowers, C. P. to J. B. Chapman 11-10-1874 (11-11-1874)
Bowers, Caroline to Leonard Brantlin Smith 10-2-1848 (10-4-1848)
Bowers, Catharine R. to L. B. Smith 1-23-1861 (1-24-1861)
Bowers, Eliza Jane to Thomas Lowry Angus 3-22-1851 (3-25-1851)
Bowers, Ellen V. to Albert L. Overall 4-27-1868 (4-28-1868)
Bowers, Maria to Wash Wils? 9-12-1873 (9-15-1873)
Bowers, Parthina to Jacob Bradshaw 9-28-1867 (9-29-1867)
Bowers, Sallie to Dabna Spencer 11-9-1874
Bowles, Amy to William P. Mears 1-17-1848 (1-?-1848)
Bowles, Eliza Jane to Lemuel M. Campbell 12-1-1841 (12-2-1841)
Boyce, Harriett to June Green 11-9-1870 (11-11-1870)
Boyce, Rose to Joshua Wright 12-27-1867 (12-28-1867)
Boyd, Amanda to George Gorden 8-23-1872 (8-20?-1872)
Boyd, Belle H. to N. Wilson Baptist 1-11-1871 (1-18-1871)
Boyd, Catherine to George Washington Barret 12-27-1870 (12-28-1871?)

Boyd, Easter to John Akin 11-2-1868
Boyd, Easter to John Akin 11-7-1868
Boyd, Fannie to Lewis Bond 12-3-1873 (12-5-1873)
Boyd, Harriet to Alex Porter 1-4-1872 (1-15-1872)
Boyd, Jane to R. H. Trobough 12-14-1865
Boyd, Martha to John Duke 12-28-1870
Boyd, Mildred L. to Sam? P. Rose 4-12-1871
Boyd, Rosetta to Albert Lane 11-21-1872
Boyd, Sallie E. to Wm. H. Strange 10-10-1866 (10-11-1866)
Boyd, Sallie to Saml. Sharp 5-11-1872 (5-12-1872)
Boyd, Tabitha to Henry Baker 10-13-1866
Bradford, Mary Ann to Peyton Dyson 10-11-1872 (10-26-1872)
Bradshaw, Ellen to John Owens 12-31-1873
Bradshaw, Henrietta B. to Solomon A. Rhodes 12-21-1846 (12-23-1846)
Bradshaw, Lucy to Phill Sadden? 12-24-1869 (1-9-1870)
Bradshaw, Lucy to Phill Sodden? 12-24-1869
Brady, L. J. to Irvin Byford 1-9-1866 (1-10-1866)
Bragg, Emaline to Harry Claiburne 9-11-1865 (9-14-1865)
Bragg, Frances Ann to Saml. A. Holmes 12-17-1851
Bragg, Lucy Ann to Caleb Field 12-27-1872 (1-1-1873)
Bragg, Lucy M. to Robert B. Turner 9-27-1869 (9-28-1869)
Bragg, Margaret E. to Henry Cobb 3-11-1844
Bragg, Martha to George W. Bell 10-2-1845
Bragg, Mary Jane to R. P. Smith 8-7-1857
Bragg, Polly to Tom Simmons 12-26-1868 (1-1-1869)
Bragg, Virginia L. to Thomas F. Scott 11-2-1870 (11-3-1870)
Branch, Grizzy Ann to William Ralph 8-4-1841
Branch, Octavia to A. D. Hooks 10-19-1865 (10-24-1865)
Branch, Olivid? P. to Peter N. Bond 5-8-1865 (5-10-1865)
Bratton, Emma C. to E. P. Walker 10-25-1870 (10-30-1870)
Breedmon, Martha R. to Wm. Martin 6-3-1868
Brigman, Rosa to James E. Scott 7-17-1873 (7-18-1873)
Brimley, Margaret A. to Isaac T. Winford 6-9-1870 (6-12-1870)
Bringle, Catharine to Alexander Wood 6-4-1846
Bringle, Crarisa C. to Barzilla C. McBride 2-3-1853
Bringle, Margaret to John Smith 1-1-1873 (1-2-1873)
Bringle, N. J. to A. Homan 12-11-1869 (12-12-1869)
Brinkley, C. D. to Charles F. Newton 9-5-1872 (9-8-1872)
Brinkley, Elizabeth to D. M. Ballard 1-6-1868 (1-8-1868)
Britt, Adaline L. to John Mason 12-9-1843 (12-?-1843)
Brodway, Phebe Ann to Alex Malone 10-13-1865
Brooks, Ann C. to Joseph H. Borum 2-9-1841
Brooks, C. E. to Augustus A. Templeton 12-3-1872 (12-5-1872)
Brooks, Dora to Benj. Fowlkes 4-1-1870 (4-3-1870)
Brooks, Louisa to Isaac Payne 1-26-1867 (2-2-1867)
Brooks, Louisa to Robert Smith 1-6-1868
Brooks, Louisa to William Brown 7-23-1867
Brooks, Martha Jane to Richard Thomas Elmore 12-9-1841
Brooks, Mollie to Lewis Connor 12-13-1872 (4-24-1873)
Brown, Amerca J. to W. H. Bowers 10-2-1865 (10-3-1865)
Brown, Anne to Henry Olive 12-19-1874 (12-20-1874)
Brown, Armenta to John Leach 4-8-1855 (4-14-1855)
Brown, Caroline to Nelson Wilie 1-7-1872 (1-9-1872)
Brown, Catharine to Amanuel Harris 12-10-1873 (12-11-1873)
Brown, Dina to Peter Thomas 10-1-1874 (10-3-1874)
Brown, Elizabeth A. to George W. Walton 12-25-1867 (12-29-1867)
Brown, Elizabeth Jane to Asa? Lenek? 2-19-1853
Brown, Emily Matilda to Asa Leach 11-28-1854
Brown, Jane to Fredrick Prehit 1-18-1867
Brown, Malissa to Washington Alston 7-8-1873
Brown, Mariah to John Patten 10-17-1874
Brown, Martha to W. H. Adams 2-12-1873 (2-13-1873)
Brown, Mary E. to S. Y. Owen 1-21-1869 (1-23-1869)
Brown, Mary J. to Joseph Dickery? 2-15-1858 (2-16-1858)
Brown, Mary to William Cannon 12-31-1866
Brown, Matilda to William Wright 6-10-1867
Brown, Patra to Tip Weaver 10-14-1874
Brown, Rebecca to Fed Hughlett 3-5-1873 (3-6-1873)
Brown, Sallie E. to Thos. J. Gray 11-23-1867 (11-24-1867)
Brown?, Mary Ann to Thoas Ralph 12-2-1843
Browne, Bettie to Wm. Brisentine 5-16-1868 (5-17-1868)
Bryant, Nancy E. to Wm. Green McClellan 11-14-1849
Bryant, Susan Ann to William F. Tilman 6-15-1866 (6-17-1866)
Budget, M. Adline to William Dueast 10-12-1857 (10-16-1857)
Buff, Eliza to J. C. Wellsman 10-10-1868
Buise, Caroline to William Davis 10-28-1842
Bumpas, Cohaly? to Ben Bell 7-28-1866 (7-29-1866)
Bumpass, Ella to Thomas Brown? 12-11-1869
Bumphass, Loveann to Dick Cothran 12-25-1873
Bunch, Jennie M. to Joseph B. Webb 12-5-1872
Bungle, Eve Ann to Flranklin Huffman 1-29-1846
Bunton, Maggie to Washington Smith 3-15-1871
Burchet, A. to P. Burchet 7-27-1870 (9-1-1872?)
Burchet, Mariah to Isaac Pryer 4-26-1870
Burchett, Laura to Guy Bynum 11-9-1871
Burkhart, Indiana M. to Charles G. Griffith 11-12-1866 (11-13-1866)
Burkhart, Safronia Evaline to James H. Fortner 8-27-1846 (9-3-1846)
Burl, Pennie to Phillip Shaw 12-5-1874
Burnes, Fannie to Andrew Jackson 8-3-1871 (8-4-1871)
Burnet, Hettie to Jim Wilson 11-7-1874 (11-9-1874)
Burns, Eliz. to Franklin Cox 11-13-1871
Burrel, Catharine to Christofer Hunt 2-22-1868
Burrel, Katie to Charles Smith 12-17-1873
Burrel, Mary to Cambridge Taylor 12-28-1869
Burrel, Maryetta to Jacob Davis 12-17-1873 (12-20-1873)
Burress, Nancy to John Elder 4-27-1842
Burton, Frances J. to James B. Hunt 12-7-1872 (12-12-1872)
Burton, Mary Ann to Daniel Adams Trobough 6-24-1846 (6-25-1846)
Buster, Frances S. to John W. Kilpatrick 11-17-1869
Butler, Elmira to James Cothran 12-18-1843 (12-21-1843)
Butler, Letty to John Griffin 9-16-1871 (9-21-1871)
Butler, Martha J. to S. P. Kirtland no dates (with 1860)
Butler, Martha to S. P. Kirkland 1-2-1860 (1-4-1860)
Butler, Mary Ann to Edmond Tho. Yarbrough 7-14-1853
Butler, Mary to Peola? Howard 12-22-1842 (12-?-1842)
Butler, Matilda to George Wood 10-7-1869
Butler, Miss A. S. to G. W. Cherry 7-18-1861 (7-19-1861)
Butler, Parthena A. M. to William McLain 8-9-1861 (8-10-1861)
Buttner?, Lucy to Daniel Mason 11-20-1872
Byars, Dicy M. to John R. Townsend 12-17-1872 (12-18-1872)
Bynum, Nancy to William Yates 8-4-1866 (8-5-1866)
Byram, Annie F. to J. D. McGrath 11-23-1874 (11-25-1874)
Byram, Ellen O. to Giles Brough 8-12-1863 (8-16-1863)
Byrd, A. A. to Jessee C. Benson 2-14-1868 (2-20-1868)
Byrd, M. R. to L. W. Hamilton 2-15-1870 (2-20-1870)
Byrd, Mrs. E. A. to J. F. Timmon 12-19-1867 (12-22-1867)
Byrd, Mrs. to John C. Caughein 10-2-1869
Byrd, V.? F. to B. L. Matthis 2-21-1866 (2-22-1866)
Byrns?, Susan C. to Jas. W. Coonts 10-15-1856 (10-16-1857?)
Cage, Canna? to Hamilton Stanup? 5-8-1869 (2-19-1871?)
Cage, Fannie to Richmond Burrell 5-9-1874
Cage, Matilda to George Bailey 1-8-1874
Cage, Sadie (Sallie?) to John Douglas Smith 7-21-1874
Caldwell, Adaline to Ben Dickson 6-3-1871 (6-5-1871)
Calhon?, Delia Elizabeth to B. L. Clark 5-25-1872
Calhoon, Fannie to W. H. Adams 1-4-1857 (1-6-1857)
Calhoon, Sallie to Jacob Cheek 1-20-1866 (1-21-1866)
Calhoun, Addie L. to Jno. D. Warmack 12-15-1873 (12-16-1873)
Calhoun, Amanda to Elyer? Tanner 1-4-1867 (1-14-1867)
Calhoun, Bettie to E. T. Wilson 8-21-1860 (8-22-1860)
Calhoun, Feebe to George Hall 10-29-1870
Calhoun, K. T. to James Mays 11-27-1871 (11-28-1871)
Calhoun, M. to N. Moore 12-22-1874 (12-24-1874)
Calhoun, Margaret J. to J. Barnett Gracy 12-9-1868 (12-10-1868)
Calhoun, Maria to Thomas Yarbro 6-2-1870
Calhoun, Martha E. to W. O. Menefee 11-14-1860 (11-15-1860)
Calhoun, Mollie J. to Samuel W. Stitt 1-10-1860 (1-11-1860)
Calhoun, Phoebe to R. Green 12-15-1866 (3-30-1867)
Calhoun, Rebecca to Dick Still 6-20-1872
Calhoun, Rener to Wm. Price 4-11-1874 (4-8?-1874) B
Calhoun, Sallie A. to J. J. Rice 12-6-1866
Calhoun, Sallie to Jacob Cheek 1-20-1866
Campbell, Elizabeth to G. W. Perry 8-8-1874 (8-17-1874)
Campbell, Frances M. to Moses Smith 3-10-1845 (3-17-1845)
Campbell, Jane Dean to William B. Baenbridge 11-15-1847 (11-16-1847)
Campbell, Jane to Saml. Alexr. Thompson 2-13-1843 (2-16-1843)
Campbell, Laura to Phillip Fraley 12-30-1869 (1-7-1870)
Campbell, Martha Ann to William J. Burris 11-7-1844 (11-9-1844)

Campbell, Mary Jane to Alexr. W. Murphy 2-5-1851
Campbell, Mary to James V. Moore 9-18-1865 (9-19-1865)
Campbell, Rosanna to Cornelius Brown 9-5-1872 (9-14-1872)
Campbell, S. E. to J. F.? Cousar 5-9-1870 (5-10-1870)
Campbell, Susan Jane to Thomas W. Coats 8-24-1841 (8-26-1841)
Cannon, Eliza to James Leach 6-24-1854 (6-26-1854)
Cannon, Elizabeth to Joshua Bailey 1-3-1867
Cannon, Julia F. to William E. Elmore 7-18-1840
Caraway, Narcissa to Joseph Collier 5-27-1859 (5-28-1859)
Carolton, Nellie to Needham H. Herron 12-27-1870 (12-28-1870)
Carother, E. C. to W. B. Reaves 3-29-1866 (4-5-1866)
Carothers, Frances to Willis McNary 6-13-1866 (6-15-1866)
Carothers, Susan to John Ross 8-8-1870
Carr, Marth J. to James Parker 3-31-1843
Carracle?, Nancey to A. W. Donnaway 12-19-1868 (12-20-1868)
Carraway, Narcissa to Joseph Collier 5-27-1859 (5-28-1859)
Carrington, D. A. to Andrew D. Flowers 2-19-1869 (2-20-1869)
Carter, Georga to R. M. Nelson 5-7-1872 (5-8-1872)
Carter, Heurin C. to Junius H. Elcan 3-2-1865
Carter, Heurin? C. to Junius H. Elcan 3-2-1865 (3-7-1865)
Carter, Martha to James D. Vaughan 12-4-1869 (12-5-1869)
Carter, Martha to W. H. McNair 2-25-1860
Carter, Martha to Z. H. McNar 2-25-1860
Carter, Mary J. to D. L. Jones 12-28-1859 (12-29-1859)
Carter, Narcissa to John A. Chapman 2-24-1869
Carter, Sarah Porter to Saml. Thomas 12-19-1873 (12-20-1873)
Caruthers, Churney to Thomas Johnson 9-11-1873
Caruthers, Leeva? to Nathan Sanford 10-2-1873
Caruthers, Margaretta A. T. to William H. Harper 11-19-1847
Casey, Tabitha to Lomax Brasher 6-6-1853 (6-7-1853)
Cash, Del to John McGuiver 3-15-1870
Caskey, Joanna to P. B. McWilliams 1-20-1869 (1-21-1869)
Caskey, M. W. to C. A. Johnson 12-31-1870 (1-5-1871)
Caskey, Margaret W. to James O. Lynn 12-31-1870 (1-2-1871)
Catten, Lida to William Boykin 11-26-1868
Catten, Mary to Frank Hall 6?-15-1867 (6-16-1867)
Cavenor, Nannie M. to George A. Walker 12-26-1870 (12-29-1870)
Cavnaugh, Nanna to T. M. Pugh 8-1-1872 (8-4-1872)
Chamber, Louisa to Henry Coward 11-17-1865 (11-18-1865)
Chamber, Martha to Dock Talley 2-25-1873 (2-26-1873)
Chambers, Margaret to Giles Smith 4-25-1873 (4-26-1873)
Champion, Matilda to Henry Deakins 8-27-1866 (8-28-1866)
Champion, Mildred N. to Josiah A. Morrow 9-3-1849 (9-6-1849)
Chaney, Mariah A. to William Carriston? 3-4-1871
Chapman, J. F. to S. T. Bowers 3-19-1874 (3-20-1874)
Chapman, Louisa to John B. Gehen 12-13-1859 (12-15-1859)
Chapman, Louisa to Robert Lamkin 4-14-1874
Chapman, Louisiana to John B. Gehen 12-13-1859 (12-15-1859)
Chapman, Nancy E. to Theodore Burtis 6-15-1866 (6-19-1866)
Chapman, Sallie J. to John J. Akin 4-18-1865 (4-20-1865)
Chapman, Sallie J. to Samuel J. Ackin? 4-18-1865
Cheek, M. J. to F. L. Smith 9-5-1871 (9-6-1871)
Cherry, Eliza K. to Richard S. Templeton 12-18-1860 (12-20-1860)
Childers, Harriet to Thomas C. McCraw 1-28-1860
Childress, Miss Minerva to L. W. Clark 11-4-1874 (11-8-1874)
Claibourne, Maria to Weddle Taylor 3-6-1871
Claibun?, Rose to John Johnson 1-28-1867 (1-30-1867)
Claiburn, Adeline to Buckham Martin 1-6-1868 (1-11-1868)
Claiburn, Sarah to Mat Winford 10-17-1869 (1-3-1869?)
Claiburn, Sarah to Mat. Winfrow? 10-17-1868
Claiburne, Betsy to Michael Hicks 3-6-1869
Claiburne, Emily to William Fletcher 1-15-1868
Claiburne, Louisa to Thos. Markham 2-1-1866 (2-7-1866)
Clanton, Patsey A. to John E. Sullinger 9-5-1868
Clanton, Patsey to John E. Sullinger 9-5-1868 (9-7-1868)
Clark, Adaline to Wm. T. Miller 1-13-1859
Clark, Amanda Malvina to Jacob Hillman Miller 12-21-1853 (12-22-1853)
Clark, Eliza to Elias D. Tarbrok 2-11-1857
Clark, Elizabeth to Morris Killingsworth 1-31-1844 (1-?-1844)
Clark, Ellen C. to William V. Goodman 9-26-1865
Clark, G.? A. to Benjamin H. Terrell 12-19-1868 (12-22-1868)
Clark, Hannah to Daniel? Smith 11-24-1869 (11-25-1869)
Clark, Julia to W. G. Upchurch ?-21-1861 (1-20-1861)
Clark, Juliann Minerva to James Harvey Armstrong 1-29-1842 (2-?-1842)
Clark, Laura Ann to Thomas Claiborne 9-24-1849 (10-4-1849)
Clark, Lizzie to Solomon Haynes 12-9-1874
Clark, Mariah L. to A. C. Hall 5-8-1866
Clark, Martha to Isaac Smith 3-1-1870 (3-2-1870)
Clark, Mary Elizabeth to Otho S. Feezor 12-21-1854
Clark, Mary to Edmond Tate 3-4-1869
Clark, Sarah Ann to John Smith 1-26-1843 (1-?-1843)
Clark, Sarah Eliza to John Dearing 1-7-18557
Clark, Sarah Jane to Wm. Wilson Morris 1-31-1866
Clark, Sarah to James Lycurgus Givin 11-11-1843 (11-?-1843)
Clark, Temperance Lucintha to Peter Juchoore? Hicks 6-20-1850 (7-3-1850)
Clay, A. P. to S. C. Harris 10-30-1867
Clay, Matilda to Thos. McIntyre 7-3-1872 (7-4-1872)
Clemant, Lavina E. to John W. Williams 6-6-1854 (6-7-1854)
Clement, Bettie to West Peete 12-25-1873
Clement, C. A. to Jesse Brown 2-7-1861 (2-12-1861)
Clement, Minerva to Grandison Calhoun 12-29-1865 (12-30-1865)
Clement, Mollie to J. W. Pinson 9-23-1872
Clement, R. to William Taylor 3-23-1866 (4-1-1866)
Clements, Candis to John Tipton 3-12-1870
Clements, Caroline to James O. Densford 4-2-1862 (4-3-1862)
Clements, E. R. to C. T. Booker 11-16-1874 (11-18-1874)
Clements, Emily to Lumon Sherrod 1-5-1867 (1-6-1867)
Clements, F. to Isaac Dyson 12-5-1871
Clements, F. to Isaac Dyson 12-5-1871 (1-6-1872)
Clements, Fannie to M. Roberts 8-17-1867 (8-18-1867)
Clements, Jenny to Owen Thomas 11-23-1866 (11-24-1866)
Clements, Lenord to M. A. Lassiter 12-17-1872 (12-19-1872)
Clements, Martha to Moses Robinson 10-17-1871
Clements, Mary A. to Thomas M. Williams 10-9-1848 (10-11-1848)
Clements, Mary A. to W. J> Roberts 11-6-1865 (12-5-1865)
Clements, Mary to Blunt Cockrill 1-10-1869
Clements, Phillis to John Wooten 1-13-1866 (1-14-1866)
Clements, Rosa to Isaac? Clark 9-7-1872 (9-8-1872)
Clements, Susan to Julius Stubbs 12-27-1866
Clements, Violet to Alfred Gibbs 3-23-1872 (3-31-1872)
Clements, Virginia E. to N. H. Elcan 7-4-1859 (7-6-1859)
Clemmit, Malina to John Richardson 11-27-1874
Clevies, Frances A. to J. V. B. Rogers 2-24-1869 (2-25-1869)
Clifton, Amanda E. to J. W. Cavenar 12-26-1870 (12-27-1870)
Coats, Bettie to Franklin Wiseman 2-18-1871 (2-19-1871)
Coats, Delitha to Benjamin Franklin Smith 12-22-1873 (12-23-1873)
Coats, Elizabeth to Lawrence Raynor 9-4-1861 (9-5-1861)
Coats, Elizabeth to Wm. Smith 3-30-1872 (4-14-1872)
Coats, Gilly Eglentine to Berry Coats 11-1-1850 (11-3-1850)
Coats, Martha to Henry Coats 10-4-1845 (10-15-1845)
Coats, Martha to L. W. Wiseman 12-1-1874 (12-2-1874)
Coats, Rosa Ann to John E. Murphey 2-7-1872 (2-8-1872)
Coats, Sarah to Lewis Grattum 3-3-1842
Cobb, Louisa to Joseph C. Brooks 11-14-1861
Cocke, Hattie to R. C. Smith 6-12-1867
Cocke, V. Carolin to Owen Turnage 10-30-1867 (10-31-1867)
Cockrill, Josephin to Alexander Dennis 1-14-1869 (1-18-1869)
Cockrill, Maria to Rihd. Sadler? 10-7-1867 (10-13-1867)
Cockrill, Sarah J. to J. C. Caulbreath 4-11-1868 (4-12-1868)
Cockrill, Sarah Y. to Charles H. Hill 10-28-1840 (10-29-1840)
Coe, Eliza to George Anderson 1-21-1874
Coe, Lovy to Julian Bumpbass 4-23-1870
Coffman, Carusa to Lewis Payton? 12-31-1873
Cole, Florrence to J. H. Jones 6-25-1867 (6-30-1867)
Cole, Martha Jane to W. J. Thompson 12-17-1860 (12-19-1860)
Cole, Mary Ann to Stephen Smith 2-3-1844 (2-8-1844)
Coleman, Charlotte to Ross Montgoery 8-23-1866 (8-26-1866)
Coleman, Dafney to Spencer Jones 8-23-1866 (8-26-1866)
Coleman, Mary to Nicholas Jones 11-13-1871
Collier, Eliza W. to William J. Hall 7-9-1850 (7-10-1850)
Collier, Martha to Robert Weatherington 9-11-1869 (9-12-1869)
Collier, Susan Elizabeth to Ephraim Hall Smith 10-16-1851
Colmer, Tommy to James C. Jackson 12-11-1869 (12-14-1869)
Compton, Margaret to Jacob Jones 12-17-1872 (12-22-1872)
Conner, Catheran to James Laird 12-19-1866
Cook, Frances to William Yarbroh 12-8-1857 (12-9-1857)

Cook, Harriet to Charles Glass 12-25-1869 (12-28-1869)
Cooke, Mariah to John Scott 2-27-1871 (3-2-1871)
Cooper, Caladonia to W. T. Harris 2-7-1874
Cooper, Charlotte to Isaac Adkisson 3-6-1843 (3-9-1843)
Cooper, Elizabeth C. to E. A. Feezor 11-27-1867 (11-28-1867)
Cooper, J. M. to S. G. McCluney 9-5-1870 (9-13-1870)
Cooper, Malinda to Michael B. Martin 10-20-1849 (10-21-1849)
Cooper, Mary to Anderson Hunt 11-21-1860 (11-22-1868)
Cooper, Mary to James McIntyre 3-20-1843 (3-23-1843)
Cooper, Susan to William H. Ticer 11-4-1858 (1-28-1859)
Corbet, L. E. to James D. Roberson 11-24-1869 (11-25-1869)
Corbet, Mary E. to Jesse G. Brown 9-23-1868 (9-24-1868)
Corder, Margaret J. to W. H. Archer 11-27-1861 (11-28-1861)
Corisar?, Eliz. Ann to Thomas L. Angus 10-12-1846 (10-13-1846)
Correthers, Laura A. to James Tucker 12-5-1857 (12-8-1857)
Corss, Henrettia to John Burrell 2-15-1873 (2-16-1873)
Cosby, Jane Ann to James C. Lanier 5-16-1854 (5-17-1854)
Cotheran, A. L. to S. M. Bell 2-17-1874 (2-18-1874)
Cotheran, Mary Jane to Lewis Harris 3-6-1872 (3-7-1872)
Cotherin, Ann to Frank Smith 12-2-1869 (12-3-1869)
Cotherun, Eldora to Saml. Polk 1-5-1870
Cothran, Mary to Isaac Crawley 2-8-1873 (2-9-1873)
Cothran, Mollie to Sam Strange 6-18-1874
Cotten, Ann to Walter Turner 12-30-1874
Cotten, Celia to Jacob Wilson 3-13-1866 (8-27-1866)
Cotten, Fannie to Jason Cotten 12-26-1868
Cotten, Sarah Carolin to Joseph Henry Dunham 12-12-1848
Cotton, Margaret E. to Wm. J. Kents 12-18-1852 (12-21-1852)
Cotton, Mary to Robt. Dickerson 6-22-1867 (6-23-1867)
Cotton, Nancy to Saml. P. Bernard 2-13-1854
Cotton, Rachel to Geo. Elam 7-2-1870
Cotton, Sallie to Daniel Hill 6-8-1872 (6-9-1872)
Couch, Evalina Pantillie? to Harvey Hughes 5-15-1843
Cousar?, Sarah Ann to James Chalmers Moore 11-5-1842 (11-8-1842)
Couts?, Cynthia to Bradford Smith 3-24-1842
Covinton, Dicy A. to Andrew Davis Flower 2-19-1869
Cowan, Ann M. to Simeon Horne 4-27-1841
Coward, Frances Eliza to Jno. Mesina Harding 12-22-1855 (1-2-1856)
Coward, Harriet to Henry Colman 12-23-1867 (12-27-1867)
Coward, Louisa to Nathan Adkins 10-22-1874 (10-23-1874)
Coward, Mary to Charles A. Weaver 12-28-1869
Cox, Eliza Jane to John J. Martin 4-1-1844
Cox, Lavina to John Ludwick 7-17-1865
Cox, Mary Jane to Perry Dawson 10-14-1872 (10-16-1872)
Cox, Parthenia Ann Melisa to James Norfleet Martin 7-8-1844
Cox, Sarah Frances to William D. Walton 2-12-1844 (2-13-1844)
Craig, Caroline to John Z. Hurt 12-4-1865 (12-6-1865)
Craig, Margaret S. to John Draffin 2-24-1855
Craig, Mary L. to John Druffin 11-19-1851
Craig, Virginia F. to John Camel? 4-10-1871 (4-11-1871)
Craighead, Ann to Edward Thomas 9-10-1872
Crain, Mary J. to James L. Cash 6-24-1873 (6-26-1873)
Crawford, Amanda to John Ewell 1-2-1854 (1-7-1854)
Crenshaw, Amanda to Yeatman Crenshaw 2-24-1870
Crenshaw, Clarinda to Charles Williams 1-21-1874
Crenshaw, Eliz. J. to Geo. C. Howard 10-28-1851 (10-29-1851)
Crenshaw, Indiana to Allen Debow Lake 11-15-1848 (11-16-1848)
Crenshaw, Julia C. to Thomas L. Garland 2-23-1865
Crenshaw, Julia to Jessee Faulk 12-20-1865
Crenshaw, Mary to Lafayette Robertson 12-28-1868
Crenshaw, Viola S. to J. S.? Winford 4-13-1857
Crenshaw, Viola S. to John S. Winford 4-13-1857 (4-16-1857)
Crofford, Josephin to Plesant Manasco 6-19-1867 (6-18?-1867)
Crofford, S. A. to Plesant Manasco 5-6-1870 (5-8-1870)
Cronk?, Rachel to Adam T. Llewelling 1-13-1856
Crouch, Mary R. to Jerome Dorsey 5-10-1855 (6-12-1853?)
Crouch, Sarah E. to George W. Pennel 1-14-1846 (1-15-1846)
Culbeath?, Carnea to Wm. Marshall 11-15-1865 (11-16-1865)
Culbreath, Annie to John D. Hopkins 10-2-1871 (10-5-1871)
Culbreath, Dicy to J. A. Ballard 2-23-1860
Culbreath, Dicy to R. M. Knox 7-1-1868 (7-2-1868)
Culbreath, Elizabeth F. to James Colwell 5-4-1860 (5-5-1860)
Culbreath, Elizabeth to James Buckley? 12-4-1843 (12-?-1843)
Culbreath, Lucy to Colemon Cooper 6-18-1870
Culbreath, Lucy to Ebenezer T. Walker 1-3-1842 (1-4-1842)
Culbreath, Martha H. to Joseph W. McCetcham 1-12-1869 (1-13-1869)
Culbreath, Mary E. to Saml. Winfree 2-26-1868
Culbreath, Mary to Archibald Pinson 1-11-1841 (1-?-1841)
Culbreath, Mollie E. to W. F. Prewett, 12-15-1874
Culbreath, S. T. to M. T. Richardson 7-16-1872 (7-20-1872)
Culbreath, Virginia to Daniel T. Lake 1-11-1855
Culbreth, Mary Frances to Joseph S. Waller 11-14-1857 (3-20-1858)
Culbreth, T. C. to L. P. Marshall 9-28-1870
Cullum, A. C. to J. J. Jones 1-4-1871 (1-5-1871)
Cullum, Eliz. Caroline Rebec to William Gillom Grace 1-13-1846
Cultin, Sarah E. to Thomas D. Pennel 12-16-1858 (12-23-1858)
Cumins, L. Jane to Wm. Taylor 1-10-1870
Cummins, Mary E. to W. P. Flowers 5-8-1871
Cup, Mary Ann to Taylor Adams 10-21-1869 (10-22-1869)
Curry, Estell to Kent H. WWhitten 9-25-1871
Curry, Jessie E. to James A. Smith 12-31-1870 (1-2-1871)
Curtis, Eliza Ann to James W. Saxton 11-21-1844
Curtis, Elizabeth to John P. Freeman 6-3-1844
Cyle, Agness to Eli Vinston 8-23-1866 (8-26-1866)
Dacus, Amanda to John D. Boswell 9-3-1859
Dacus, Elizabeth Jane to John Boswell 2-11-1847
Dacus, Frances to Daniel Buford Boswell 9-27-1848 (9-28-1848)
Dacus, Hester Ann to Franklin Huffman 10-3-1859 (10-4-1859)
Dacus, Martha L. to John Davis Boswell 12-28-1854
Dacus, Mary B. to J. G. Sherill 8-8-1860
Dacus, Rebeca A. to F. M. Knight 11-22-1860
Dacus, Viney to Peter M. Wilson 1-12-1869
Dagling, Elizabeth to William Ralph 11-7-1866 (11-8-1867?)
Dale, Catharan E. to John A. Haines 10-15-1870 (10-16-1870)
Dalle?, Willie Helen to Robert H. White 3-23-1871
Dalton, Mary Ann to George Simpson 1-9-1854 (1-12-1854)
Daniel, Harriet to Thos. Parker 8-1-1868 (8-3-1868)
Daniel, Manerva to Zachariah Harrison 1-31-1857 (2-5-1857)
Daniel, Mary A. to Robert A. Walker 5-8-1873 (5-3?-18730
Daniel, Tillie A. E. to William J. Prince 4-6-1867 (4-9-1867)
Daniels, Louisa C. to Jesse G. Brown 2-27-1871 (2-22?-1871)
Darby, Cecilia Beverly to William A. Old 1-30-1847 (2-?-1847)
Darby, Mary Elizabeth to Norman Reynolds 6-26-1850
Darby, ____ Vanhook to John Wesley Clark 11-24-1842 (12-?-1842)
Darr, Lucy to Peter Long 12-9-1840
Davenport, Bettie to W. H. Fisher 7-22-1871
David, Arelia to John McKenzie 5-10-1861 (7-8-1861)
David, J. A. to John W. Webb 6-17-1871 (6-19-1871)
David, V. C. to W. F. Jones 12-17-1868 (12-3-1869?)
Davidson, D. Ann to James Starnes 3-13-1866 (3-14-1866)
Davidson, Elizabeth Wade to James Timbs 12-21-1853 (12-22-1853)
Davidson, Ellen C. to Jabus Timms 12-28-1859 (12-29-1859)
Davidson, Julia C. to Z. C. Cullen 8-27-1860 (8-28-1860)
Davidson, Mary Valentia to Wm. Carroll Marsh 12-21-1853 (12-22-1853)
Davidson, Mildred to Chas. Delashmet 11-18-1867 (11-21-1867)
Davidson, S. E. to John D. Moore 8-2-1872 (8-6-1872)
Davis, Annie to Andrew Foley 10-14-1874 (10-15-1874)
Davis, D. E. to W. F. Jones 12-17-1868 (1-7-1869)
Davis, Eleanor B. to Adam Dean Campbell 12-3-1855 (12-4-1855)
Davis, Eleanor C. to William C. Hart 1-28-1850
Davis, Eliza Ann to Wm. McKinstry 12-16-1858
Davis, Elizabeth Jane to Marcus H. Cullum 1-27-1845
Davis, M. C. to Thomas Carson 10-11-1865
Davis, M. E. to Franklin Hertsfield 2-12-1872 (2-13-1872)
Davis, M. F. to William Payne 9-6-1865 (9-7-1865)
Davis, Manerva A. E. to Saml. M. Williams 2-11-1857 (2-12-1857)
Davis, Marth E. to J. C. Clayton 10-21-1865 (10-25-1865)
Davis, Martha A. E. to Wm. G. Grace 5-1-1855
Davis, Martha Helen to Rufus T. Basheres 7-24-1843
Davis, Mary Susan to Joseph L. Roberts 12-8-1852 (12-9-1852)
Davis, Melvina to John A. M. Covington 6-11-1857
Davis, Nancy Jane to John Tinnen 2-7-1859
Davis, O. C. to J. G. McCain 1-26-1862 (1-29-1862)
Davis, Ofilia to Jerry Omara 1-8-1867
Davis, S. M. A. to J.R. Culbreath 6-20-1874
Davis, Salina M. to James M> Hill 12-27-1859 (12-28-1859)
Davis, Salvina? M. to James McHale 12-27-1859
Davis, Sarah Adiline to Wm. Carroll Davis 9-4-1854 (9-6-1854)

Davis, Sarah Jane to Thomas? James Wiley 8-10-1854
Davis, Siller to Rubin Davis 11-5-1874 (11-8-1874)
Davis, Susan Ann to J. Lambkins 8-8-1873 (8-9-1873)
Dawson, Eliza Janie to Absolam Hendricks Evans 10-8-1853 (10-9-1853)
Dawson, Elizabeth Jane to W. L. Baskins 8-1-1866 (8-10-1866)
Day, Cathran to Napolion Pete 3-26-1866 (3-31-1866)
Day, Miss Emma C. to Dr. A. Perry 11-12-1860 (11-13-1860)
Day, S. P. to M. Perry 2-6-1866
Deakin, Harriet V. to Jas. H. Cook 11-14-1856 (11-19-1856)
Deakins, Ann Eliza to David H. Woods 12-8-1847 (12-?-1847)
Deakins, Indiana to Josiah A. Monroe 3-23-1852 (3-25-1852)
Deakins, Mary E. to David H. Wood 12-17-1850 (12-19-1850)
Deakins, Sarah Ann to David M. Parish 2-12-1853 (2-16-1853)
Dean, Susan A. to James M. Jimmerson 11-26-1873 (12-3-1873)
Deason, Eliza Ann to James Nichols 7-19-1846
Dehart, Mary Bryant to William B. Densford 10-13-1849 (10-14-1849)
Delancey, S. L. to R. S. Ford 2-23-1874 (2-26-1874)
Delancey, Sarah E. to Joseph W. Earwood 9-18-1867 (9-22-1867)
Delaney, Mary J. to W. W. McKinny 8-3-1872 (8-4-1872)
Delashmeit, Mariah W. to John L. Turnage 7-1-1865
Delashment, Lavina to P. C. Alexander 11-11-1862 (11-13-1862)
Delashment, Mary F. to Wm. M. Eldridge 1-23-1865
Delashmet, Adaline G. to Andrew J. Loyd 1-16-1872 (1-17-1872)
Delashmet, Elzabeth to William Mears 11-21-1848 (11-22-1848)
Delashmet, Marth J. to Saml. R. Timberlick 5-6-1867 (5-14-1867)
Delashmet, Martha A. to George W. Haynie 5-29-1852 (5-30-1852)
Delashmet, Sarah Margaret to John Craig 8-2-1871 (8-3-1871)
Delashmet, Susan D. to Wm. J. Cullam 12-13-1869 (12-14-1869)
Delashmit, Nancy E. to Robert H. Ralph 8-8-1871 (8-10-1871)
Dellahunty, L. A. to Joseph B. Harrell 11-17-1868 (11-18-1868)
Deming, Ive Ann to George M. Nevils 2-11-1871 (2-12-1871)
Dennis, Sarah A. to Benj. K. Simmons 2-17-1868 (2-18-1868)
Densford, Amanda to John Adams 4-6-1866 (4-7-1866)
Densford, Julia to Wm. D. Erwin 6-4-1866 (6-12-1866)
Densford, Sallie to Mat McElmore 12-12-1872
Dentenac, Manda to Thomas Lewis 8-15-1867
Desmond?, Julia M. L. to Samuel B. Hurt 7-2-1842 (7-16-1842)
Dewease, Maggie to J. N. Leach 12-18-1874 (12-22-1874)
Dickason, arion to Ned Graham 11-26-1869 (11-27-1869)
Dickens, Emaline to Louis Fisher 3-20-1866 (3-24-1866)
Dickens, Henrietta to Wm. Shackleford 12-16-1868 (12-25-1868)
Dickerson, Mary E. to John Rowland 8-22-1850
Dickerson, Mary E. to Robert B. Batte 10-17-1866 (10-25-1866)
Dickerson, Mary Janice to Albert Martain 7-12-1871 (7-21?-1872?)
Dickerson, Nancy J. to Columbus F. Gay 6-22-1867
Dickey, Nancy to L. B. Smith 5-11-1874 (5-13-1874)
Dickson, Cora to Daniel Wiley Payne 11-12-1867 (11-14-1867)
Dickson, Fannie to John Randolph 5-15-1867 (5-18-1867)
Dickson, Martha Ann to Charles Strong 1-21-1857 (1-22-1857)
Dickson, Mollie to R. C. Thompson 12-28-1869 (12-30-1869)
Dillahenty, Laura to Saml. Helm 2-24-1872
Dillahunty, E. to R. N. Harrel 11-6-1865 (11-15-1865)
Dillahunty, Lucinda to R. C. Young 3-19-1874
Dillahunty, Martha to A. R. Wylie 9-12-1870 (9-13-1870)
Dillahunty, Sallie to J. L. Jamison 12-15-1874
Dillihunty, Susan to Robert Gee 6-15-1859 (6-?-1859)
Dinkins, _____ to S. H. Hawkins 5-6-1868
Dinwoody, Dilly to Malica C. Bright 1-24-1848
Dinwoody, Marget to Albert Williams 9-19-1859
Dison, Sallie to George Washington 8-21-1873
Dixon, Amanda to Covey Moore 12-1-1873 (12-3-1873)
Dobson, C. C. to James Morgan 12-20-1870 (12-22-1870)
Dobson, Martha Jane to Robert Smith 12-11-1867
Dodson, Sarah Benton to Saml. Clements 8-9-1851 (8-10-1851)
Dogget, Eliza to Wm. Runnels 5-5-1869 (5-9-1869)
Doldon?, Mary C. to E. F. Walker 9-14-1859
Donohoo, Margaret to John Needham 10-24-1867
Dosson, JSane to _____ Martin 5-26-1863 (5-28-1863)
Dots, Holland to Edward Tarrey 12-25-1874 (12-27-1874)
Douglas, Bettie to William Sanford 1-17-1867
Douglas, Dilcey to Alex Hall 2-14-1866
Douglas, Eva L. to Jno. K. Russel 5-19-1869
Douglas, Susan J. to Thomas J. Haynie 12-31-1866 (1-1-1867)
Douglass, Ann to Henry Smith 12-30-1865
Dowdy, Charlotte to Erasmus Darwin Edwards 8-27-1844
Dowell, Emaline to Edmond Carter 12-4-1873
Downing, Sarah L. to Richd. Vaughan 8-4-1868
Downing, Susan A. to M. V. B. Harris 5-5-1871
Draffin, M. J. to W. B. McCoy 5-5-1873
Draffin, Margaret J. to J. W. Pinner 1-3-1874 (1-15-1874)
Driver, Elizabeth to M. S. McCall 9-21-1871
Driver?, Mary Vanburen to Josiah Washington Bandy 8-28-1852
Drummond, Franca? J. to J. B. Burton 4-3-1868 (4-5-1868)
Drummond, W. to James McKeown 2-8-1869 (2-10-1869)
Drummons, Ann H. to H. H. Joyner 11-5-1866 (11-6-1866)
Drummons, Drucilla D. to William E. Clements 12-19-1843 (12-21-1843)
Dumis, Sarah to Thos. Davidson 12-2-1874
Duncan, L. Jane to A. W. C. Pittman 10-21-1872 (10-24-1872)
Duncan, S. C. to W. H. Howell 5-28-1873 (5-29-1873)
Dunlap, Ann J. to Wm. Elison 1-27-1868 (1-30-1868)
Dunn, A. B. to John Kennedy 12-4-1872
Dunn, Elizabeth J. to John R. Patten 11-2-1857
Dunn, Frances to Isaac Leftwich 12-24-1870
Dunn, Mary to George Holland 2-24-1874
Dunn, Rebecca to William Martin 12-27-1873 (12-28-1873)
Durham, Rebecca J. H. to O. H. P. Wood 5-7-1840
Duveast, Rhoda to Samuel Forbess 12-18-1854 (12-26-1854)
Dyer, M. J. to Henderson Hemp no date (with 12-1874)
Dyson, Eliza to Gilbert Hill 10-5-1871 (10-6-1871)
Dyson, Fannie to Watkin? Smith 11-9-1872 (11-15-1872)
Dyson, Milly to Lemuel Shelton 8-18-1866
Easley, Eliza to Bynum Adkison 5-31-1858 (6-1-1858)
Easley, Mary C. to John A. Moore 10-4-1842
Easley, Mary to James Adkison 11-20-1869 (11-23-1869)
Easley, Sarah J. to William M. French 1-1-1874
Easley, Sarah to Andrew Lamar 8-1-1867 (8-2-1867)
Easley, Susan A. M. S. to Joshua N. Brunson? 9-14-1840 (9-15-1840)
Easly, S. A. to A. L. Forbess 1-8-1872
Eaton, Catherin to Ezekal Butler 4-3-1872 (4-4-1872)
Eckford, Nancy to Jas. P. Thompson 11-10-1865 (11-12-1865)
Eddie, Kate to James Browning 4-27-1872 (4-29-1872)
Edwards, Amey to Bob Wilson 11-14-1874
Edwards, Elizabeth to E. A. Walker 8-18-1857 (8-20-1857)
Edwards, Laura Ann to Thomas Parsons 8-16-1850 (8-20-1850)
Edwards, Mary Love to James Henry Caraway 12-28-1844 (1-2-1845)
Edwards, Sallie to Esquire Cothran 2-20-1873 (2-21-1873)
Elam, Ann to Jefferson McCain 8-9-1867 (8-10-1867)
Elam, Ann to L. Wright 3-17-1866 (3-18-1866)
Elam, Kitsy to John McGee 9-27-1872 (10-16-1872)
Elam, L. J. to J. S. Mayes 4-1-1867 (4-2-1867)
Elam, Margaret to JSames A. Knight 11-13-1866
Elam, Mary to Jacob Dyson 5-21-1866 (5-22-1866)
Elam, S. A. to W. R. Slate 11-13-1866 (11-14-1866)
Elcan, Hettie to Ike Taylor 3-10-1873
Elder, Eliza Jane to Ben Mitchel 3-31-1873 (4-3-1873)
Elder, Lorania C. to Wm. Franklin Elder 8-18-1851 (8-19-1851)
Elder, Mary to Newton Dickson 2-28-1850
Elder, Missouri to Mosel? Bellar 3-1-1869 (3-3-1869)
Elkin, Mary to William Jones 9-7-1868 (9-10-1868)
Elkin, Sallie to Profeit Taylor 3-3-1869
Elkins, Mary to Allen Wethington 6-21-1853 (6-23-1853)
Elliot, Harriet to Griffin Ellis 1-5-1866 (1-27-1866)
Ellis, Ann to Alexander Still 12-26-1873 (12-29-1873)
Ellis, Hanna to Alex Simonton 10-7-1873 (10-9-1873)
Ellis, Sibbey to John H. Parrot 8-15-1850 (8-18-1850)
Ellison, Fannie to Woodson Knight 5-16-1870
Ellison, Susan A. to J. A. Watson 10-27-1874 (10-28-1874)
Elmore, Ann to P. Green Upchurch 10-16-1873
Elmore, Eliz. Lucretia to Saml. Crawford Sanford? 11-22-1855
Elmore, M. C. to J. J. Weaver 11-7-1867 (11-8-1867)
English, Margaret to C. L. Barnes 1-8-1873 (1-9-1873)
English, Margaret to David Owen 3-9-1866
English, Margaret to James McCormack 3-20-1865
English, Mariah to Allen Louisen 9-7-1866 (9-9-1866)
English, Martha J. to Thos. Alston 3-3-1874 (3-26-1874)
Epperson, Mary A. to James H. Yarbro 1-20-1870
Epps, Elizabeth to Jack Bivens 3-15-1871 (4-10-1871)
Epps, L. B. to James Ings? 12-12-1874

Erwin, Anna to John Wiley 11-16-1867 (11-20-1867)
Erwin, Mary J. to Thos. P. Bowden 7-1-1874
Erwood, Rachel Ann to Pleasant M. Long 9-20-1873 (9-21-1873)
Evans, Elizabeth to Terrell Shankle 1-1-1842
Evans, Ellen to George Alston 1-4-1871
Evans, Margaret to Thomas Hamilton 12-30-1873 (1-1-1874)
Evans, Mary to Joshua Thomas Mitchell 8-16-1847 (8-17-1847)
Ewell, Julia Ann to A. W. Murphey 12-20-1869 (12-21-1869)
Ewell, Rebecca to W. A. J. Hartsfield 3-5-1857
Ewell, Susan E. to Edward Shankle 9-4-1855 (9-6-1855)
Ewill, Martha Jane to Jesse F. Blount 1-11-1851 (1-12-1851)
Fagan, Nancy to Albert Thompson 1-26-1870
Fairfax, Emma H. to James Landen 12-17-1869
Falanigan?, Winnie L. to William Parker 6-22-1871
Farington, Theodocia E. to Thomas J. Ross 5-13-1858
Faris, Ann to Charles Henry Hart 1-31-1844 (2-8-1844)
Faris, Harriet Jane Eliz. to John Allen Quimmly 9-26-1853 (9-27-1853)
Faris?, Elizabeth Ann to Saml. Woodfin Pilkington 12-3-1851
Farmer, M. J. to James Boyd 12-20-1858 (12-22-1858)
Farmer, Martha E. to James H. Jamison 4-23-1857
Farmer, Mary M. to William Staret 1-10-1867
Farmer, O. C. to R. F. Eperson 10-24-1868 (10-25-1868)
Farmer?, Janie Frances to Kenneth B. Lanier 1-13-1856 (1-31-1856)
Farrar, Fannie to Burton L. Smith 12-19-1868
Farrar, Rosa P. to Benjamin B. Benson 8-14-1848 (8-?-1848)
Farrington, A. C. to James Stone 1-2-1866 (1-3-1866)
Farrington, Z. T. to James C. Hill 2-6-1867
Farris, Martha V. to A. A. Aycock 10-22-1864 (9-26-1864)
Farriss, Sarah F. to Thos. D. Pennel 8-10-1861 (8-14-1861)
Farrow, Mary Jane to Elias Smith 6-5-1868
Faucett, Ella? to Migugol? Adams 10-30-1869
Faulk, Alabama to Albert Jordan 12-21-1867 (12-22-1867)
Faulk, Caroline to George Phillips 1-1-1874 (1-2-1874)
Faulk, Jane? to John K. Robinson 10-28-1841
Faulkner, Eliz. Agnes to Wm. Druffin Strain 4-8-1851
Faulkner, Margaret A. to Thos. Cowser 12-24-1866 (12-25-1866)
Faussett, Mary O. to John E. Hanna 1-10-1867
Faussette, E. C. to J. C. McLuster 7-10-1873 (7-11-1873)
Feezor, Caroline to Smith M. Bandy 12-20-1851 (12-28-1851)
Feezor, Christena to James C. Jones 12-24-1849
Feezor, E. A. to A. J. Harris 10-2-1865 (10-3-1865)
Feezor, Margaret to Thomas A. Maxwell 8-27-1866 (8-29-1866)
Feezor, Martha F. to Joseph F. Wiseman 11-16-1865
Feezor, Martha V. to Cyrus C. Rice 1-30-1859
Feezor, Mary A. to J. H. Stevens 1-3-1865
Feezor, Mary E. to Robert P. Collier 5-29-1845
Feezor, S. L. to F. Flemming 10-12-1870 (10-13-1870)
Feild?, Sarah to Fed Bales 2-9-1867
Femins?, Mary to John W. Edwards 5-10-1861
Ferguson, Mary to Robert Young 3-12-1856 (3-13-1856)
Ferrell, M. T. P. to Wm. B. Bowles 12-3-1864 (12-4-1867)
Field, Caroline to M. Van Davelt? 1-18-1871 (1-19-1871)
Field, Clarisa to Willis Stevens 1-14-1874
Field, Fannie Ann to John McCan 4-8-1870
Field, Farrie Ann to John McCan 4-8-1870
Field, Lucey to Henry Clay Davis 9-22-1874
Field, Mary Catherine to Fras. M. Green 11-15-1853 (11-16-1853)
Fields, Kate to Phillip Buggs 8-30-1873 (8-31-1873)
Fields, Lucy to Henderson Cowan 2-14-1874
Fields, Sallie to William Wilson 8-4-1873 (8-9-1873)
Fields, Sinora to Joseph Smith 5-24-1871
Fields, Tempe to Aubner Tinsly 2-21-1871
Fink, Louisa to Charles Williams 5-7-1873
Finty?, Miss Jane to Aux? W. Gravy 3-13-1869 (3-17-1869)
Fisher, Annie L. to James B. Hamilton 10-24-1867
Fisher, Elizabeth Glover to Gabriel J. Slaughter 3-6-1849
Fisher, Emma F. to George J. McBride 1-20-1869 (1-21-1869)
Fisher, Lusten to Bill Hemp 1-5-1869 (not executed)
Fisher, Rosa to Gerrit DeVries 8-12-1872 (9-1-1872)
Fitzgerill, Emmer to A. W. Dickerson 2-14-1872
Flanakin, J. F. to A. J. Montgomery 5-7-1868
Flanakin, Martha to Robert E. Tycen 10-3-1857
Flanakin, Mary Jane to Jeremiah Manasco 7-6-1857
Flanakin, Nancy C. to William Griffee 1-11-1860
Flaniken, Sarah to Wm. Brown 7-3-1841 (10-17-1841
Flanikin, Mary R. to Hubbard Ferrell 5-26-1855 (5-31-1855)
Fleming, Amanda F. to J. E. Smith 10-24-1874 (10-25-1874)
Fleming, Lenny to F. J. Sherrill 11-4-1868
Fleming, M. A. to W. H. Moten 7-16-1867 (7-18-1867)
Fleming, M. E. to Downey Fleming 12-25-1871
Fleming, Margaret to J. C. Rhodes 1-23-1861 (1-24-1861)
Fleming, Nancy Catharin to John A. Goss 2-4-1857
Flemming, Elizabeth to Louis Sanford 12-17-1865 (12-28-1865)
Flemming, Frances F. to C. F. Slack 9-8-1866
Flemming, Susan L. to Jno. D. Reid 1-1-1866
Flinn, Mary to Pleasant B. Williams 2-5-1847
Flower, Hannah to Henry Cotheran 1-13-1866
Flower, Mary T. to Mike Green 12-25-1868 (12-26-1868)
Flowers, Lizzie W. to R. Fenner Johnson 5-20-1868 (5-21-1868)
Flowers, Sarah Jane to R. A. jr. Parker 5-24-1858 (5-25-1858)
Flowers, Sophia C. to Geo. Washington Cook 12-21-1851 (not executed)
Flowers, Sophia Cotten to William Dunham Fisher 1-19-1852 (1-20-1852)
Forbess, Margaret C. to John C. George 12-19-1870 (12-22-1870)
Forbess, Mary E. to Wm. Henry Joyner 2-27-1866 (3-1-1866)
Forbess, Sarah Ann to Washington Joyner 7-21-1868 (7-23-1868)
Forbus, Margaret to Sterling Harris Pinner 12-22-1845
Ford, Ann Rebecca to Bolivar C. Wesson 11-22-1848 (11-23-1848)
Ford, Elizabeth to Robert A. Rose 7-19-1869 (7-20-1869)
Ford, Emily to Thoas Thompson 1-24-1849
Ford, Emmer to Thomas Dickerson 1-8-1873
Ford, Marth to Z. A. Flanigan 2-13-1867 (2-15-1867)
Foreman, Sallie to Jessee Hunt 12-29-1866
Forest, Mary M. to William P. Miller 10-5-1858 (10-6-1858)
Forrest, Mary Elizabeth to R. R. Moore 12-5-1874 (12-8-1874)
Forsyth, Jane to Joseph Hagans Strain 1-26-1854
Forsythe, Mary E. to Francis J. Sherrill 11-15-1871
Forsythe, Sarah to John Hurley 1-4-1869
Fortner, Nancy Eleanor to Lovod Stevens 1-20-1858
Fortner, S. Evolin to Isaac W. Owen 3-24-1862
Fortner, Susan A. to Simpson Hastings 8-21-1844 (8-?-1844)
Foster, Eliza Ann to Samuel B. Miller 2-19-1842 (2-27-1842)
Foster, Hannah Jane to Henry Clay VanLien 6-15-1848 (6-24-1848)
Foster, Margaret to Nelson McCauley 4-23-1874
Foster, Permelia to Wm. Hunley Townsend 2-10-1855 (2-14-1855)
Foster, Sarah L. to John Booker Payne 12-2-1863 (12-3-1863)
Foster, Sindey to Isham Sitton 4-24-1874
Foster, Sindy to Isham Litten 4-23-1874 (4-25-1874)
Franklin, Jane to Green Adams 3-3-1874
Franklin, Martha Frances to John Faulkner 3-24-1854 (3-29-1854)
Freeman, Fredonia Olivia to Regis Dunwood 2-16-1853 (2-17-1853)
Freeman, Indiana to Jefferson Shantly 9-17-1866 (9-19-1866)
Freeman, Marilyn to James White 7-5-1851 (7-?-1851)
Freeman, Martha A. to Wm. Carson 2-2-1859 (2-3-1859)
Freeman, Mary E. to Thomas C. McCraw 2-22-1865 (2-23-1865)
Freeman, Mary Jane to James S. Bryant 8-7-1843
Freeman, Mary to Thomas C. McCraw 3-14-1868
Freeman, Nanny to John C. Weisheiver 8-15-1870 (8-16-1870)
Freeman, Sallie to David J. Baskins 7-12-1864 (7-13-1864)
Freeman, Sarah Sopornia? to John Adams Stokes 8-6-1851 (8-7-1851)
French, C. A. to N. W. Grimes 1-17-1861 (1-20-1861)
Fry, Elizabeth E. to Peter E. Hall 8-16-1860
Fuller, Martha E. to L. J. Beavers 9-21-1872 (9-22-1872)
Fults, Violet Ann to Armistead Boyd 2-2-1869
Furnandez, Candis to Richard Wood 9-19-1867 (9-21-1867)
Futhery?, Rosa to J. R. Tenny 1-27-1868 (1-29-1868)
Futhey, Louisa to Andrew Gaither 12-20-1870
Futhey, Nancy to John Hunter 2-13-1850
Gainer, Sallie to Ned Richardson 5-8-1872
Gaither, Tobitha A. to Jacob H. Sink 12-2-1848 (12-6-1848)
Galaway, Ann to Bryant Hill 9-24-1869 (9-25-1869)
Galbreath, Caroline to Abner Clements 8-2-1858 (8-3-1858)
Galbreath, Dicy to J. A. Ballard 2-23-1860
Galbreath, Sally to John E. Sullivan 9-23-1867
Galbreath, Susan L. to A. J. Clements 4-4-1870 (4-5-1870)
Gamewell, Jacinda? to Isham G. McNeal 9-6-1867 (9-14-1869?)
Gammelle, C. to Rasmus Taylor 10-13-1871
Gann, Matilda to Rainy Neron? 11-21-1871

Gant, Jennie to Isaac Payne 10-9-1874
Gardner, America Jane to Thomas B. Winford 10-13-1841
Gardner, Elizabeth to Peter Scott 7-28-1858 (8-1-1858)
Garland, Fannie to Elijah Beats 12-23-1873
Gary, Mrs. to John Taylor 12-1-1863
Gay, Nannie to Thos. Hays 1-4-1871
Gehan, Cordelia to William S. Herring 10-23-1849 (10-24-1848?)
Gendren, Rebecca Ann to Andrew Stevens 8-20-1845 (8-21-1845)
George, A. S. to J. C. McBride 11-4-1865 (11-7-1865)
George, Elizabeth B. to William H. Fuller 12-29-1844
George, Martha to James S. Walker 12-10-1868 (12-15-1868)
George, Mary Jane to W. A. Woodson 9-17-1856 (9-18-1856)
George, Polina C. to William H. Gurley 11-12-1840 (11-18-1840)
George, Sarah to Pleasant K. Larimore 5-18-1847 (5-20-1847)
Gibbons, Elizabeth to Henry Lebdor 4-8-1850
Gibbs, Cylvia to Charles Lemes? 5-26-1866 (5-27-1866)
Gibson, America to Saml. Cooper 3-6-1869 (3-9-1869)
Gibson, Sarah E. to James Dodson 9-8-1846 (9-9-1846)
Giffrey, Zilpha to Balam Lundy 3-9-1867 (3-12-1867)
Giles, Mary Margaret to Wade Henry 10-30-1849 (11-1-1849)
Gilham, Mollie to George Dickerson 1-19-1872
Gilhan, Harriet to Moses Morris 1-1-1871? (1-1-1872)
Gilland, Florence to Harrison Smith 9-5-1872
Gilleland, Sarah A. F. to Johnathan (Norman?) Williams 10-7-1873 (10-9-1873)
Gillum, Mary to ____ Wallace 5-25-1867
Gillum, Matilda to Saml. Adkins 1-11-1873
Gillun, Harriet to Rufus Howard 5-25-1867
Givens, Harriet to Robt. Morgan 8-20-1870
Glass, Artemisia to Isaac Terrell 1-25-1856
Glass, Jones to S. A. Dewees 11-2-1874 (11-4-1874)
Glass, Malissa J. to John H. Hightower 1-30-1869 (2-4-1869)
Glass, Mary A. to Wm. A. Yarbrough 11-12-1851 (11-13-1851)
Glass, Mary to Jacob Scurry 11-8-1873
Glass, Sarah Ann to Henry Cannon 8-12-1858
Glass, Sarah to James Orr 2-24-1869 (2-25-1869)
Glass, Silvia to Moses Harris 7-17-1869 (7-18-1869)
Glass, T. to John Kelly 10-24-1874 (10-29-1874)
Glisson, Eveline to Tobe Thompson 12-10-1867 (12-12-1867)
Glover, Eliza to John Cooper 1-24-1868 (1-25-1871?)
Goforth, Adaline M. to Milson? D. ____ 9-29-1842
Goforth, Margaret to William Trantham 1-11-1845 (1-13-1845)
Goforth, Martha to A. A. Myres 2-22-1860
Goforth, Mary to Erasmus Rose 12-20-1853 (12-21-1853)
Goforth, Mary to John Lenoir Gray 8-10-1852
Goforth, Sarah E. to M. B. Harrison 1-19-1870
Goheen, Helen to Reuben Fletcher McFarland 9-30-1850 (10-2-1850)
Golden, Mary A. to J. H. McClain 1-31-1870 (2-1-1870)
Gooch, Mollie E. to John L. McCalla 1-3-1870 (1-4-1870)
Gooddin, Ally to Lewis Jones 1-27-1868 (1-30-1868)
Goodman, B. L. to S. B. Turner 12-21-1869
Goodman, Josephine H. to William Turner 3-23-1871
Goodman, Martha A. to W. D. Nickleson 11-15-1865
Goodman, Mary A. to Jas. H. Petty 5-21-1867
Goodman, R. to Chas. Taylor 1-1-1872
Goodman, Sallie O. to D. H. Smith 5-2-1871 (5-3-1871)
Goodman, Sallie to Saml. Collins 12-24-1874 (12-25-1874)
Goodman, Sue to Thos. Angus 1-23-1869 (1-26-1869)
Goodnoe, Mary Elizabeth to HGenry Wisener? 2-13-1844 (2-16-1844)
Goren, Frances J. to Jesse Kinney 11-23-1859 (11-24-1859)
Gorin, Frances Jane to James Payne 12-17-1850
Gornet?, Julia Ann to Henry W. Cotton 6-28-1869
Goss, Eleanor to Richmond Winkler 1-13-1841 (1-14-1841)
Goss, Sarah to William Walker Hutchinson 4-12-1844 (4-15-1844)
Grace, Eliza Violet to Wilson Billings 5-3-1851 (5-4-1851)
Grace, Evaline to Rufus Wsh. Myers 1-18-1853
Gracey, Maney to Daniel Webster Chamber 1-27-1866
Gracy, Martha A. to David Wood 4-19-1855
Graham, Julia Ann to Henry Washington Cotton 6-28-1869 (7-1-1869)
Granderson, Katy to John Blackwell 11-17-1873
Grant, Betsey to Peter Glass 10-8-1869 (10-9-1869)
Grant, Margaret J. to Canter B. Ralph 9-12-1855
Grant, Margaret J. to Johnathan B. Faulk 11-24-1874 (11-25-1874)
Gray, C. D. to J. S. Kerkpatrick 12-6-1873
Gray, C. V. to C. A. Johnson 12-1-1874
Gray, Jennie to Sandy Alston 12-16-1873
Gray, Martha J. to Saml. Ray 7-16-1870 (7-17-1870)
Gray, Martha S. H. to Wm. F. Staton 6-3-1867 (6-6-1867)
Gray, Mary E. to Wm. Pool 5-8-1854 (5-9-1854)
Gray, Rachel to Wm. Alexr. Kent 11-29-1851 (12-3-1851)
Gray, Sophia to Jesse Kirkman 10-27-1871 (10-28-1871)
Green, Ann E. to S. E. Johnson 5-30-1859
Green, Aubanett to A. M. Phillips 10-7-1867 (10-10-1867)
Green, Caroline to Henry Hall 1-7-1869
Green, Eliza F. to James P. Parker 1-4-1868 (1-5-1868)
Green, Eliza Jane to Thomas Hickerson 12-29-1869
Green, Elizabeth to Bart Bledsoe 2-12-1873 (2-13-1873)
Green, Ellen to Jas. Gooden 12-1-1869 (12-4-1869)
Green, Fannie S. to Chas. P. Noell 9-23-1873 (9-24-1873)
Green, Harriet A. to Peyton jr. Dyson 7-16-1870 (7-17-1870)
Green, Hollen Applewight to John N. Hall 3-5-1842 (3-8-1842)
Green, Laura to William Field 12-27-1870
Green, Lily to Henry Magee 10-23-1873 (12-16-1873)
Green, Marier to Leroy Jones 12-28-1865
Green, Martha to Anthony Walton 4-17-1872
Green, Martha to Bob Butts 3-2-1872 (11-20-1872)
Green, Mary C. to W. E. Person 2-19-1862
Green, Mary to Armistead Lake 7-1-1867?
Green, Mollie to G. W. Barnett 8-11-1874 (8-13-1874)
Green, Rachal to Rubin Snelling 12-10-1870
Green, Sallie Ann to John Uriah Green 3-29-1865 (3-30-1865)
Green, Sarah Adeline to David Henry Limbarger 3-1-1865
Green, Susan A. to Brother M. Jones 3-12-1860 (3-20-1860)
Green, Susan J. to Booker Jones 3-12-1860
Green, Susan to Wm. O. Taylor no date (with 1868)
Greenfield, Bettie to Robt Linden 12-28-1874
Greer, Annis to Z. Williams 7-6-1869
Gregg, Sallie M. to John G. Whitson 3-30-1872
Gregory, Ruby Elmira to Wm. Jasper Prince 9-12-1860 (9-13-1860)
Gregory, Sarah Jane to Thomas Gregory 10-13-1870 (10-14-1870)
Griffith, Eliza E. to Wm. J. Rice 12-21-1868 (12-22-1868)
Griffith, Jane C. to Bassel Jeanes 3-6-1870 (5-9-1870)
Griffith, Nancy to Robert J. Flanakin 9-9-1867
Grigg, Bettie to Byrd Danniel 5-3-1873
Griggs, Betty to Byrd Daniel 5-3-1873 (5-4-1873)
Grigsby, Harriet to Coleman Barmer? 3-12-1874
Grimes, Henrietta to Saml. Crosby 12-28-1868
Grimes, Mary to Derry Cooper 11-23-1870 (11-27-1870)
Grimes, Mary to Elijah Shelton 9-10-1866 (9-16-1866)
Grimes, Pattie E. to George F. Grimes 2-25-1873 (2-26-1873)
Grimes, Tennessee E. to N. T.? Akin 11-10-1874 (11-11-1874)
Grishom, Candis to Solomon Gordon 9-14-1846 (9-17-1846)
Grooms, Jane to E. R. Hatch 6-28-1841
Gross, Nancy Jane to W. T. Valentine 7-21-1865
Guardner, Rebecca to Ezekil Bennett 6-4-1855 (6-7-1855)
Guinn, Amanda to W. C. Huffman 11-30-1873 (12-2-1874?)
Gustins?, Ann Savanna? to James Irwin Carn? 1-5-1843 (1-5-1843)
Hadly, M. to Jeff Conner 1-4-1872
Hafter, Martha E. to Charles W. Hafter 4-16-1872
Hainie, Caroline c. to W. R. Slate 12-7-1858 (12-9-1858)
Hall, A. to Wm. Nealey 12-18-1874 (12-19-1874)
Hall, Adalin to Stevens Davis 1-7-1865 (6-10-1865)
Hall, Alice to Anthony Bernard 3-27-1869 (3-28-1869)
Hall, Ann E. to George Fowler 2-11-1867 (2-17-1867)
Hall, Annie to J. G. Young 1-15-1873
Hall, Carolin W. to J. B. Danniel 12-20-1865
Hall, Catharine Clamentine to Edward Holister Green 7-17-1851
Hall, Ceelin Ethalinda to Enos Alexander Sherrill 4-7-1845 (4-16-1845)
Hall, Clarissa to Lewis Haywood 6-16-1867
Hall, Cornelia W. to J. B. Daniel 12-20-1865
Hall, E. E. to Wm. E. Sherrill 2-8-1866
Hall, Eliza J. to John C. McCauley 11-8-1855 (11-16-1855)
Hall, Elizabeth R. to James Leander Stitt 8-9-1854
Hall, Emaline to George Ross 2-24-1866
Hall, Fannie to Melvill Vaughn 3-9-1869 (3-11-1869)
Hall, Fannie to Robt Winn 11-1-1873 (11-2-1873)
Hall, H. A. to W. L. Buford 8-2-1859 (8-3-1859)
Hall, Henritta to James Hunt 6-17-1871
Hall, Jane to George Anderson Johnson 5-5-1873

Hall, Jane to Loyd Lassater 3-14-1867 (3-17-1867)
Hall, Katie E. to W. S. Davie 9-29-1874 (9-30-1874)
Hall, L. S. to F. W. Hill 12-12-1872
Hall, Martha to Alfred Thomas 3-12-1873 (4-5-1873)
Hall, Mary E. to James J. Hall 1-2-1866
Hall, Mary E. to Jas. J. Hall 1-2-1866
Hall, Mary N. to William S. Coward 10-10-1865 (10-11-1865)
Hall, Mary to Geo. Morrison 12-2-1865
Hall, Mattie A. to Smith Buford 2-6-1866 (2-7-1866)
Hall, Nancy M. to John D. Bryant 8-19-1867
Hall, Winny to Henry Stevens 12-28-1870 (12-29-1870)
Hall, __ane to Benj. Bernard 9-9-1865
Hamilton, A. J. to M. T. Bird 11-20-1871
Hamilton, Amanda to Williamson McClelland 7-12-1859
Hamilton, Margaret to Alexander A. Montgomery 12-29-1856 (12-30-1856)
Hamilton, Mary M. to Robert F. Garret 1-23-1871 (1-25-1871)
Hamilton, Mary to Williamson McClelland 11-28-1854
Hamilton, Susan to Jas. Tool 7-26-1874 (7-29-1874)
Hammon, Mary to Robert A. Pool 2-10-1869
Hammond, Marteller Ann to Sidney R. Timms 10-16-1867 (10-19-1867)
Hanegin, Sarah Ann to W. B. Robinett 5-9-1846 (5-12-1846)
Hanley, Lottie T. to W. M. Dickerson 1-26-1858
Hanlin, Gracy to Wm. Hall 12-30-1871
Hanly, Nancey to Samuel Davis 4-5-1861
Hanna, Emalin to Chas. Kilpatrick 2-22-1872
Hanna, Rosetta J. to John A. Yarbro 10-13-1866 (10-16-1866)
Hannah, M. J.? to W. A. Loyd 12-12-1866 (12-13-1866)
Hannah, Martha J. to Henry Moore 5-15-1855 (5-16-1855)
Hannis?, Sarah C. to John N. Timms 4-9-1867 (4-10-1867)
Harden, Fannie to Rubin Beasley 3-30-1867 (4-2-1867)
Harley, Alice J. to Jno. C. Ellam 11-20-1871
Harmon, Emeline to Alfred Conelly 12-26-1874 (12-27-1874)
Harper, Isadora to William H. Cullim 12-21-1871
Harper, Luler to J. D. Cullens 10-28-1868
Harper, Phillis to Anderson Williams 12-28-1868 (12-30-1868)
Harper, Susan to George Chamber 10-16-1874 (10-17-1874)
Harris, Amanda to Robt. Boyce 10-28-1871 (11-2-1871)
Harris, Bettie to Archer Rayond 10-2-1869
Harris, Cassa to Friday Payne 2-5-1870
Harris, Colorado to Robert Gutherie 11-4-1854 (11-5-1854)
Harris, Costinza Missouri to Doctor Wesley McFarlane 12-18-1844 (12-19-1844)
Harris, Delilah to Jesse B. Lindsay 8-3-1843
Harris, Eady to Frank Walker 12-16-1867
Harris, Eady to Frank Walker 8-12-1867
Harris, Florence to James Jones 5-13-1874
Harris, Georga to Willis Johnson 12-17-1873
Harris, Jane C. to Ben Calhoun 1-5-1871
Harris, L. to P. R. Mitchel 1-30-1872 (1-31-1872)
Harris, Laura to J. A. Mason? 10-26-1871 (10-27-1871)
Harris, Livina to Francis Williams 7-30-1870
Harris, Lucy to Mingo Bernard 12-27-1871 (12-28-1871)
Harris, Malinda to John E. Smith 4-10-1848 (4-15-1848)
Harris, Manerva F. to William H. Rollins 6-1-1867 (6-2-1867)
Harris, Margaret L.? to William Henry Wilson 4-16-1840
Harris, Martha V. to Jas. McWherter Faris 2-4-1856
Harris, Martha to Daniel Williams 2-25-1846 (2-26-1846)
Harris, Mary Matilda to Richard S. Barret 12-22-1847
Harris, Mary to Albert Clay 12-28-1870 (12-29-1870)
Harris, Mary to Ed. Jeruiza? Max 9-11-1869 (9-15-1869)
Harris, Mary to George Rollins 3-9-1871
Harris, Mary to Green Jones 1-1-1874
Harris, Nancy to A. J. Covdy? 10-15-1874
Harris, Rosetta to Peter Lark 1-18-1872 (1-20-1872)
Harris?, Becky to Boyd Calhoon 12-29-1865 (1-14-1866)
Harrison, Amanda to Robert Guthrie 11-26-1855 (11-29-1855)
Harrison, Charlett to Charles Claiburne 3-22-1869 '
Harrison, Emer to Cyrus Gibbs 2-15-1867 (2-16-1867)
Harrison, Frances America to Geo. Gideon Coats 9-2-1846 (9-3-1846)
Harrison, Jane to Samuel Roe 6-24-1851 (6-26-1851)
Harrison, Mary to Frank Lamar 8-1-1867 (8-2-1867)
Harrison, Nancy Emaline to Samuel Darby Simons 7-22-1845 (7-?-1845)
Harrison, Nancy J. to William Wiseman 12-17-1860
Hart, Elizabeth to Isaac Clark 12-27-1866 (12-13?-1866)
Hart, Lizzie to Isaac Clark 12-29-1866
Hart, Louisa to Aleck Eaton 2-15-1867
Harte?, Adaline to Jordan Walker 3-15-1872
Hartfield, Rachel M. to Silas Luttrell 9-25-1867 (9-26-1867)
Hartsfield, Frances E. to Alex Murphy 2-7-1859 (2-10-1857)
Hartsfield, Frances Malvina to Chas. David McCoy 12-22-1853 (SB 1852?)
Hartsfield, Julia Ann to Oliver P. Kelley 7-14-1847
Hartsfield, Louisa J. to Alfred McGuire 2-12-1842 (2-15-1842)
Hartsfield, Martha C. to sDaniel M. Myers 12-28-1843
Hartsfield, Martha F. to Jacob Hartsfield 1-3-1873 (1-5-1873)
Hartsfield, Rachael A. to Jacob C. Menes 7-3-1858
Hartsfield, Rachael to Jessee Hill 12-5-1860
Hartsfield, S. C. to Edward Shankle 6-4-1860 (6-14-1860)
Hartsfield, Sallie A. to James Yewell 1-15-1862 (1-16-1862)
Hartsfield, Sarah Elizabeth to Peter P. Wood 7-7-1869 (7-8-1869)
Hartsfield, Sarah to James L. Bailey 12-20-1851 (12-21-1851)
Harwell, Eliza to Robert Bragg 8-6-1868
Hassler, Anne to John M. Smithson 11-7-1872
Hatch, Roasina to James H. Lauderdale 6-2-1841
Hatchell, Sarah F. to Thos. J. Smith 2-19-1870 (2-20-1870)
Hatton, M. A. to J. B. Turnage 1-12-1874 (1-14-1874)
Hawkins, Caroline to Moses Mitchell 12-19-1873
Hawood, Ellen to Pomp Calhoun 8-15?-1871
Hay, Nancy to John Lee 4-19-1873
Haye, M. E. to W. T. Dickerson 12-10-1867
Hayley?, Eliza to Henry Hamilton 1-18-1871
Haynes, Bettie to Sandy Wilson Downing 5-13-1874 (5-14-1874)
Haynie, Elizabeth Catharine to LaFayette Hill 10-13-1847
Haynie, Jane to Peter Martin 10-20-1866 (10-21-1866)
Haynie, M. A. to John W. Murphy 5-11-1869
Haynie, Martha Ann to James Henry Cockrell 10-13-1847
Haynie, Mary C. to John Jarrett Peebles 2-24-1852
Hays, Amelia Ann to W. F. Drappin 10-7-1856
Hays, Cora to Henry Burchett 5-7-1870
Hays, Lettie to James M. Jones 9-24-1872 (11-24-1872)
Hays, M. E. to James Bulger 1-30-1862
Hays, Mary D. to Joshua L. Sturgis 3-14-1861
Hays, Nancy to Zackary A.? Henly 10-13-1855 (10-14-1855)
Haywood, Famia to Fred Wm. Wilson 11-9-1871
Heart, Sarah Virginia to Philip D. Bowles 10-27-1846 (10-28-1846)
Heffman, Bettie to J. A. Lynn? 12-31-1870
Helms, Martha C. to John Tims 12-13-1871 (12-14-1871)
Helperin?, Martha to James C. Nelson 3-20-1860
Hemphill, Catharine to Henry Burlison 2-15-1868 (2-6?-1868)
Hemphill, Ellen to Jacob Angus 1-17-1871 (1-18-1871)
Hemphill, Sallie to Ed Overall 1-31-1871 (2-1-1871)
Henderson, Jane to Isham Garret 3-8-1867 (3-9-1867)
Henderson, Janie to George Graves 8-5-1867 (8-6-1867)
Henderson, Mary Ann to James Miles Burkhart 8-15-1843 (8-18-1843)
Hendren, Sarah J. to James Stewart 11-7-1866
Hendron, Elizabeth J. to Josephus Crenshaw 1-28-1850
Hendron, Martha E. to James O. Henry 9-26-1855
Henley, Louisa to Josiah Ward 6-8-1843
Henry, Louisa to Swinson? Gardner 4-13-1843 (4-15-1843)
Henry, Mary A. to Francis Marion Lee 10-9-1848 (10-12-1848)
Herrell, Mrs. L. J. to T. D. Lane 12-17-1873
Herrin, Ellen to Samuel Lowe 5-10?-1868
Herrin, Mollie to James Pierce 10-25-1871 (10-26-1871)
Hightower, Elizabeth to John P. Good 4-21-1873 (5-1-1873)
Hightower, M. J. to E. G. Berges 12-15-1873 (12-16-1873)
Hightower, N. J. to S. F. P. Glass 12-20-1871 (12-21-1871)
Hightower, N. J. to W. C. Worley 12-12-1874 (12-27-1874)
Hill, B. M. to John G. Matthews 12-18-1872
Hill, Cle. to Willis Lowe 12-22-1870
Hill, E. F. to Sidney Martin 8-24-1872 (8-25-1872)
Hill, Eliza to Austem Wright 2-27-1871 (2-28-1871)
Hill, Ellen to Lewis Rutherford 10-21-1869 (10-22-1869)
Hill, Indiana to John F. Williams 9-19-1865 (9-20-1865)
Hill, Indianna to John F. Williams 9-19-1865
Hill, Jane to James L. Adkins 2-3-1847 (2-10-1847)
Hill, Jane to John Upchurch 7-20-1867 (7-21-1867)
Hill, Laura to Richard Green 3-2-1872 (3-5-1872)

Hill, Lizzie to Jas. Neeley 3-14-1874
Hill, Louisa A. P. to Robert Thompson Foster 12-20-1847 (12-23-1847)
Hill, Louisa to Abe W. McCrutchen 2-2-1869 (2-3-1869)
Hill, Lucey A. to R. P. McClenny? 3-21-1868 (3-24-1868)
Hill, Lucy to Milton Walker 9-12-1873
Hill, M. J. H. to W. H. White 10-15-1863
Hill, M. J. to John W. Martin 11-25-1873 (11-15-1873?)
Hill, Margaret L. to Robert L. McFadden 7-24-1866
Hill, Margaret Leventen to Charles Strong Dickson 1-31-1849 (2-1-1849)
Hill, Marth to Adkin Hughlette 12-28-1866 (12-29-1865)
Hill, Mary Jane to Derastus Baldock 12-26-1853 (1-2-1854)
Hill, Mary to Arch Morgan 3-15-1867 (7-4-1867)
Hill, Mary to Hughey Hickine 6-23-1860
Hill, May Eller to Robert Beriam 11-28-1871 (11-29-1871)
Hill, Miss M. E. to Heb. C. Morrison 3-28-1861
Hill, Miss Peggy to Hibrey? Cage 12-2-1865
Hill, Nancy C. to J. Richardson 1-7-1860
Hill, Nancy P. to John A. Stokes 11-28-1861
Hill, Sallie to John C. Rutherford 12-18-1873 (12-17?-1873)
Hill, Sallie to John W. Fallin 1-7-1874
Hill, Sarah Elizabeth to John P. Townsend 3-16-1852 (3-17-1852)
Hill, Silusla? H. to Peter Vaughn 4-4-1867
Hill, Susan G. to Bailey Sanford 1-6-1865
Hill, Vina to George Boyd 8-8-1873
Hilliard, S. J. to Thadius H. Boykin 10-10-1860
Hindman, Hellen to James Caskey 12-8-1861
Hindman, Roxanne W. to James M. McCheshire 9-18-1850
Hindman, Sarah S. to G. N. McCormick 1-22-1861 (1-23-1861)
Hinds, Mary to Jacob Shankle 7-20-1853
Hise, Julia Ann to Pinkney Wortham 3-26-1868
Hite, Frances Jane to John Campbell 3-6-1869 (3-7-1869)
Hitower, Amanda to W. H. Guthrie 6-17-1871 (6-22-1871)
Hitower, Fannie to W. Archer 4-8-1874 (4-5?-1874)
Hobs, M. E. C. to E. J. Weever 12-17-1874
Hoffler, Elizabeth Trotman to Charles D. Walker 2-11-1850
Hoffler, Martha Caroline to Spencer Thomas Hart 6-1-1844 (6-6-1844)
Hoke, Mary Magdalin to Kinchin Pace 5-6-1851
Holland, Mary to William Gibbson 1-17-1851 (1-20-1851)
Holland, Nancy to Jerry Sherrill 3-2-1874
Holley, Eliza to John Thos. Yancy 12-23-1867 (12-25-1867)
Holloway, Violet to Jas. Dick Bragg 8-3-1871 (8-4-1871)
Holmes, Anna W. to Thos. F. Patterson 10-25-1866
Holmes, Emma to David Hays Cummins 8-14-1843
Holmes, Harriet to Phillip Adkins 4-2-1866 (4-7-1866)
Holmes, Julia A. to John N. Hill 2-19-1866 (2-20-1866)
Holmes, Sarah Rebecca to William Minor Hall 8-7-1849 (8-8-1849)
Holmes, Susan to Lewis Williams 9-30-1871
Holsouser?, Eurind to Wm. L. Burlerson 12-20-1853
Holsowser, Catherine to John J. Philips 8-16-1866 (8-17–1866)
Hood, Jane E. to Micado Murchison 2-4-1841 (3-15-1841)
Hood, Sarah to George W. White 1-16-1844 (1-18-1844)
Hooks, Ann M. to John M. Siler 2-2-1848
Hooks, Caroline to Thomas Fitzgerald 10-11-1853 (10-12-1853)
Hooks, Mary A. to James R> McCall 4-23-1846 (5-25-1846)
Hopper, Martha Susan to James Goodram Adams 2-9-1849 (2-15-1849)
Hopper, Welthy Ann to David Ewing White 5-26-1855 (5-27-1855)
Horn, _____ E. to John G. Joiner 3-1-1864 (3-2-1864)
Horne, Rachel E. to William B. Jackson 12-18-1849 (12-20-1849)
Horne, Susan E. to Isham B. Roberts 9-18-1848 (9-19-1848)
Houston, C. H. to James B. Forbiss 2-25-1859 (2-28-1859)
Houston, Clerisa H. to James P. Forbiss 2-25-1859 (2-28-1859)
Houston, Delilia to William Williams 11-13-1872 (11-27-1872)
Houston, Sarah to Johnathan Keathley 12-28-1859 (12-29-1859)
Houston?, Mary Frances to Mussintyre? Sloane Mathews 11-10-1842
Howard, A. C. to M. Bragg 5-21-1870 (5-22-1870)
Howard, Ann Rebecca to Jesse S. Cothran 11-14-1840 (11-19-1840)
Howard, Catharine to Hana? Miller Larimore 5-31-1853
Howard, Chainey to Thomas Jones 10-3-1874
Howard, Emaly to Thomas Beaver 11-8-1873
Howard, Henrietta to James Rhodes 4-28-1868 (5-2-1868)
Howard, Joanah to Columbus Hogan 9-11-1871
Howard, Joanah to Frank Robertson 7-31-1868 (8-1-1868)
Howard, Joanna to Wm. Stricklun 11-10-1866
Howard, M. F. to A. P. Parker 5-30-1871 (5-31-1871)
Howard, Martha M. to William Bragg 12-29-1869 (12-30-1869)
Howard, Ophelia P. to Geo. W. Wynne 6-21-1871 (6-22-1871)
Howard, Rebecca J. to G. W. Winn? 6-10-1863
Howard, Susan to Richd. Archer 2-25-1869
Howell, Gray to Wm. F. Ayers 4-15-1858
Howell, Mary W. to John C. Forbess 5-23-1845 (5-25-1845)
Howerton, Caroline Winiford to William Henry Wooten 12-14-1841
Howerton, Mary C. to Thadeus A. Alexander 1-19-1858 (1-20-1858)
Hudson, Cyntha V. to John Y. Prince 5-8-1862 (5-11-1862)
Hudson, Mary E. to Henry H. Hudson 1-25-1866 (1-30-1866)
Hudson, Mattie E. to W. H. Cocke 12-18-1871 (12-19-1871)
Huffman, Eliza to W. G. Miller 12-9-1856 (12-11-1856)
Huffman, Julia A. to N. R. McCormick 8-29-1855
Huffman, L. A. to H. C. Dacus 11-7-1874 (11-10-1874)
Huffman, M. C. to O. S. Feezor 2-23-1874
Huffman, Martha Ann to J. R. Morrasett 1-8-1872 (1-9-1872)
Huffman, Mary to R. R. Simonton 2-8-1870
Huffman, Mary to William G. Harris 1-7-1867 (1-13-1867)
Huffman, Nancy J. to F. M. Harris 4-3-1871 (4-4-1871)
Hughes, Elizabeth Caroline to William B. Turnage 6-5-1843 (6-6-1843)
Hughleette, Jane to Calvin Harris 6-18-1870
Hughlett, Emma to Geo. Wilson 1-18-1868 (1-19-1868)
Hughlett, Martha to Louis Kennedy 12-27-1865
Hughlett, Martha to Needhan Kilpatrick 9-28-1872
Hughlette, Emmer to Erwin? Yarbro 6-8-1867
Huison?, Miss Jane to D. M. Twisdale 12-12-1865 (12-13-1865)
Hult?, M. E. to M. L. Keene 12-16-1874
Hunley, Joice to John Gross 2-16-1841 (2-17-1841)
Hunn?, Sallie B. to J. H. Bailey 12-12-1868 (12-10?-1868)
Hunt, Dora O. to W. G. Poindexter 11-16-1872 (11-20-1872)
Hunt, Elizabeth T. to R. B. Sommerville 1-9-1853 (1-12-1853)
Hunt, Emma to William Winn 4-13-1874
Hunt, Emma to Wm. Winn 4-13-1874
Hunt, Fannie S. to Nat M. Kimbrough 5-20-1867 (5-22-1867)
Hunt, Laura to Robert M. Drummons 8-4-1865 (8-5-1865)
Hunt, Martha A. to H. H. Elcan 7-10-1865
Hunt, Martha Maria to Jeptha Hogue 2-24-1847 (2-25-1847)
Hunt, Mary Jackson to Wm. R. Clements 9-9-1854 (9-14-1854)
Hunt, Polly to Patrick Richerson 1-13-1866
Hunt, S. E. to W. D. Cash 3-23-1869 (3-24-1869)
Hunt, Sallie Anderson to Wm. Little Tarry 4-4-1850 (4-10-1850)
Hunt, Sissee to Lawson Williamson 1-31-1870
Hunt, Tempe to Joseph Rice 1-3-1866? (1-5-1867)
Hunt?, Sallie B. to Thos. H. Poindexter 11-16-1872 (11-20-1872)
Hunter, Anna J. to G. C. Pinkston 2-8-1871
Hunter, Mary S. to John S. Wright 2-1-1865 (2-2-1865)
Hunter, S. E. to A. W. Shaw 1-29-1869 (1-30-1869)
Hurt, Mattie C. to R. E. Aikens 1-1-1866 (1-4-1866)
Hurt, Sarah E. to J. F. Tinnen 8-10-1861 (8-14-1861)
Hurt, Virgina C. to Jessee Wright 10-11-1873 (10-13-1873)
Hurt?, Ann Elizabeth to John Hendin? Crouch 3-7-1853 (3-8-1853)
Huston, Adaline to Wm. Turner 7-15-1871
Hutcherson, Eliza to Arthur Torbiss? 12-10-1842 (12-15-1842)
Hutchinson, Mary Carolin to Richard Trotter 9-3-1867
Hutchinson, Sarah A. to William W. Goss 12-22-1847 (12-25-1847)
Hutton, Mary to Aderson Laremore 2-27-1869 (3-4-1869)
Hytower, Charlotte to James Coats 1-24-1860 (1-26-1860)
Innis, Nancy J. to Thomas Gross 4-7-1870
Irby, R. J. to C. R. Black 12-12-1866 (12-20-1866)
Irvin, M. J. to A. H. Irvin? 2-11-1860
Isom, Caroline to G. G. Howell 8-8-1863 (8-9-1863)
Ivey, Elizabeth A. to Daniel T. Lake 4-4-1861
Ivey, S. T. to M. Fletcher 12-14-1864 (12-18-1864)
Ivy, N. M. to A. A. Porter 10-25-1865 (11-6-1865)
Jackson, A. to James R. Miller 1-11-1865 (1-12-1865)
Jackson, Adaline to Calvin Upchurch 2-24-1873 (2-26-1873)
Jackson, Adeline to John Winn 2-2-1871
Jackson, Agnes to Dick Bradford 12-7-1870
Jackson, Clara A. to David K. Crenshaw 10-19-1853 (10-20-1853)
Jackson, Eliza Jane to Tho. B. Trobough 3-16-1850 (3-19-1850)
Jackson, Eliza to Jonas Dyson 12-27-1870 (12-28-1870)

Jackson, Florenc to Wm. Taylor 9-17-1868 (9-18-1868)
Jackson, Isabella to R. S. Strong 4-12-1870 (4-13-1870)
Jackson, Julia C. to Richard Morning Epperson 5-27-1843 (5-30-1843)
Jackson, Louise to Albert Bragg 1-11-1871? (2-11-1872)
Jackson, Malissa to Allen Jones 5-10-1873 B
Jackson, Malissa to Phillip Ferbury 10-12-1867 (10-13-1867)
Jackson, Maria to Isaac Rhodes 12-16-1874
Jackson, Mariah to Henry Vaughn 12-26-1867
Jackson, Mary to David Holms 9-8-1874
Jackson, Nellie to Willie Maclin 11-11-1874
Jackson, Rachel to Lemuel Williams 10-9-1852 (10-12-1852)
Jackson, Sallie to Dallas Tipton 8-13-1868
Jacob, Maud Hunter to Henry Smith 4-18-1873
Jacobbs, Nancy C. to J. V. Robb 9-4-1869
Jacobs, Mary A. to W. P. Malone 5-21-1870 (5-22-1870)
James, Fidelia to Thomas Washington Dinwoody 5-19-1842
James, Mary Louisa to Thomas M. Daniel 8-28-1849 (9-6-1849)
James, Sarah E. to John W. Price 5-9-1860 (5-15-1860)
Jamison, Lethia to John Vaughn 11-12-1870
Jamison, M. E. to H. W. Benson 12-16-1873 (12-17-1873)
Jamison, Mary E. to W. W. McBride 1-27-1857 (1-28-1857)
Jamison, Mary to Thornton Parish 8-12-1870 (8-13-1870)
Jarson?, Mildred A. to Wm. Ashurst 3-6-1873 (3-7-1873)
Jeans, Mary to Robert B. Jones 3-11-1861
Jenkins, Elizabeth to Thomas Kern 5-24-1841 (5-26-1841)
Jenkins, V. C. to M. L. Delashmut 10-14-1871 (10-19-1871)
Jett?, Amanda to Andrew Macklin 10-23-1865 (10-29-1865)
Jiles, Leutitia to Richmond Vaughn 10-4-1873
Johnson, Amanda Ann to William Pullin 3-5-1868
Johnson, Amanda J. to Thomas J. Hill 3-21-1870
Johnson, Angeline to Jerry Evans 8-19-1872 (8-5-1873)
Johnson, Annie to Jim Hemp 12-24-1874
Johnson, Anny to James Mills 8-30-1866
Johnson, Beckey to Charles Taylor 12-28-1869
Johnson, Clarisa Ann to Rufus Goodman 12-19-1866
Johnson, Emma to George Sherrill 12-25-1873
Johnson, Hanna to Ruffin Jackson 12-?-1866
Johnson, Lessie? to Ben Lyons 11-27-1867
Johnson, Lucinda E. to James W. Ralph 8-5-1854 (8-27-1854)
Johnson, Maggie to Lewis Wilson 12-24-1875 (12-24-1874?)
Johnson, Margaret to John Taylor 1-5-1870
Johnson, Margaret to W. Sulfrige 12-31-1872 (1-2-1873)
Johnson, Maria to Solomon Richards 11-21-1871
Johnson, Mary to Ben Alston 1-24-1870
Johnson, Mary to Evans Read 1-4-1873 (1-6-1873)
Johnson, Mary to George W. Cox 6-23-1855 (6-26-1855)
Johnson, Parelee to Henry Lauderdale 11-12-1874
Johnson, S. M. to J. W. Ballard 6-29-1868 (7-1-1868)
Johnson, Sarah to John W. Starnes 12-2-1867 (12-4-1867)
Johnston, Elizabeth Susannah to James Franklin Harper 4-3-1844 (4-4-1844)
Johnston, Hannah to Osborn Rhodes 9-12-1867 (9-22-1867)
Joice, Ann Eliza to Arthur F. Wooten 5-14-1842 (5-15-1842)
Joice, Cordelia Ann to James Henry Bowers 1-12-1846 (not executed)
Joiner, Elizabeth to William Capehart 11-28-1853
Joiner, Nancy to Jordan Fields 11-14-1872 (11-15-1872)
Jones, Alethia Munford to William Branch Booker 9-18-1852 (9-23-1852)
Jones, Caroline to Jacob M Davis 3-2-1866 (5-30-1866)
Jones, Deffilue? to John Whiteman 12-23-1870
Jones, Delpha to James M. Mullens 5-28-1873
Jones, Dorothy Ann to Samuel J. Rose 5-27-1847 (5-28-1847)
Jones, Elisabeth to James Wass? 8-22-1868 (8-23-1868)
Jones, Eliza to Edmond Rose 11-24-1866
Jones, Elizabeth L. to James L. Quin 9-23-1873 (9-25-1873)
Jones, Frances to John Woods 3-25-1874 (3-26-1874)
Jones, Hanner to Booker Reid 3-10-1874
Jones, Jennie to John W. Wiley 9-30-1871 (10-1-1871)
Jones, Josephine to N.L. Lyles 4-7-1873 (4-10-1873)
Jones, L. A. to W. F. Cowen 12-20-1871
Jones, Laura to R. J. Flanigan 8-26-1874 (8-27-1874)
Jones, Lyda to Louis Scurry 1-11-1866
Jones, Maattie to James Williams 1-1-1873 (1-2-1873)
Jones, Margaret A. to Samuel S. Hurt 12-22-1863 (12-21?-1863)
Jones, Mariah to Nathan Martain 1-25-1873 (1-28-1873)
Jones, Martha to Joseph Johnson 7-8-1872
Jones, Mary C. to James A. Bower 1-12-1867 (1-15-1867)
Jones, Matilda to Ephran Fraizar 6-15-1865
Jones, Matilda to Ephriam Feazur 6-15-1867 (6-16-1867)
Jones, Milly to Lee Cotten 7-2-1872 (7-13-1872)
Jones, Miss M. B. to Jas. W. Lemmon 2-5-1866 (2-8-1866)
Jones, Nancy Jane to Stephen B. Johnson 4-27-1847 (4-30-1847)
Jones, Serilda Ann to George W. W. Crouch 5-7-1860 (5-8-1860)
Jones, Susan J. to J. M. Stroud 7-24-1871 (7-26-1871)
Jones, Susan to Jack Harper 2-7-1870
Jones, Susan to Jackson Smith 10-17-1874 (10-20-1874)
Jones?, Ester to Sam Dick 1-5-1869
Jordan, Paulina to Isaac N. Kelley 12-18-1848 (12-24-1848)
Joyce, Cordelia to Joseph McGowan 11-7-1854
Joyce, Mary to A. J. Montgomery 2-5-1866 (2-8-1866)
Joyner, Elizabeth to G. H. Stevens 10-24-1856
Joyner, Jane to J. M. Stephens 11-26-1874 (11-27-1874)
Julian, Martha Ann to Jno. Bettis 6-4-1864 (6-5-1864)
Keenan, Mrs. Nancy M. to James A. McGee 5-16-1860
Keeth, Ceralda to James Wilson 12-13-1872
Keller, Susan to B. F. Baines 2-25-1874 (3-1-1874)
Kelley, C. A. to A. A. Kelley 1-1-1874
Kelley, D. A. to P. G. Kelley 12-14-1870 (12-15-1870)
Kelley, Elizabeth E. to James McClerkin 11-8-1856 (11-11-1856)
Kelley, Lucinda to John Cummins 3-24-1851 (4-3-1851)
Kelley, Mahala Jane to Robt. Mathews Wallis 3-11-1856
Kelley, Martha to Absolum H. Evans 6-30-1847 (7-1-1847)
Kelley, Mary A. E. to T. L. Faulkner 10-7-1873 (10-9-1873)
Kelley, Sarah Elenor to James M. Terry 9-20-1858 (9-21-1858)
Kelly, Arrilla to James C. Bradford 9-2-1868 (9-31-1868)
Kelly, Malinda J. to John B. Baskins 12-16-1868
Kelly, Martha Ann to James M. Ward 12-8-1841
Kelly, Martha C. to Willis A. Wilson 3-21-1868
Kelly, Rebeca to Steven Terry 1-3-1853 (1-25-1853)
Kelly, Sarah C. to Lemuel Williams 8-31-1867 (9-3-1867)
Kendrick, Ann to Benjamin Pippin 10-30-1861
Kennedy, Martha to William Vincent 1-1-1871
Kenney, Laura Ann to Wm. Cannon Flemming 4-13-1854 (4-15-1854)
Kennon, Mary H. to Henry L. Elcan 9-1-1865 (9-7-1865)
Kent, Fanny to Phil Pain 8-25-1870
Kent, Judith Ann to Garrett Cooper 8-18-1849 (8-22-1849)
Kerr, Msaggie W. to George T. Kinny 12-23-1873 (12-24-1873)
Killingsworth, Martha to William M. Gardner 3-24-1847 (3-?-1847)
Killingsworth, Piety to Jesse Applewhite 4-10-1843 (4-12-1843)
Killy, Elizabeth to Henry Richardson 2-20-1868 (2-25-1868)
Kilpatrick, Margaret J. to James Futhey 11-17-1869 (11-18-1869)
Kilpatrick, Marth J. to James C. Nelson 3-22-1860
Kilpatrick, Mary to Sam Jones 9-14-1872
Kimbro, Miss R. S. to A. Ravenall 1-7-1861 (1-8-1861)
Kimbro, Nancy to Andrew Taylor 9-6-1869
Kimey, Mary Margaret to William Justice 12-20-1856 (12-23-1856)
Kindle, Cordie to Davie Davis 4-16-1873 (4-17-1873)
King, Margaret E. to A. W. Dumas 1-27-1869
King, Martha to Thomas Hankison? 6-29-1852 (7-1-1852)
Kinney, E. C. to A. G. Street 5-7-1870 (5-9-1870)
Kinney, Elvira to Dennis Slaughter 9-23-1851 (9-25-1851)
Kinney, F. M. to W. E. Smith 12-10-1872 (12-11-1872)
Kinney, Frances M. to William H. Davis 7-23-1857
Kinney, M. J. to J. C. Street 8-2?-1871 (8-3-1871)
Kinney, Susan to J. M. Terry 7-2-1874
Kinny, J. E. to O. O. Wiseman 12-22-1873 (1-7-1874)
Kirk, M. R. to S. R. Thompson 12-10-1873
Kitchen, Eliza to Elijah Brown 2-26-1855 (2-27-1855)
Kitchen, Lucy C. to Pleasant Manasco 6-30-1860 (7-5-1860)
Kitchen, Mary M. to James Manasco 6-30-1860 (7-7-1860)
Kitchum, Ruth Ann to J. W. David 7-4-1870 (7-7-1870)
Kluigh, Sarah Jane to C. A. Allen 10-29-1856 (10-30-1856)
Knight, Elizabeth to Wm. Parrot 6-27-1858
Knox, Eliza C. to David A. Cherry 5-31-1854 (6?-1-1854)
Knox, Shelley to J. T. Newsom 12-26-1872
Koonce, Amanda to Taylor Neeley 11-26-1874
Koonce, Eliza M. to W. M. Burns 12-18-1859 (12-21-1859)
Kulbeth, Mary to Tho. Evans Gray 9-16-1851 (9-17-1851)
Kulbreath, Rosanna to Chas. Wm. Webb 12-19-1850
Kurts, Lorina to Jas. Monroe Locke 1-2-1856

Lacey, Mattie to Smith Maclin 1-25-1871
Lacy, Lucy to Henry Hastings 7-6-1867
Ladd, Elisa to T. J. Briggs 2-19-1870 (2-24-1870)
Ladd, Elizabeth to W. H. Hise 9-4-1874 (9-6-1874)
Ladd, Mary to John Mauzy 8-21-1872 (8-25-1872)
Lake, Elvira to Jesse Thomas Faris 10-23-1848 (10-24-1848)
Lake, Mary Susan to Elisha B. Ray 1-27-1852 (1-28-1852)
Lake, Rena to Isaac Rhodes 12-10-1868
Lamb, Amanda J. to John T. Douseford 2-17-1858 (2-18-1858)
Lamb, E. J. to T. J. Whitson 9-17-1861 (9-18-1861)
Lamb, Eliza M. to John Henry Deakins 9-19-1849 (9-20-1849)
Lamb, Elizabeth to John Bowen? Wiseman 12-12-1846 (12-24-1846)
Lamb, Erena to James Franklin Young 9-2-1844 (9-4-1844)
Lamb, Mahalah to Daniel W. Hering 12-6-1847 (12-22-1847)
Lamb, Mary C. to W. A. Martin 9-5-1859 (9-6-1859)
Lamb, Mary Frances to Edward Joseph Mariner 3-8-1850 (3-11-1850)
Lamb, Paulina A. to Joel Currin Parish 2-18-1849 (2-22-1849)
Lambert, Ann E. to W. E.? Rodgers 9-21-1864 (10-25-1864)
Land, Susan to John D. Erwin 9-29-1847 (9-30-1847)
Lane, Mary E. to John A. Freeman 8-25-1866 (8-28-1866)
Lane, Mary to Daniel Taylor 11-27-1870
Lane, Susan to W. H. Davis 1-19-1871
Laremore, T. A. to J. H. Shaf 7-27-1874 (7-29-1874)
Larimore, Amanda to J. P. Keaton 2-25-1868
Larimore, Elsey to James A. Calhoon 9-17-1840 (10-15-1840)
Larimore, Nancy to J. W. Barnet 2-11-1868 (3-3-1868)
Larimore, W. P. to W. N. Myers 2-18-1873 (2-20-1873)
Larrimoore, M. to Joe Hall 12-17-1874
Las?, Milly to Jos. R. Owen 1-23-1869 (1-24-1869)
Lasseter, Lucinda C. to James H. Galbreth 2-5-1866 (2-18-1866)
Lathan, Sarah to James Gross 1-10-1855 (1-11-1855)
Lauderdale, Betsy Ann to John Ford 4-14-1866
Lauderdale, Clara H. to Josiah H. Lauderdale 4-4-1866 (4-4-1865?)
Lauderdale, Eliza J. to James A. Hill 7-31-1867 (9-1-1867)
Lauderdale, Pecella to Hilary Cage 3-5-1869
Lawthon, Sarah to Wash Anderson 3-13-1869 (3-14-1869)
Laxton, J. C. to William Bennett 7-19-1873 (7-20-1873)
Laxton?, Sarah E. to Thomas McMallen 1-26-1870 (1-27-1870)]
Leach, Arminta H. to James Drummonds 1-4-1862 (1-5-1862)
Leach, Eliza to A. J. Bowden 11-20-1853
Leach, Elizabeth to Green B. Young 11-14-1849
Leach, Emily to Marcus Henry Hartsfield 12-26-1849
Leach, Harriet Ford to Hosea Carroll Brown 9-22-1852
Leach, Nancy Ann to Benjamin F. Hartsfield 8-8-1855
Leach, Nancy to Thornton Rhodes 10-4-1851 (10-5-1851)
Lemmon, Sarah Irene to James Iredell Hall 12-26-1849 (12-27-1849)
Lewellen, Margaret to John Ballard 7-9-1866 (7-12-1866)
Lewellen, Martha J. to John S. Silvers 5-11-1858
Ligon, Ann Jane to Christopher Col. Sharp 9-6-1854
Ligon, C. E. to J. F. Hall 2-4-1873 (2-9-1873)
Ligon, Harriet to Louis Sanford 4-17-1868 (4-18-1868)
Ligon, Sue H. to M. Bell 5-16-1865 (5-17-1865)
Linder, Parale to George W. Smith 2-14-1872
Lindsay, Mary E. to A. T. Ikard 1-1-1869 (1-5-1869)
Lindsey, Mary E. to John W. Jenkins 9-17-1872 (9-19-1872)
Linn, Mattie J. T. to L. L. Webster 7-13-1874 (7-15-1874)
Linn, Sarah J. to James G. Hindman 2-1-1858 (2-2-1858)
Linsey, Mattie E. to Charles H. Warren 12-22-1874
Lippman, Maria to Ned? Barret 10-9-1868 (10-12-1868)
Littlejohn, Melvinia to William Richardson 1-4-1873
Litus, Rachel to John Dickson 7-20-1867
Livingston, Mary Luellen to Henry Fry 8-22-1874 (8-23-1874)
Lock, L. A. to John Kurts 12-21-1858
Locke, Emily Jane to John Holland 6-11-1844
Locke, Maggie to J. B. Kelly 2-16-1874
Locke, Virginia C. to Wm. Pleasant Pewitt 4-25-1852
Locket, Nerva to John Somerville 2-16-1874 (2-25-1874)
Lodgings, Sarah Jane to F. M. McAlilly 7-27-1858
Logan, Elizabeth to Jerry Robinson 1-12-1872 (1-17-1872)
Logan, Louisa to John Ingram 9-18-1873
Logan, Mary to T. S. Baker 10-24-1874 (10-25-1874)
Long, Harriet to Macal Beavers 1-14-1868 (1-16-1868)
Long, Margaret to H. W. Beaver 5-1-1862
Long, Permelia to Saml. J. Marsh 6-20-1859 (6-21-1859)
Lorimore, Vicey to Henry Small 2-8-1872
Lowe, Felia to Johnson Bernard 8-7-1872 (1-16-1872?)
Lowe, Nancy to Dan Smith 12-7-1871 (12-9-1871)
Loyd, M. A. to J. H. Hamby 5-24-1873 (5-25-1873)
Loyd, Martha to William Obrien 1-29-1867 (1-31-1867)
Luckado, Cardelia to William Edwards 8-21-1868
Lummicons, Martha to John J. Bius? 6-24-1868 (6-25-1868)
Lunford, Tennessee to Dabney Smith 1-14-1873 (1-16-1873)
Lunsford, Amanda Jane to James C. Wharton 6-7-1842 (6-9-1842)
Luster, Catherin to John Somerville 3-22-1869 (3-24-1869)
Lyle, Cordelia T. to Charles H. Welch 12-22-1868 (12-24-1868)
Lyles, Mary Martin to John B. Parsons 9-30-1853 (10-2-1853)
Lyn, Ann Willis to Cornelius Yates 5-3-1870
Lynn, Adaline to Alexander Morrison 3-16-1869 (3-6?-1869)
Lynn, N. E. to R. M. McCallie 10-5-1868 (10-6-1868)
Lyon, Susan to Edward Bannon 12-23-1873
Mabene, Maria to Thomas Gray 5-4-1872
Maburn, Nancy to Peter Vincent 1-3-1871 (1-14-1871)
Macafee, Jane to Charles Manasco 1-10-1866
Macke?, M. M. to A. B. Griffin 8-7-1871 (8-8-1871)
Macklin, Anna L. to Jack Fields 12-26-1868 (1-20-1870)
Macklin, Indy to Richard Edwards 12-20-1867
Macklin, Mary to George Roberts 12-19-1867
Macklin, Sallie to Wedly Taylor 9-6-1866
Maclin, Aggny? to Alfred Craig 12-14-1867 (12-21-1867)
Maclin, Easter to William Maclin 2-27-1874
Maclin, Eliza S. to Wm. F. Brodnax 5-15-1865
Maclin, Frances to Wesley Jones 12-21-1869
Maclin, Frankie to Wm. Taylor 1-28-1870
Maclin, Gracey to James Jones 12-7-1874
Maclin, Harrit to George Reddick 12-31-1870 (1-2-1871)
Maclin, Jennie to Ed Peete 12-26-1870
Maclin, Jenny to Claiburn Whitley 7-18-1868
Maclin, Lily to Beverly Johnson 7-26-1867 (7-27-1867)
Maclin, Louisa to George Maclin 4-8-1870
Maclin, Mary F. to P. E. Northern 3-4-1874 (3-5-1874)
Maclin, Rhode to David Whitley 6-16-1866 (6-17-1866)
Maclin, Sina to David Burrel? 12-23-1872 (12-26-1872)
Maclin, Smith Ann to Levi Cannon 2-27-1867
Maclin, Sophia to Beverly Johnson 12-24-1869 (12-27-1869)
Maddocks, Mary Ann to Moses Fletcher 10-12-1852 (10-14-1852)
Mailey, Elizabeth Ann to Joshua M. Miller 7-28-1845 (8-1-1845)
Mainer, Sarah to Joseph Sutton Rainer 3-22-1842 (10-?-1842)
Maley, Jane to S. R. Smith 6-20-1872
Maley, Julia Ann to Gideon G. McGee 8-23-1857
Maley, Larisa A. W. to E. B. Daniel 6-8-1858
Maley, Margaret F. to Robert H. Ralph 2-17-1870 (2-20-1870)
Maley, Patienc to Tilman McGee 1-17-1868
Maley, Sarah E. to Alfred A. Myers 9-13-1855
Maley, Sarah to J. M. Daniels 1-31-1871 (2-2-1871)
Maley, Virginia to Walter Napier 11-23-1872 (11-24-1872)
Malone, Bettie A. to Wm. G. Ray 11-15-1852 (11-18-1852)
Malone, E. G. to W. H. Mattice 7-19-1873
Malone, Edna E. to L. A. Scarbrough 3-21-1866 (3-22-1866)
Malone, Katie A. to John G. Scarbrough 4-1-1872 (4-2-1872)
Malone, Leaner to John Williamson 2-23-1867 (2-28-1867)
Malone, M. B. to W. H. Murphey 1-17-1870
Malone, Malinda to Edwin Anderson 1-13-1869
Malone, Mildred E. to Charles E. Smith 9-20-1853 (9-22-1853)
Malone, Sarah Elizabeth to Jacob Roland 10-29-1874 (10-31-1874)
Malone, Susan A. to T. W. Winn 10-23-1856
Malugin, Susan to Edward Upton 1-17-1872
Maly, Louisa J. to Thomas Myers 8-17-1869
Manasco, Mary E. to John Wesley Stanus 9-6-1860 (9-13-1860)
Manasco, Mary M. to H. C. Starnes 3-7-1865 (3-8-1865)
Manasco, Mary to James W. Turnage 12-16-1868 (12-17-1868)
Manasco, Matilda C. to W. H. Archer 2-8-1871
Manasco, Nancy Ann to James Tedwell 7-3-1867 (7-4-1867)
Manaslk?, Mary to James W. Oumage? no date (with 1868)
Manly, Rebecka Frances to Henry Martin Turnage 12-30-1857 (12-31-1857)
Mariner, Eliza Jane to Erasmus kSydenham Campbell 6-1-1844 (6-4-1844)
Markham, Elenor H. to Jesse M. Claiborn 5-4-1859
Markham, Elizabeth to John Caldwell 10-4-1851
Markham, Susan to James Burgess 9-8-1855 (9-10-1855)

Marsh, Martha E. to W. T. Davidson 12-28-1869 (12-30-1869)
Marsh, Mary E. to James F. Davis 10-23-1866 (10-24-1866)
Marsh, Mary L. to Wm. R. Hunt 2-7-1871 (2-9-1871)
Marsh, Missouri A. to Jonathan Snider 1-15-1849 (12-24-1848?)
Marshall, A. to Samuel Maclin 9-30-1871 (10-6-1871)
Marshall, Eliza P. to Thos. C. Crawford 2-9-1871
Marshall, Lydia Frances to John W. Walker 12-13-1847 (12-?-1847)
Marshall, Martha L. to R. H. Murphey 9-30-1865
Marshall, Salina to Frank Johnson 12-30-1874
Marshall, Sarah Jane to Uriah Pinckney Yarbro 1-15-1853 (1-20-1853)
Martin, Hanna? to J. M. Flemming 2-8-1870
Martin, Jane to ____ Wiseman 1-26-1874 (1-28-1874)
Martin, Parthenia H. M. to Shelton D. Taylor 10-11-1846
Mason, C. D. to D. A. Davis 10-25-1865 (10-26-1865)
Mason, Hanna to Frank Holloway 1-10-1872 (1-15-1872)
Mason, Olivia to Georg W. Bonner 2-6-1854 (2-7-1854)
Mason, Veria to Alexander Taylor 12-23-1874
Massey, Martha to John Stearns no date (with 1862)
Massey, Rebecca J. to James H. Morterson? 2-20-1843 (3-15-1843)
Maston, Senith Elizabeth to John Manasco 4-22-1874 (4-23-1874)
Maten, Rosa V. to George W. Whitlock 6-29-1869 (7-1-1869)
Mathews, Edith to Allen Thompson 12-28-1872
Mathews, Emeline to Ben Mathews 12-17-1874
Mathis, Emma to Clink Rhodes 12-25-1871 (12-26-1871)
Mathis?, Prefom? to Charles Christopher Freeman 7-17-1843 (8-18-1843)
Mattice?, S. E. to J. B. McDaniel 7-19-1873 (7-23-1873)
Maurring?, Annie to A. P. Smith 12-1-1869
Max, Hariet L. to M. F. Hartfield 1-3-1870 (1-5-1870)
Maxwell, Mary Eliza to James J. Maxwell 9-26-1867 (9-27-1867)
Maxwell, Mollie to James Bringle 2-14-1872
Maxwell, Nancy to Jas. T. Winburn 9-22-1855
Maye, Sarah to Johnathan Bough 8-25-1866
Mayfield, Nancy Jane to J. W. Davis 12-12-1859 (12-13-1859)
Mayo, Laura J. to William G. Cockrill 3-18-1867 (3-14?-1867)
Mayo, Meter to Frank Toliver 12-28-1869 (1-1-1870)
McBride, Amanda Minerva to Wm. Alen Lawrence? 3-12-1856 (3-13-1856)
McBride, Louvina A. to Thomas Forbess 7-16-1866 (7-18-1866)
McBride, Marth E. to James Stevens 4-3-1867
McBride, Martha J. to Robert A. Rice 1-?-1867 (1-16-1867)
McBride, Mary Eliz. to Peter Simpson Jackson 12-3-1855 (12-6-1855)
McBride, Mary J. to Evander McNair 11-23-1860 (11-27-1860)
McBride, Nancy Emily to A. M. Duncan 3-12-1856 (3-13-1856)
McBride, Nancy J. to J. J. Laxton 2-2-1870 (2-3-1870)
McBride, Paula? to Sam Hughes 5-20-1874
McBride, Rachel L. to Robert M. Green 9-7-1867
McBride, Sina to A. Laremore 8-1-1872 (8-4-1872)
McCain, Amanda to Belfast Strong 1-19-1869 (1-21-1869)
McCain, Amanda to Tom White 8-1-1874
McCain, Caroline to Alfred Strong 12-2-1865 (12-7-1865)
McCain, Eliza H. to A. J. Wilson 12-15-1857
McCain, M. E. to J. W. Lynn 6-2-1869 (6-3-1869)
McCain, M. J. to J. A. Moore 12-3-1866 (12-4-1866)
McCain, Margaret G. to Alexander J. McQuiston 12-16-1845
McCain, Martha A. to John J. Faulkner 11-25-1867 (11-26-1867)
McCain, Martha Jane to Jonathan Calvin Davis 9-13-1854
McCain, Mary C. to Joseph A. Dickson 9-15-1855
McCall, Abby to Abner Vincent 12-7-1868 (12-20-1869?)
McCall, Sallie A. to Alfred A. Langstaff 11-13-1871 (11-15-1871)
McCall, Susan to Vernas? Sherrod 12-29-1866
McCalla, Charlotte Ann to John B. Gooch 1-11-1870
McCalley, Jane E. to George W. Banner 12-30-1868 (1-2-1869)
McCamack, May J. to John Tuikler 12-17-1856
McCanla, Jane H. to William Paden 4-27-1840
McCarrol, Martha to Mathew Walt 1-12-1869 (1-28-1869)
McCarroll, Eliza to W. C. Boswell 10-1-1864 (10-2-1864)
McCarroll, Nancy to Wm. L. Wilson 9-8-1854 (9-14-1854)
McCauley, Elizabeth M. to John Voss 12-12-1849
McCauley, Mary Hood to James Carroll Taylor 1-8-1845 (1-9-1845)
McClamick, Maggie D. to E. Z. Simmons 11-23-1870
McClannohan, L. R. to John T. Z. Marshall 11-26-1867 (11-28-1867)
McClellan, Mary Coffy to David Alexr. Brunson 1-12-1846 (1-13-1846)
McClellan, Permelia Jane to John Menasco? 3-8-1852
McClelland, Sallie to Saml. Payne 2-17-1866
McClelland, Susan to James Spencer Smith 2-9-1853 (2-15-1853)
McClenahan, Nannie to Francis Thomas 1-14-1869 (1-20-1869)
McClenahan, Sallie to S. W. Bedingfield 11-9-1874 (11-11-1874)
McClerkin, Elizabeth to Alexander Hindman 3-26-1860 (3-29-1860)
McClerkin, Martha H. to Robert P. Harper 5-17-1841 (5-18-1841)
McClerkin, Mary E. to W. R. McLaughlin 3-7-1874 (3-18?-1874)
McClerkin, Sarah Ann to Wm. H. Thompson 12-1-1873
McCluhen, Mary Jane to John A. Moore 11-31-1857 (12-1-1857)
McClurkin, Nancy Jane to Augustus P. Moffatt 2-6-1850
McCommack, Mary to Arche English 9-23-1868 (9-24-1868)
McConnell, Bell to Albert Cooper 10-30-1872 (11-1-1872)
McCormack, E. J. to J. J. Garret 12-17-1872
McCormick, Harriet N. to John S. Frierson 2-5-1855 (2-8-1855)
McCormick, R. B. to Jas. L. McLintock 5-6-1867
McCoy, Frances M. to John H. Wood 6-18-1856 (6-19-1856)
McCoy, Mary Margaret to Craddock Vaughan 1-20-1846 (1-21-1846)
McCoy, Sarah Fina to G. W. Payne 3-22-1860
McCrare?, Mary to James L. Wright 9-1-1853
McCraw, Anne? to ____ Tycer 5-18-1863
McCraw, Bettie to Thomas H. Lamkin 4-1-1869
McCraw, Elizabeth to Thos. C. McCraw 10-26-1861
McCraw, Martha D. to John Craig 6-26-1866 (6-28-1866)
McCraw, Mary Elizabeth to Zachariah Tyre 2-9-1842
McCraw, Orlenia to Alfred H. Ralph 8-6-1855 (8-16-1855)
McCraw, P. Ann to A. L. Forbiss 12-6-1859 (9-8-1859)
McCraw, Patsey W. to Littleton W. Trobough 5-29-1844
McCraw, Penelope to Richard Turner Wright 11-18-1848 (11-20-1848)
McCraw, Penelopee Ann to L. A. Forbiss 12-6-1859
McCreight, Harriet R. to Robert Miller 9-5-1848 (9-7-1848)
McCreight, Mary Ann to Wm. James Strong 9-25-1850 (9-26-1850)
McCreight, Mrs. M. A. to J. H. Blanchard 6-21-1866
McCuller, Nancy to Jo Brown 12-30-1873
McCullough, Charlotte J. to John L. Duncan 2-18-1873 (2-20-1873)
McCullough, Nancy Ann to W. H. Grigsby 11-16-1872 (11-19-1872)
McCullough, Susan L. to John M. Hobbs 8-18-1874 (8-20-1874)
McCullough, T. J. to R. W. Bailey 12-1-1873
McCulough, Sarah to William Wilson 12-31-1857
McDaniel, Axie to J. P. Wall 12-22-1873
McDaniel, M. M. E. to Wm. C. Baird 8-25-1873 (9-4-1873)
McDier?, M. A. to H. W. McQuiston 2-26-1870 (3-1-1870)
McDill, H. E. to R. W. McLaughlin 5-25-1871 (5-30-1871)
McDill, Mary A. to Charles B. Simmonton 10-15-1866 (10-16-1866)
McDonald, Catharine to Moore Stevens 12-24-1849
McDouggle, Catharine to James McDonald 11-23-1869 (11-25-1869)
McDowell, R. A. to Horace Posey 11-10-1870 (1-14-1871)
McFadden, Bettie to Peter Menken 7-23-1874 (7-24-1874)
McFadden, Callie H. to Jacob Silvertooth 2-14-1871
McFadden, Miss Mollie to N. C. McFadden 1-29-1862
McFadin, Susan F. to Wesley A. Burnett 10-12-1858
McFarland, Jennetta L. to John B. Knox 3-7-1848 (3-?-1848)
McFarland, Mary A. to Charles W. Fultin 6-7-1848 (6-?-1848)
McFarlane, Rebecca to James D. Wesson? 1-14-1844 (1-16-1844)
McFerin, Nancy Jane to John Applewhite 2-16-1841 (2-20-1841)
McFerren, Ellen to John Ramsey 6-9-1869
McGill, Mattie to Andrew McNeal 11-1-1873
McGowan, Elizabeth to William Tennant 10-25-1850 (10-27-1850)
McGregor, Columbia W. to C. R. Harris 1-4-1865
McGregor, Elizabeth to J. W. Harris 7-15-1851
McGregor, K. F. to O. E. Martin 2-10-1874
McGregor, Mary Fannie to John L. Payne 2-6-1861 (2-7-1861)
McGregor, Mary to James Wright 1-?-1871) (1-19-1871)
McGregor, Mitty to Tyler Harris 1-3-1867
McGregor, Sarah to Thos. B. Kent 1-13-1866
McGrogan, Martha Burton to Wm. Henry Hill 2-8-1859
McGuice, Jerusha Ann Jane to Milton A. Coats 11-7-1857 (11-10-1857)
McGuier, J. W. to Henry L. Harris 12-23-1874
McGuin, America F. to W. Wilkins 5-4-1859
McGuin, Susan to Landon B. Yarbrough 3-31-1846 (4-3-1846)
McGuire, Ann E. to W. L. Peeler 12-19-1865
McGuire, Emly to Alex. W. Fradle? 5-18-1854
McGuire, Minerva Jane to Robert W. Smith 1-24-1852 (1-28-1852)
McGuire, N. M. to J. E. Dobson 1-3-1865
McGuire, Sarah E. to Wm. H. Griffith 10-20-1860 (10-21-1860)

McGuise, Eliza to John G. Mears 12-24-1856 (1-1-1857)
McIlwaine, Mary M. to W. L. Stegall 4-16-1872
McIlwaine, Sallie to H. J. Long 5-22-1871 (5-23-1871)
McIlwaine, Tersa to R. L. Beaves 2-20-1873
McIntosh, Emily to Henry Frazier? 3-24-1870 (3-30-1870)
McIntosh, Mariah J. to William H. Walton 11-25-1869
McIntosh, Samuella to Jacob F. Smith 10-24-1867
McIntyre, Mary to George Evans 9-6-1841
McKenny, Mary J. to J. C. Mills 5-6-1868 (5-7-1868)
McKenon, Nancy to Felix Robertson David 1-25-1842 (1-26-1842)
McKinney, Frances to John Wayman 8-18-1841
McKnatt, Martha E. to Samuel H. Trim 9-10-1872
McLain, Nancy to Louis McQuistian 9-16-1865
McLeary, Elizabeth E. to Cyrus W. Weller(Miller?) 9-1-1840 (9-2-1840)
McLennahan, H. J. to Lynn Boyaknir 1-20-1871 (1-22-1871)
McLennan, Elizabeth to F. B. Adkins 3-7-1860 (3-8-1860)
McLinn, Frances to Laudin Davis 5-5-1871
McLister, Cy to John Horton 4-25-1866
McMin, Sarah O. to Robert S. Bird 12-16-1867 (12-18-1867)
McMinns, Mary Jane to Tho. Jefferson Kelley 7-20-1850
McMullin, M. E. J. to J. W. Koonce 4-8-1874 (4-9-1874)
McMullins, Matilda J. to John W. Koonce 12-23-1867
McNair, Martha to Robert L. Walker 4-24-1865
McNat, P. F. to J. H. Bird 11-8-1872 (11-12-1872)
McNilly, Mollie to F. Hifield 6-17-1874
McQLuiston, Martha to Robert B. Harper 9-9-1847
McQuisten, Elizabeth to James M. Wright 3-20-1841 (3-23-1841)
McQuister, Eliza to Cornelius Bond 1-23-1866
McQuiston, E. W. to J. C. Castles 12-12-1870 (12-15-1870)
McQuiston, Eliza A. to Andrew J. Wright 1-29-1868 (1-30-1868)
McQuiston, Jennette to William D. Strain 12-17-1847
McQuiston, M. Bettie to J. Linsey Baird 12-6-1870 (12-8-1870)
McQuiston, Margaret E. to R. P. Straing 11-22-1870
McQuiston, Margaret to Robert Simonton 9-4-1855
McQuiston, Martha to John Ready McDaniel 5-5-1851
McQuiston, Nancy Jane to William Baird 3-5-1844
McQuiston, Nancy to Henry Simonton 7-3-1871 (7-4-1871)
McQuiston, Rachel to James Jordan 6-1-1866 (6-3-1866)
McQuiston, Sarah Isabella to Saml. Dunn Dickson 10-9-1850
Mcquiston, Mary Ann to D. H. McQuiston 8-31-1870
Mears, Lucinda to Andrew Montgomery 5-19-1849 (5-20-1849)
Mears, Mary E. to T. M. Morrison 6-18-1861 (6-19-1861)
Mears, N. W. to N. A. Sullivan 11-25-1871 (11-30-1871)
Meeler, Eveline to Ben Ellis 2-14-1874 (2-15-1874)
Melugin, Annie E. to Simon dP. Driver 10-18-1869 (10-19-1869)
Menafee, Mary Jane to Lewis Stevens 5-5-1871 (5-7-1871)
Menascoe, Mary L. to David C. Booth 5-7-1866 (5-11-1866)
Menefee, Florence S. to Green W. Smitheal 10-27-1870
Merrill, J. to G. W. Sargent 4-5-1871 (4-9-1871)
Merrit, Catharine to N. H. Boswell 10-12-1865 (11-6-1865)
Mickelberry, Martha to Robert T. Fortner 3-29-1851 (3-30-1851)
Mila, Elizabeth to Clark C. Deson 11-27-1844 (11-28-1844)
Miller, Aanda to Ben Wooten 1-20-1869
Miller, Adaline to Richard Green 11-9-1872
Miller, Alva to A. W. Druse? 1-24-1871 (1-25-1871)
Miller, Annie A. to John D. Thompson 2-21-1865 (2-22-1865)
Miller, Annie to Andrew Collins 5-21-1874
Miller, Eliza A. to William B. Simonton 12-18-1866 (12-19-1866)
Miller, Eliza M. to John F. Miller 10-26-1869
Miller, Eliza to John Baird 1-29-1868
Miller, Eliza to Thos. C. Horne 10-5-1870 (10-10-1870)
Miller, Indiana to William Clark 1-20-1866
Miller, J. A. to T. J. Forbess 12-21-1870 (12-22-1870)
Miller, Jane to Jackson Pinkston 8-26-1871 (8-29-1871)
Miller, Jane to John Pool 1-29-1868
Miller, Jane to Peter Read 7-7-1866
Miller, Lucinda to Gilbert Wylie 2-13-1873
Miller, M. A. to W. M. Nichols 1-11-1865 (2-6-1865)
Miller, M. E. to E. S. Ellis 1-17-1872 (1-18-1872)
Miller, M. to Anthony Ross 12-29-1869 (12-30-1869)
Miller, Margaret to Benj. Tho. Adkins 10-2-1850
Miller, Margaret to Henry Smith 1-12-1846 (1-15-1846)
Miller, Margaret to James Buttery? 12-16-1871 (12-17-1871)
Miller, Martha A. to John Simonton 5-18-1847 (5-21-1847)
Miller, Mary to D. A. Merrill 12-29-1856
Miller, Mary to Maurice Mitchell 9-5-1849 (9-9-1849)
Miller, Minerva to Jack Tipton 6-22-1867 (6-23-1867)
Miller, Mollie J. to J. W. Campbell 10-20-1871 (10-26-1871)
Miller, Nancy E. to John W. Wilie 7-31-1855 (8-2-1855)
Miller, Nancy to Richard Green 4-18-1874
Miller, RAchel to Edward Radford Crouch 8-12-1844 (8-15-1844)
Miller, Susan A. to George W. Turner 10-31-1854 (11-2-1854)
Miller, Susan to Albert Smith 2-21-1873 (2-22-1873)
Miller, V. Ann to Austin Peete 1-14-1873
Mills, Martha A. to Jessee F. Dawson 1-18-1871 (1-19-1871)
Mills, Mary E. to Saml. J. Mills 8-28-1865
Mills, Rosa Ann Jane to W. D. Dawson 12-?-1869 (12-19-1869)
Minor, Sallie to Jos. Cotherane 1-5-1866 (1-27-1866)
Mitchell, Adeline B. to Isaac Morrison 1-8-1849
Mitchell, Elizabeth to Willia G. Wright 2-8-1844 (2-27-1844)
Mitchell, Julia L. to William M. Tinnen 12-11-1858 (12-12-1858)
Mitchell, Laura to James T. Shankle 8-24-1869 (8-29-1869)
Mitchell, Maggie to T. P. Martin 10-9-1874 (10-10-1874)
Mitchell, Margaret to Jacob Gordon 1-20-1870
Mitchell, Mary D. to J. H. Wilson 9-29-1872
Mitchell, Milly to Isaac Griffin 1-20-1870
Mitchell, Sarah M. to Samuel L. Taylor 10-31-1860
Mitchell, Tennie E. to James W. Mathis 9-5-1867
Moffit, Harriet to Cal Coward 12-30-1874 (12-31-1874)
Moffit, Martha to K.? Strong 11-15-1871
Monroe, Sarah Clementine to Thomas Morrison 3-6-1844 (3-7-1844)
Monroe?, Elizabeth to George W. Miller 3-9-1841 (3-10-1841)
Montgomery, Adelia to Granville Runnels 4-29-1871 (5-2-1871)
Montgomery, Artemisia Ann to Lawrence Page 2-1-1851 (2-6-1851)
Montgomery, Martha to Thomas Hamilton 5-16-1857 (5-18-1857)
Montgomery, Mary N. to William Cozby 5-5-1866
Montgomery, Nancy M. to T. S. Vaughan 9-7-1870
Montgomery, Polly to Louis Taylor 12-24-1867
Montgomry, Sallie to Washington Downing 1-6-1869 (1-8-1869)
Moore, Eleanor K. to Minor B. Davidson 1-4-1842
Moore, Elizabeth to Mack Drummons 12-4-1843 (12-13-1843)
Moore, Elizabeth to Peter Perkins Smith 6-6-1845 (6-15-1845)
Moore, Elizabeth to Robert McCullough 10-29-1851 (10-30-1851)
Moore, Ellen to Archibald Marshall 10-13-1854 (11-1-1854)
Moore, Elvira to Robt. McComb McEwin 11-15-1850
Moore, Eugenie P. to Jerry Manasco 2-27-1871 (3-1-1871)
Moore, Fannie C. to Jas. Dickey 5-12-1869
Moore, Jane to John J.? McCorkle 4-27-1840 (5-5-1840)
Moore, Judith to John Townsend 5-2-1868
Moore, Julia to Wm. Boner 12-23-1858 (12-30-1858)
Moore, Leana to John Gross 5-30-1865
Moore, Leanah to Robert Cooper 11-18-1861
Moore, Leanna to Thomas Cowan? 5-5-1842 (5-12-1842)
Moore, Leer to George Jones 4-17-1871
Moore, M. D. to J. M. Bragg 1-7-1873 (1-9-1873)
Moore, Margaret Jane to John Cox Custer 12-3-1850 (12-8-1850)
Moore, Margaret to James Dickey 12-25-1861
Moore, Margaret to Jonathan A. Nelson 8-17-1846 (8-18-1846)
Moore, Mariah Tucker to Mingo Johnson 1-19-1872 (1-20-1872)
Moore, Mary E. to Jas. J. Faulkner 10-7-1856
Moore, Mary L. to John Pierce 5-8-1841
Moore, Mary L. to Melvil A. Moore 11-17-1869 (11-18-1869)
Moore, Nancy A. to Jonathan Spencer 9-3-1860 (9-5-1860)
Moore, Nancy A. to Jonathan Spencer 9-5-1860
Moore, Nancy C. to Samuel Tims 2-18-1845 (2-19-1845)
Moore, Penni? to Wm. Brown 1-11-1871 (1-15-1871)
Moore, Rachal to Albert Avery 12-17-1869 (12-18-1869)
Moore, Rebecca to Bill Prier 2-12-1874 (2-13-1874)
Moore, Sallie Ann to Wm. Hollaway 9-9-1857 (9-21-1857)
Moran, Cathrine to Alford Smith 5-27-1854 (5-28-1854)
Morents?, Angeline Jane to John Mailey? 4-5-1843 (4-6-1843)
Morgan, Elizabeth to Joshua Sherrod 12-24-1866 (12-29-1866)
Morgan, Fannie to J. B. Kent 9-23-1865
Morgan, Harriet to Wm. Tipton 8-11-1866
Morgan, Lu to Robert Eaton 11-23-1869
Morgan, Rosina to Dick Tipton 11-16-1865
Morris, Sarah A. to John W. Pool 6-1-1872
Morrisett, Catharine F. to G. A. Huffman 1-8-1872 (1-9-1872)
Morrison, Emerline to James Simmons 11-28-1868 (11-30-1868)

Morrison, Julia E. to Joseph G. Delashmeit 7-1-1865
Morrison, Laura to Needham Kilpatrick 6-3-1869 (6-4-1869)
Morrison, Mary A. to Samuel W. Hudleston 9-3-1872
Morrison, Matilda to A. Harris 1-4-1869 (1-8-1869)
Morrison, Nancy Caroline to Jacob Wallace 1-19-1854
Morrison, Nannie E. to W. T. Morgan 12-11-1874
Morrison, Susanna to Henry Lynn 7-3-1869
Mosby, Sarah to Stark Anerson? 8-16-1870 (9-4-1870)
Moss, Lucy E. to P. A. Bourn 10-11-1870 (10-12-1870)
Moss, Rachell to Peter Burrell 11-12-1873
Moss, Sarah to James Weatherford 7-21-1865 (7-26-1865)
Moss?, Sophia? to J.? W.? Markham? 11-26-1862
Motley?, Florence E. S. to J. C. Banden 8-21-1869
Mounts, Angeline J. to Robert Evans Cloud 1-17-1843 (not executed)
Muligin, S. J. to J. S. Bashears 12-23-1874
Mullin, Lou to Robt. Scarimon? 6-3-1867 (6-1?-1867)
Munford, Ermine to John G. Hall 5-29-1872
Munford, Sallie E. to Geo. D. Holmes 1-18-1866
Murphey, Mary E. to T. H. Harris 10-24-1874 (10-5?-1874)
Murphey, S.B. to R. G. Goodman 11-18-1869
Murphey, Sarah A. to Joseph Harris 9-1-1869 (9-9-1869)
Murphey, Sue to William Dyson 3-31-1873 (4-1-1873)
Murphy, Hager to Frank Bernard 2-6-1871 (3-5-1871)
Murphy, Margaret to ____ Addison Cooper 5-22-1843
Murphy, Mary E. to Alfred H. Goodman 10-29-1866
Murphy, Nancy Ann to Joshua M. Miller 7-8-1847
Murphy, Sallie to Sidney Kincaid 10-1-1874
Murren, Harriet to James C. Pewitt 12-23-1840 (12-24-1840)
Murrin, L. P. to John Gacy 11-24-1867
Murrin, Mary Ann to Bryan Tillman 6-17-1865
Murry, Mary C. to Washington H. Wade 5-9-1841 (5-18-1841)
Myers, Bettie A. to Alfred Page 7-24-1871 (7-26-1871)
Myers, Elizabeth ANn to Daniel Payne 9-3-1849
Myers, Everline to William Page 7-5-1866
Myers, L. A. to W. H. Francis 8-8-1866 (8-9-1866)
Myers, M. F. to M. H. Hartsfield 9-29-1866 (9-30-1866)
Myers, Margaret E. to George S. Cates 12-23-1873
Myers, Maria to Jeremiah Bowden 11-15-1853
Myers, Martha F. to F. W. Evritt no date (with 12-1861)
Myers, Minerva Jane to Geo. Washington Walton 3-21-1849
Myers, S. E. to J. H. Howard 5-10-1871 (5-11-1871)
Myers, Sallie E. to William A. Fortner 12-17-1866 (12-16?-1866)
Myers, Susan to Marcus H. Hartsfield 11-30-1853 (12-1-1853)
Myres, Susan R. to Russell Goforth 3-16-1859
Neel, Isabla? to William Fitch 11-27-1874
Neel, Martha to Henry Bell 11-1-1869
Neil, M. A. to G. T. Scott 5-26-1869
Nelson, Christina to Washington Johnston 1-12-1869 (1-19-1869)
Nelson, Delia Ann to John Lanier 12-6-1873
Nelson, Elizabeth J. to W. M. Allen 12-22-1858
Nelson, Elizabeth to W. M. Allen 12-22-1858
Nelson, Louisa to Allen Trass? 1-26-1867 (2-18-1867)
Nelson, Martha J. to James M. Hill 11-13-1866 (11-16-1866)
Newman, Elizabeth Frances to Joseph Allen Green 3-4-1845
Newman, Ellen Rose to John Ambrose Wheelock 9-19-1850
Newman, Mary Fannin to James Rose 10-28-1856 (10-29-1856)
Newsom, Mary E. to George W. Bonner 7-21-1865
Newton, Fanny E. to Henry C. Bowers 8-22-1865 (8-23-1865)
Newton, Georgia Ann to John B. Yancey 12-18-1868 (12-20-1868)
Newton, Hester M. L. to Andrew Yarbro 1-17-1868 (2-6-1868)
Nichols, Anne to Vaulentine Yates 6-21-1841
Norquist, Anna Ereka to John Landerstedet 9-6-1873
O'Bryan, Mary to Mulucky? O'Conor 6-7-1871 (6-8-1871)
Oaks, America W. to Jesse V. Mullins 8-29-1860 (8-31-1860)
Odom, Martha Jane to Wesley Cup 6-25-1857
Oliphant, Rebecca Ann to A. F. Ducast 2-2-1859 (2-3-1859)
Olipshaw, Rabecca to A. F. Dueast 2-22-1859 (2-3?-1859)
Oliver, Mary Cathrine to Wilson Wm. Coats 3-18-1854 (3-19-1854)
Oliver, Sarah Ann to Solomon Coats 12-8-1853
Ore, A. D. to J. C. Coleman 3-22-1873 (3-25-1873)
Ore, Elizabeth F. to William H. Yager 3-18-1867
Orr, Eliza to W. C. Grimes 4-22-1873 (4-23-1873)
Orr, Lavinia to Authen J. Levto? 2-9-1869
Orr, Susan to John B. Thompson 5-25-1870 (5-26-1870)
Orshin?, Juley Ann to Solomon McBride 5-20-1864 (3?-21-1864)
Orwell, Mary Ann to Isaac Lainn? 1-19-1847
Osborn, Dona to William Thompson 5-3-1871
Osborne, Susanna L. to Robert J. Morris 9-29-1849 (10-1-1849)
Ovnall?, Susan America to David Cannon Slaughter 7-15-1850 (7-?-1850)
Owen, Ann H. to James Wilkins 7-19-1855
Owen, Eleanor W. to Hiram H. Ralph 12-8-1846 (12-10-1846)
Owen, Elizabeth J. to S. J. Bringle 4-28-1860 (4-29-1860)
Owen, Ellen to Allen Martain 2-25-1869
Owen, Emily to Thomas Coleman 9-23-1871
Owen, Frances to James W. B. Dannil 1-29-1868
Owen, Holly to Henry Dorch 12-28-1868 (12-31-1868)
Owen, Louisa Adaline to Benjamin H. Ligon 11-22-1841 (11-26-1841)
Owen, Margaret Jane to James J. Furgerson 10-10-1855 (10-11-1855)
Owen, Martha J. to James J. Furguson 1-15-1867 (1-22-1867)
Owen, Mary to James P. Overall 1-22-1867 (1-23-1867)
Owen, Mary to Robert Bell 8-10-1870 (8-11-1870)
Owen, Mollie to Patrick Bynum 3-26-1868
Owen, Nancy to John Goforth 1-19-1867
Owen, Nancy to John Goforth 1-19-1867 (1-20-1867)
Owen, Nancy to Young Gray 10-21-1851 (10-23-1851)
Owen, Peggy to Smith Miller Feezor 6-18-1846
Owen, Rebecca to Saml. E. Stevenson 4-24-1866 (4-29-1866)
Owens, Matilda Elizabeth to Allen Martin 9-15-1868
Owens?, Luvenia to Sip Field 11-15-1869 (11-15-1869)
Pace, A. E. to F. T. Read 12-18-1871 (12-20-1871)
Pace, Alvin A. to Isaac Lavell 8-21-1874 (9-8-1874)
Pace, Eliza to Charles C. Freeman 1-16-1860
Packard, S. H. to John Corbet 10-5-1858
Paden, Rachel to D. Smith 9-23-1871 (9-26-1871)
Page, Fannie to John Roe 8-29-1874 (8-30-1874)
Page, Martha A. to John Q. Bradley 11-17-1869
Palmer, Caroline A. to William D. Smith 7-25-1868 (7-26-1868)
Parham, Julia A. to ___thas W. Dodson 8-11-1868
Parish, Frances to Enos Lamb 2-5-1849
Parish, Lucinda to Perley James 5-11-1846
Parker, Annie Eliza to Charles Taylor 12-23-1873 (12-26-1873)
Parker, Eliza to Hector McNair 2-14-1852 (2-15-1852)
Parker, Mary Ann to Henry Travis 9-14-1848 (9-?-1848)
Parker, Mary Ann to Wm. M. Maser 9-27-1855
Parker, Mary to Jerry Edmonds 12-25-1874
Parker, Susan to Adam Douglas 6-14-1873 (6-15-1873)
Parrish, Mildred A. to Benj. A. Mosley 10-7-1867 (10-16-1867)
Parsons, Elizabeth to Wm. J. Brimley 2-23-1857 (3-8-1857)
Parsons, Indiana to Joseph O. Freeman 5-14-1859 (5-16-1859)
Parsons, Mary to Saml. Jones 9-8-1857
Parsons, Matilda M. to Jesse Palmer 4-15-1843 (4-16-1843)
Partlow, Mary Ann to Lucien Mayo 12-21-1859 (12-22-1859)
Partlow, Nancy J. to Lucian Maye 5-31-1866
Partlow, Uminie to James Williams 9-11-1873
Paten, Martha A. to Saml. McNaire? 5-3-1867
Patterson, C. P. to J. T. Morgan 10-30-1869 (11-3-1869)
Patterson, Maryana to William Freeman 1-17-1870 (1-18-1870)
Patterson, Mooney to Andrew Walker 9-9-1869 (9-11-1869)
Payne, Ann to Moses Adkins 1-7-1874 (1-8-1874)
Payne, Georgeanna to James Blaydes 12-25-1873
Payne, Laura A. to John F. Miller 4-11-1871 (4-12-1871)
Payne, Maggie to Daniel Hayden 9-21-1869 (9-24-1869)
Payne, Malinda E. to James E. Bloyde 4-33-1866
Payne, Mary to J. R. Manasco 9-24-1861 (9-27-1861)
Payne, Rachel S.? to James F. Dickson 11-22-1865 (11-23-1865)
Payne, Rebecca to Scott Smith 12-3-1872 (12-4-1872)
Payne, Rose to John Evans 12-21-1867 (12-26-1867)
Peacock, Sarah to John J. Sawyers 9-27-1867 (9-28-1867)
Pearce, Caralin to Barton Luster 3-3-1868 (3-4-1868)
Peeler, Martha to George Coats 1-23-1866
Peeler, Sarah E. to E.B. Whitley 12-31-1866 (1-1-1867)
Peete, Ann to Ferry Peete 12-23-1865 (12-25-1865)
Peete, Minerva to Richard Cooper 2-21-1867 (2-23-1867)
Peete, Rhody Ann to Lenard Clement 6-1-1866 (6-2-1866)
Peete, Sallie to Richard E. Bullington 12-27-1869
Peete, Susan to Robert Green 3-22-1869 (3-?-1869)
Pendergrass, Frances Eleanor to James K. Schooley 1-1-1850
Pennel, Ellen M. to Bird L. Mathews 6-3-1861 (6-5-1861)
Pennel, M. E. to W. D. Cash 1-21-1874 (1-24-1874)

Pennel, Mary Jane to H. Sullivan 10-23-1856 (11-3-1856)
Pennel, S. E. to G. B. Cash 12-7-1868 (12-9-1868)
Pennell, Massey Lavinia to Joseph B. James 5-18-1849 (not executed)
Pennell, Massey Lavinia to Walter Archer Coleman 10-30-1849 (11-2-1849)
Pennington, Annie E. to E. W. Fight 12-23-1865
Penny, Sarah B. to C. T. Archer 2-20-1869 (2-24-1869)
Penson, M. E. to Mathew M. Lawton? 1?-30-1868
Perkinson, Ann Branch to John W. Hudson 9-27-1841 (9-28-1841)
Perkinson, Eliz. Anderson to Edmund Booker 6-29-1846 (7-2-1846)
Perry, George to Hugh House? 6-1-1869 (6-2-1869)
Person, Martha Ann to Nelson Avant 1-23-1872 (1-28-1872)
Peter, Nancy to Adam Boyd? 12-1-1865 (12-3-1865)
Petit, Lizzie E. to James Gunter 5-18-1872 (5-22-1872)
Pettey, Rebecca D. to George S. Wright 2-26-1861
Pettie, Laura B. to Wm. B. Robinson 3-8-1870 (3-10-1870)
Petty, Elizabeth M. to N. Bryan 11-26-1853 (11-27-1853)
Petty, Mrs. Mary A. to James E.? Nicholson 10-21-1874
Petty, Orlina Jane to Robert Lowry 12-29-1855 (1-5-1856)
Pewitt, Ann Eliza to Green Smith 2-15-1865
Phelps, Ellen to Lawrence Alston 3-28-1874
Phelps, Lucisa N. to John Morison? 8-12-1856 (8-14-1856)
Phelps, Neadis Isis to Milton Hunt 9-27-1847 (9-30-1847)
Phelps, Susan M. to Ily D. Turnage 10-26-1847 (11-10-1847)
Philips, Mary N. to Alfred C. Rucker 11-4-1854 (11-8-1854)
Phillips, Catheran to Jasper Moore 3-1-1867 (3-16-1867)
Phillips, Flavia to John V. Ryan 3-30-1871 (4-4-1871)
Phillips, Lemess? to Solimon Vincent 12-25-1867
Phillips, Lousanna to John Kelly 3-11-1854 (3-12-1854)
Phillips, Martha to Samuel Allen 1-17-1868
Phillips, Susan E. to John Thomas Rose 2-14-1854
Pickard, E. C. to W. J. Faires 4-28-1857
Pickard, Irena R. to Henry M. Loveene? 7-2-1872 (7-4-1872)
Pickard, Mahala to W. H. Wooten 9-24-1861
Pickard, Margaret to Washington Singleton 2-28-1872 (3-9-1872)
Pickard, Mary J. to J. D. Easley 2-13-1860 (2-14-1860)
Pile, Lucinda to Henry Moore 6-25-1869
Pilkington, Ann Eliza to James Osburn Hint? 12-9-1851 (12-10-1851)
Pinkston, Mary E. to H. F. Nelms 3-5-1870 (3-6-1870)
Pinner?, Jane to Alfred Young 12-7-1852
Pinson, Eliza Elin to P. B. Johnson 11-7-1874 (11-8-1874)
Pinson, Estella Ann to Wm. Campbell Norton 9-7-1852
Pinson, Laura to James H. Hunley 10-25-1872
Pinson, Nancy to J. A. Thomas 1-10-1870
Pinson, Nancy to J. A. Thomas 1-10-1870 (1-13-1870)
Pitt, Mary to William H. Winn 3-1-1865 (3-3-1865)
Plumley, Mary E. to John W. Bucham 5-30-1872
Plummer, Looky to Wm. Maclin 12-20-1871
Poff, Frances to J. W. Henderson 2-20-1867 (2-21-1867)
Polk, Eliza to Calumbus Hogan 12-1-1869 (12-2-1869)
Polk, Harriet to Thomas Jackson 10-17-1874 (10-28-1874)
Polk, Rachel to Prit Drane? 12-3-1868 (12-4-1868)
Pool, Ann to John Smith 9-26-1870
Pool, Bammer to George Maburn 9-7-1871 (9-9-1871)
Pool, M. E. to L. W. Trobough 5-21-1862?
Poor, Sarah A. to J. J. Lowry 7-17-1860 (7-19-1860)
Powell, Nelley A. to Isaac Copland 12-23-1867 (12-31-1868?)
Powell?, Amanda L. to Jones J. Williams 12-21-1841 (12-27-1842?)
Power, Henrietta Christmas to James Faulk 10-28-1843 (11-2-1843)
Power, Sarah Christmas to William Culbreath 4-23-1849 (4-26-1849)
Prewett, Louisa Lavinia to Joseph Lewis Gardner 2-1-1846
Prewitt, Elizabeth to Wm. Simmons 12-23-1852
Prewitt, Mary Elizabeth to John R. Wormath 10-23-1874 (10-24-1874)
Price, Sarah to Robert Joyner 12-28-1868 (12-3-1869?)
Prince, Cynthia P. to Anderson Fry 6-1-1870 (6-9-1870)
Prince, Lilly Ann to A. J. Massey 2-3-1871
Prince, Martha E. to J. B. Englihs 11-27-1858
Probusaugh?, Mary E. to G. C. Crider 10-2-1871 (10-?-1871)
Proctor, Louisa V. to W. A. Davis 11-22-1873 (11-27-1873)
Proctor, M. E. to W. S. Erwood 1-8-1872 (1-9-1872)
Pugh, Mary E. to Leopold Buhse? 8-22-1874 (8-26-1874)
Pullen, Laura L. to R. G. McLewain 11-18-1858 (11-23-1858)
Pullim, Everline to Giles Smith 10-27-1866 (10-28-1866)
Pullim, July to Noah Stevenson 12-16-1865
Pullims, Julia to Noah Stevenson 12-16-1865 (12-26-1865)
Pullin, Mary A. to J. J. McDow 10-30-1865 (11-1-1865)
Punch?, Martha Jane to Philip S. Winn 1-11-1843
Purvis, Ann Elizabeth to James Hooper Cotton 4-2-1853 (4-4-1853)
Putman, M. S. to W. B. Dean 8-5-1870 (8-7-1870)
Pyles, Adeline to Mathew Cullison? 10-26-1867 (11-4-1867)
Quimmly?, Mary to William Shadrach Starling 7-20-1846 (7-30-1846)
Quinaly, Patsey Safroney to Relix Grundy Hallum 10-22-1846 (10-26-1846)
Quinby, Nancy J. to David Goss 7-12-1859
Ralph, America J. to M.W. Taylor 4-16-1857
Ralph, Cathrine to Albert Goodman 4-11-1872
Ralph, Eliza to Peter P. Wood 4-12-1849
Ralph, Elizabeth to James K. Farmer 7-30-1841 (8-3-1841)
Ralph, Jane to William Werter Angus 7-16-1849 (7-17-1849)
Ralph, Jetty F. to James H. Owen 4-16-1857
Ralph, Margaret to David Adams 9-30-1873 (10-1-1873)
Ralph, Mary A. to Wm. O. Wiseman 8-14-1852
Ralph, Mary Ann to Henry Beavers 12-19-1846 (12-25-1846)
Ralph, Mildred J. to Michael Beaver 4-21-1853
Ralph, Nancy Jane to Henry Windiss 4-21-1847 (4-22-1847)
Ramsey, Martha to Calvin Tucker 2-17-1845 (2-20-1845)
Randolph, Mary to Jefferson McCann 4-5-1873 (4-11-1873)
Ray, Bettie to P. C. Thompson 11-2-1863
Ray, Mary Frances to John Leroy Hutchison 2-24-1853
Ray, Nancy to Saml. W. Hutcherson 12-27-1873 (12-31-1873)
Ray, Riller to Asa Kingkade 10-12-1867 (10-30-1867)
Read, Adalin to Harrison Gaines 1-15-1872 (1-18-1872)
Read, Elizabeth M. to William T. Erwin 11-25-1869
Read, Mary to William Gibson 5-8-1871
Read, Mary to William W. Winford 12-30-1868
Read, N. J. to John T. Read 12-30-1869
Reatherford, Bettie J. to John W. Shelton 1-30-1861
Reatherford, Georgia Ann to W. R. M. Logan 12-28-1859
Reaves, Jone? to Moses Johnson 1-4-1871
Reece, Adaline to James Ingram 4-4-1873 (4-5-1873)
Reece, Bettie to James Rudd 2-26-1873 (2-27-1873)
Reed, Irene to George Butler 10-12-1866
Reed, Martha to C. L. Reed 9-11-1866 (9-19-1866)
Reed, Matilda to Henry Strong 12-19-1866
Reed, Rachael E. to William R. Kimbro 7-16-1858 (7-17-1858)
Reese, Ardinia? to John C. Blackburn 4-28-1841 (5-4-1841)
Reeves, J. M. to J. F. Burkhart 8-29-1860 (9-4-1860)
Reeves, Sarah to Lawson Taylor 8-13-1870
Reid, Martha Ann to John B. Thompson 12-24-1861
Reynolds, Minirva to Jesse S. Byrd 11-21-1860
Rhodes, Alice A. to Elam F. Thomas 9-3-1844
Rhodes, Amanda? S.? to Allen Harvell 11-28-1867
Rhodes, Bettie to John Fowler 3-13-1873
Rhodes, Fannie to Lee Miller 1-9-1873
Rhodes, Frances D. to John Staritt 5-16-1865
Rhodes, Frances E.? to John Garrett 5-16-1865 (5-17-1865)
Rhodes, Jack Ann to George Washington 8-6-1870 (8-7-1870)
Rhodes, M. E. to O. E. Hamilton 10-26-1868 (10-29-1868)
Rhodes, Mary J. to D. H. Smith 2-6-1869 (2-7-1869)
Rhodes, Mary to Washington Maclin 1-19-1868 (1-20-1868)
Rhodes, Nancy to Henry McClanahan 3-31-1871 (4-1-1871)
Rice, Ann Eliza to George Holmes 7-27-1847 (7-?-1847)
Rice, Eliza G. to Hugh T. Hanks 3-17-1865 (3-18-1865)
Rice, Hariet L. to S. R. Smith 2-27-1866 (2-28-1866)
Rice, Harriet to Robt. Coachman 6-28-1867
Rice, Margaret to William McBride 2-7-1847
Rice, Martha A. A. to Wm. D. Walton 4-16-1856
Rice, Mary A. to Alfred W. Owen 10-30-1865 (11-2-1865)
Rice, Mary to John Stevens 11-6-1866
Rice, Mona Agnes to John Madison Butler 7-17-1843 (7-19-1843)
Rice, R. H. to J. H. Flowers 11-13-1860
Rice?, Harriet Anderson to John Walter Morehead 7-12-1843 (7-18-1843)
Rich, Rosa J. to C. A. Bringle 1-2-1871 (1-5-1871)
Richard, Isabell to James Townsend 2-9-1867
Richards, Easter to John Harris 6-27-1866
Richards, Elizabeth to Samuel Neal 4-13-1841
Richardson, Amanda to Logan Clark 3-2-1869 (3-3-1869)
Richardson, Ella to James Hill 2-3-1870
Richardson, Harriet to Henry Williams 12-28-1868 (12-30-1868)

Richardson, Jane to Cyrus A. Allen 2-27-1849
Richardson, Jane to Thomas W. Skiles 12-20-1858
Richardson, Lizzie to Robert Gordon 5-8-1872
Richardson, Martha Jane C. to James McLillie 8-7-1871 (8-8-1871)
Richardson, Martha to Clark Brown 1-3-1871 (1-5-1871)
Richardson, Mary to Aaron Hutcheson 8-31-1869
Richardson, Sarah Ann Eliz. to Henry James Mailey 5-16-1843 (5-18-1843)
Richarson, Mary Ann to Daniel Friel 4-2-1870 (9-29-1872?)
Richerson, Milley R. to Calvin Huston 7-2-1873
Rigsby, Galaney to Alexander Williams 10-18-1847 (10-19-1847)
Rigsby, Hester Ann Hamilton to Henry Jackson Dacus 1-20-1852 (1-22-1852)
Riley, E. V. to G. A. Dunn 12-14-1874 (12-15-1874)
Rivers, Mary A to Charles C. Churchill 7-8-1857 (7-15-1857)
Rlayner, Ann to Robert Smith 3-8-1867 (3-9-1867)
Roach, Lucinda to Samuel Roberts 3-15-1852 (3-22-1852)
Roan, Christina E. to John B. Pullin 10-30-1865 (10-31-1865)
Roan, M. R. to F. T. Billing 11-25-1868 (11-26-1868)
Roane, Henrietta to Andrew J. Whitley 8-25-1851
Roane, S. J. to R. F. Williams 1-1-1872 (1-4-1872)
Roark, Mary Jane to Allen Nealey 12-2-1844
Robbs?, Sallie to Ben Morgan 7-17-1871
Roberson, Jane C. to John C. Ford no date (with 1861)
Roberts, Gabella Ann to Jordan Jamison 1-13-1870
Roberts, M. L. to J. W. jr. Drummon 6-2-1873 (6-4-1873)
Roberts, Mahala J. to George Lewellen 8-1-1861
Roberts, Malinda J. to George W. Redditt 11-6-1866 (11-8-1866)
Roberts, Martha Jane to Albert Ambrose Kelley 10-27-1855 (10-29-1855)
Roberts, Mary Ann to William Daniel Rice 7-26-1847 (7-?-1847)
Roberts, Nancy to George Chisam 12-4-1869
Roberts, Sarah Eliz. to Perley? James 10-25-1852 (10-31-1852)
Roberts, Sarah to Alexander Bell 9-16-1871
Roberts, Susan to Solaman Richardson 7-18-1874 (7-22-1874)
Robertson, L. J. to J. N. Cooper 7-27-1874 (7-29-1874)
Robertson, Margaret Ann to John D. McClanahan 10-17-1840 (10-22-1840)
Robertson, Mary E. to John Pool 5-12-1870
Robertson, Mary O. to Ridley Clifton 4-30-1860
Robertson, Mary to Billy Hall 4-1-1867 (4-3-1867)
Robertson, Shelley to Marshal Herring 15-18-1858
Robinson, Aggy to Allen Faulk 5-7-1869
Robinson, Aggy to Allin Faulk 5-7-1868
Robinson, Amy to Sam Adkins 2-14-1867
Robinson, Eliza F. to James B. Turnage 12-3-1866 (12-4-1866)
Robinson, Laura A. to Calvin Angel 2-12-1866 (2-1?-1866)
Robinson, Mary to Thomas Jefferson Allen 1-17-1843 (not executed)
Robinson, Narcissa to Saml. M. Woods? 1-13-1844 (1-18-1844)
Robinson, Sallie to Thomas McQuiston 12-19-1870 (12-24-1871?)
Robinson, Sarah to Joseph J. Fellows 2-6-1847 (not executed)
Robinson, ary to Lewis W. Miller 5-13-1844 (5-17-1844)
Robison, Nellie to Henry Joseph 5-29-1867
Rodger, Martha T. to John D. Glakin? no date (with 1867)
Rodgers, Bettie to W. L. Irbey 9-26-1866
Rodgers, Elizabeth W. to Richard T. Payne 5-1-1854 (5-6-1854)
Rodgers, Martha F. to John D. Flanigan 3-13-1867
Roe, A. E. to J. H. Coates 7-21-1871 (7-26-1871)
Roe, Cynthia C. to Newton W. King 10-15-1868 (10-18-1868)
Roe, Elizabeth to Jas. Abner Billings 11-21-1855 11-21-1855
Roe, Lucy Ann to J. C. N. Glass 11-11-1858
Roe, Martha to Jno. W. Young 8-4-1874 (8-12-1874)
Roe, Mary M. to J. B. Coates 11-18-1871 (11-21-1871)
Roe, Matilda J. to D. L. Glass 8-31-1859 (9-1-1859)
Roe, Sarah M. to Thos. Wood 12-11-1865 (12-13-1865)
Roe, Sharlott to Spinia? Billings 9-3-1856
Rogers, Lucy kA. to A. F. Phillips 11-18-1871
Rogers, Margaret C. to George Richardson 9-4-1873 (9-14-1873)
Roil, Janie Ann to Henry Culbreath 3-31-1870 (4-1-1870)
Rooks, Nancy to Anderson J. Barns 1-26-1842 (1-?-1842)
Rose, Amanda to George P. Collinsworth 9-6-1873
Rose, Amanda to Robert E. Whitley 1-6-1869
Rose, Amanda to Sandy Bledsoe 12-20-1867 (12-27-1867)
Rose, Amelia to Anthony Jones 7-29-1873 (8-14-1873)
Rose, Catherine to Wesley Woolfirk 4-4-1873 (4-8-1873)
Rose, E. A. R. to John Donely 6-29-1870
Rose, Ellen Conway to Richard James Jones 1-7-1850 (1-10-1850)
Rose, Jane to Albert Smith 1-18-1869 (1-19-1869)
Rose, Mary Eliza to John J. Philips 6-23-1857 (6-24-1857)
Rose, Mary L. to Joseph Etherly 4-15-1868 (4-18-1868)
Rose, Nancy J. to Haywood Stevens 12-17-1851 (12-18-1851)
Rose, Patti W. to John Green Hall 12-21-1871
Rose, Sallie to Ed Dickson 3-21-1872
Rose, Sarah Ann to John James Philips 7-25-1849 (8-1-1849)
Ross, Betty to Wody Driver 5-13-1871 (5-15-1871)
Ross, Willie to Jesse Wright 11-21-1872 (11-22-1872)
Roton, Mary Ann to Michael Wesley Hoke 10-21-1851
Roulker?, Eleanor H. to R. G. Goodman 8-7-1866
Rousan, Clara to Robt. P. Sullivan 5-29-1867 (5-30-1867)
Russell, Martha to William Stutham 5-30-1849 (5-31-1845)
Russell, Pearl F. to Elizah C. Shaw 8-23-1873 (8-24-1873)
Rutherford, Louisa to James Madison Leach 7-17-1849
Rutherford, Sallie B. to Saml. R. Shelton 5-4-1857 (5-5-1857)
Ryan, Amelia Vanclaire? to Jas. Henry Claiborn 10-26-1852
Saddler, Maggie to David E. Haynie 1-10-1871 (1-11-1871)
Sadler, Emily to Frank Gaise 4-4-1867 (4-6-1867)
Sadler, Mary G. to John L. Haynie 12-19-1872
Sadler, Mary to Aaron Pullin 11-26-1865 (11-6?-1865)
Sadler, P. A. to Henry Palmer 3-23-1867 (3-30-1867)
Salliers, Mattie J. to W. M. Hurley 8-15-1874 (8-16-1874)
Sample, Nancy to Richard A. Abnathy 3-8-1873 (3-9-1873)
Samuels, Sylva to Edwin Chambers 10-10-1868
Sanders, Emaline to Richard Davis 1-8-1870 (1-9-1870)
Sanders, F. A. E. to J. A. McCraw 12-7-1870 (12-8-1870)
Sanders, Martha B. to L. A. Childress 4-15-1865 (5-28-1865)
Sanders, Nancy S. to Jessee R. Chapman 5-8-1873 (5-14-1873)
Sanders, Sarah to T. W. Vaughan 4-15-1865 (5-24-1865)
Sanford, Fannie S. to James R. Alexander 12-8-1858
Sanford, Mary Jane to John Uriah Green 4-7-1853
Sanford, Mary to Shirley Fisher 2-14-1874 (2-15-1874)
Sanford, Priscilla to George Goodram Townsend 11-10-1842
Sanford, Sarah Ann to Marcus C. Green 3-23-1848
Sanford, 'Amanda? to Thomas? Hall 1-20-1869 (1-21-1869)
Sanford, kSina to Thos. Aldridge 1-11-1866 (1-13-1866)
Sasser, Bettie to Isaac Cranbury 3-7-1868 (3-8-1871?)
Saunders, Gyaura? to Geo. W. Pate 10-28-1874
Saunders, Mollie to William Wright 12-18-1872
Saunders, Sarah to Tom Cotton 2-10-1872 (2-11-1872)
Sawyer?, Malinda to John Owen 12-26-1868 (12-27-1868)
Sawyers, M. J. to George W. Shelton 10-13-1873
Sawyers, Sallie to August Wakefield 4-17-1869 (4-18-1869)
Scales, Margaret to J.B. Parsons 3-13-1872
Scales, Sarah J. to Andrew J. Curtis 1-25-1870
Scheen, Martha Ann to Thomas Tims 9-11-1858 (9-12-1858)
Schooley, Ellen F. to W. B. Russell 3-4-1869 (3-7-1869)
Schrigs?, Louiza to William Elder 7-6-1861 (7-9-1861)
Scot, Sarah to Allen Williams 3-13-1858 (3-14-1858)
Scott, Catharine E. to Wm. H. Leach 12-10-1860
Scott, Catharine R. to F. A. Enochs 8-30-1869 (9-16-1869)
Scott, Eliza to Andrew Brown 3-7-1872
Scott, L. J. to Richard Tredway 9-21-1869 (1-1-1870)
Scott, Minnie to George Tucker 7-1-1867 (7-6-1867)
Searcey, Elizabeth E. to John W. Smith 12-4-1866 (12-5-1866)
Searcey, Nancy Jane to Wylie Stevens 6-3-1855
Searcy, Mary D. to B. F. Mitchel 5-19-1866 (5-25-1866)
Seay, Martha Jane to Robt. J. Murphy 11-6-1852 (11-7-1852)
Sexton, Jane to Francis McLain 7-25-1866 (8-20-1866)
Sexton, Malinda to Mansel Cooper 4-25-1844 (5-28-1844)
Shankle, Amanda to William H. Billings 7-17-1868 (7-19-1868)
Shankle, Ellen to G. L. Huffman 11-20-1871 (11-21-1871)
Shankle, Fannie to Am? Downing 1-17-1867
Shankle, Franky Jane to William Joseph Roe 8-17-1867 (8-18-1867)
Shankle, Nancy to Munro Kelley 8-12-1873
Shankle, V. L. to James G. Riley 1-1-1866
Sharp, Adaline L. to David T. Holloway 7-24-1855
Sharp, Ann Jane to James M. Barrett 4-3-1861
Sharp, Catharine to Pleasant Davis Benson 1-11-1850 (1-16-1850)
Sharp, Elizabeth to J. W. Hays 9-26-1870 (9-27-1870)
Sharp, Margaret J. to John J. Hall 3-15-1841 (3-18-1841)
Sharp, Mary to Sterling S. Roane 4-28-1841 (4-27?-1841)

Shaw, Jane E. to Richard Dillon 2-20-1867
Shaw, Margaret N. to J. S. Wright 1-29-1869 (1-30-1869)
Shaw, Margaret to John Bennett 5-8-1840 (5-12-1840)
Shaw, Martha to Daniel E. Shaw 11-24-1865 (11-?-1865)
Shaw, Nancy to George Wilkins 4-28-1857 (4-29-1857)
Shaw, R. to U. P. Lynn 1-9-1871 (1-10-1871)
Shaw, Sallie to Burgis Merrill 1-20-1864 (1-7?-1864)
Shaw, Sarah J. to Robt. W. Fenton 2-20-1867 (2-21-1867)
Shaw, Sarah J. to Robt. W. Fenton 2-26-1867 (2-27-1867)
Sheffield, Mary L. to James R. Sharp 3-12-1850
Shelton, Ella A. to C. C. Poindexter 11-15-1873 (11-18-1873)
Shelton, Indiania to John Wood 7-27-1868
Shelton, Isabella to John B. Moore 11-18-1847
Shelton, Judy to Ephreham Hawk 12-16-1871 (12-17-1871)
Shelton, Mary to Fagan Westbrooks 3-6-1867
Shelton, Mary to W. A. Steven 9-18-1869 (9-19-1869)
Shelton, Mary to W. A. Stevens 9-18-1869
Shelton?, Mary M. to John A. Vincent 2-14-1843
Shenault, Emma to S. W. Faulk 10-19-1872 (10-24-1872)
Shepard, Elizabeth to Rufus Hill 12-16-1870 (12-17-1870)
Shepard, Emmer to Isaac Eaton 4-10-1871
Shepard, Sallie E. to Thomas J. Morris 4-?-1871 (5-1-1871)
Shepherd, Martha Ann to Jesse D. Strayhorn 3-10-1873
Shepherd, Octavia to Lum? Tho. Moore 12-19-1855 (12-20-1855)
Sherill, Martha to Wm. Hall 10-14-1865 (2?-14-1865)
Sherrell, Leah to Andrew Adams 3-17-1866 (3-25-1866)
Sherrid, Celia to Moses Smith 8-4-1866
Sherril, Laura] to Geo. W. Hall 12-29-1865 (1-3-1866)
Sherril, Martha to Wm. Hall 10-14-1865
Sherrill, Anna E. to John A. Cary 12-22-1874 (12-23-1874)
Sherrill, Elizabeth M. to Joseph Forsyth 11-13-1866 (11-15-1866)
Sherrill, Flora to Leroy Smith 10-6-1870
Sherrill, Harriet to Furgus Alston 1-7-1874
Sherrill, Isa L. to J. G. Adams 12-4-1873
Sherrill, Lizzie to Alex Johnson 6-19-1869 (6-20-1869)
Sherrill, Siller to Alex Stitt 7-20-1872
Sherrod, Caroline V. to John W. Durant 11-2-1844
Sherrod, Catharin to Moreau P. Estes 11-27-1867
Sherrod, Eliza Rufina to Joseph D. Whitley 12-16-1854
Sherrod, Martha Ann to Adam Dabney Clements 5-3-1847 (5-6-1847)
Sherrod, Mary S. to John C. Jacobs 5-9-1859 (5-10-1859)
Sherrod, Nia to Jno. G. Sherrod 12-26-1865 (12--29-1865)
Sherrod, Tempa to Noah Bond 2-10-1866 (2-15-1866)
Shoaf, Christinea to J.E. Davis 11-25-1874
Shultz, Delila M. to Harvey C. Starnes 6-1-1867 (6-2-1867)
Siler, M. T. to W. P. Brown 8-2-1873 (8-3-1873)
Siler, Mary Ann to James C. Lake 11-25-1857 (11-26-1857)
Siler, Mary to James R. Sharp 11-10-1858
Siler, Nancy to Cirus Wright 3-1-1867 (3-2-1867)
Simeton?, Margaret A. to R. T. Wilson 2-24-1866
Simmons, Ellen to Ben Sommerville 10-18-1870
Simmons, M. J. to W. E. H. Hill 12-12-1870 (12-15-1870)
Simmons, Mary Ann to Tom J. Pewett 10-27-1861 (10-29-1861)
Simon?, Louisa A. to ____ Crofford 6-19-1864 (6-21-1864)
Simonton, Leticia to Wm. Ross? McCain 2-13-1856
Simonton, M. E. to J. C. Moffet 9-20-1870
Simonton, Margret to E. P. Lucado 6-28-1856 (7-11-1856)
Simonton, Martha Jane to Albert Gallatin McCuin 7-25-1850
Simonton, Sallie to C. F. Strong 9-25-1860 (9-26-1860)
Simpson, Martha A. to Walker Turnage 3-27-1844 (3-28-1844)
Simpson, Martha Ann to Jesse Simpson 7-31-1872 (8-1-1872)
Simpson, Martha S. to Hugh M. Lynn 4-9-1862
Simpson, Mary G. to John Wright 7-31-1872 (8-1-1872)
Simpson, N. D. to H. H. Bate 11-24-1873 (11-25-1873)
Simpson, Nancy to John T. Dowell 3-13-1843 (3-15-1843)
Simpson, Polly Ann to S. Stevens 9-29-1856
Simpson, Sarah to John B. Davis 10-12-1846 (10-15-1846)
Sims, Elsie Manna to Moses Trigg 12-31-1873
Siser?, Margaret to Lawrence Stephens 12-4-1854 (12-15-1854)
Sitner, Harriet to John George Boyd 3-19-1872
Slass, V. T. to Plesant Manasco 11-2-1868 (11-4-1868)
Slaughter, Lucy A. to James R. Fallin 1-18-1871
Slaughter, Mary C. to John C. Garland 4-21-1868
Slaughter, Susan Eliz. to James Jefferson Culbreath 1-20-1851 (1-23-1851)
Sloss, Amanda to Wm. C. Reynolds 1-13-1857 (1-22-1857)
Sloss, Rebecca A. to Jessee Lockett 3-4-1861 (3-17-1861)
Small, Pleasan to Milus Alexander 2-28-1867
Smith, Albertine to Thomas Kinney 5-25-1846
Smith, Allace to Joshua Small 5-12-1873
Smith, Allice to Ephm. Smith 1-2-1868
Smith, Amanda Jane to Mark Vanderbilt 10-23-1845
Smith, Amanda to Edmond Swain 8-28-1868 (8-29-1868)
Smith, Amanda? to Geo. Golston 12-15-1866 (12-16-1866)
Smith, Angaline to John M. Harris 10-25-1872 (10-27-1872)
Smith, Ann L. to Frank Milton 12-27-1865
Smith, Ann to Bob Macklin 5-13-1869
Smith, Ann to James Goodwin 6-20-1870
Smith, Anner to Isham Goodman 11-28-1868
Smith, Bettie to Joseph Marshall 10-12-1867
Smith, Caroline to George Fitze 3-15-1873
Smith, Catharine H. to William Wilkins 7-14-1852 (7-15-1852)
Smith, Catharine to John Wilson 12-28-1868 (12-31-1868)
Smith, Catherine E. to Chas. G. Smith 1-13-1870
Smith, Catherine E. to Gaml.? C. Dickey 4-3-1871 (4-20-1871)
Smith, Chainey to Butler Williams 9-12-1871 (9-16-1871)
Smith, Claway? to George Gibson 4-29-1868
Smith, Darcus to Frank McLemore 12-12-1870 (12-15-1870)
Smith, Delia Ann to George Smith 7-1-1868 (7-19-1868)
Smith, Delia to Wm. Trout no date (c. Sep 1866)
Smith, Donna to Spencer Goodman 3-29-1871 (4-4-1871)
Smith, Drusilla to Bob Harris 12-15-1871
Smith, Eliza Clewellyn to Cowell? Culbreath 8-3-1841 (8-5-1841)
Smith, Eliza J. to C. W. Flanakin 1-23-1858 (2-4-1858)
Smith, Eliza T. to Jack Smith 1-4-1869
Smith, Elizabet Ellen to Robert G. Jamison 10-21-1869
Smith, Elizabeth to Alexander Rhodes 8-19-1869
Smith, Elizabeth to Sidney Hall 4-4-1870 (4-10-1870)
Smith, Ella? to Bill Woods 10-4-1873
Smith, Ellen to Asa Margan 10-28-1865
Smith, Emaline to W. Hill 10-16-1873 B
Smith, Emeline to Henry Jones 11-26-1869
Smith, Emeline to Thomas Kinney 9-26-1855
Smith, Emeline to W. H. D. Dickens 1-12-1868 (1-2-1868)
Smith, Emerline to Clay Yarbro 12-25-1866
Smith, Emily to Silas McCullough 8-19-1871
Smith, Evaline H. to John T. Douglass 1-21-1842
Smith, Evaline to Wm. Ray Whitlock 2-5-1849 (2-8-1849)
Smith, Fannie to Green Anderson 12-22-1869
Smith, Fany to John Scott 6-19-1869
Smith, Frances to Andy Hall 6-6-1873 (6-14-1873)
Smith, Frances to James McClelland 9-22-1859
Smith, Hannah to Alexander Smith 5-10-1852
Smith, Hannah to Wade Gaines 4-16-1874 (4-23-1874)
Smith, Harriet J. to J. M. Witherington 1-27-1866 (1-28-1866)
Smith, Harriet to Columbus Jenkins 11-11-1873 (11-12-1873)
Smith, Harriet to Cyrus W. Hutchison 12-16-1849
Smith, Hellen to J. W. Myers 4-2-1874
Smith, Henrietta to Nathaniel Wortham 4-29-1852
Smith, I. J. to J. K. McClerkin 3-28-1871 (3-29-1871)
Smith, Isabella F. to John H. Barret 12-14-1870
Smith, Isabella to Whit F. Alston 2-10-1873 (2-12-1873)
Smith, Jane M. to Thomas M. Williams 5-25-1861
Smith, Jane to Wm. Hemphill 12-20-1871
Smith, Julia C. to H. W. Beaver 10-29-1873 (11-3-1873)
Smith, Julia to George Alston 11-29-1866 (11-30-1866)
Smith, Kezir? to William Campbell 1-30-1866 (1-31-1866)
Smith, Laura E. to Needham Stevens 12-15-1874 (12-16-1874)
Smith, Laura to Louis Gray 12-10-1870
Smith, Lizzie to Jordon Hart 5-28-1870
Smith, Louisa Ann to Andrew Jackson Douglass 12-21-1846
Smith, Louisianna C. to John C. Pace 2-25-1847 (3-?-1847)
Smith, Lucinda C. to John J. Sherrod 5-13-1857
Smith, Lucretia Jane to Thomas J. Hill 4-16-1869 (4-18-1869)
Smith, Lucy Ellen to Saml. P. C. Johnson 2-5-1844
Smith, M. J. to J. W. Payne 2-20-1871 (3-7-1871)
Smith, Malinda to George Howerd 8-17-1872
Smith, Margaret Ann to Elijah Robert Himey 8-20-1857
Smith, Margaret Ann to Wm. Franklin Archer 12-5-1849
Smith, Maria to Charles Winn 2-23-1866 (2-24-1866)

Smith, Mariah J. to Wm. H. Harrison 4-3-1868 (4-4-1868)
Smith, Martha Ann Frances to James T___ 12-10-1842 (12-15-1842)
Smith, Martha H. to C. G. Griffith 12-13-1858 (12-15-1858)
Smith, Martha S. to Moses Vaughan 11-20-1865 (11-22-1865)
Smith, Martha W. to Charles J.? Fisher 12-3-1868 (12-9-1868)
Smith, Martha to Harrison Malone 11-8-1872
Smith, Mary C. to John Brassell 10-24-1871
Smith, Mary E. to Absolum T. J. Humphreys 10-7-1844 (10-24-1844)
Smith, Mary E. to G. L. Kinney 12-16-1873 (12-17-1873)
Smith, Mary E. to Isaac Winfield 10-9-1872
Smith, Mary J. to Columbus Blasingame 4-14-1874
Smith, Mary Jane to G. W. Jones 6-10-1861 (6-11-1861)
Smith, Mary L. to John P. Taylor 6-2-1858
Smith, Mary to Henry Brown 12-30-1871
Smith, Mary to Ivason Booser 9-28-1871
Smith, Mary to J. B. Parsons 6-9-1866 (6-10-1866)
Smith, Mary to Kelley Goodman 11-3-1866 (11-4-1866)
Smith, Mary to Washington Ligon 1-17-1874 (1-4?-1874)
Smith, Matilda to Charles Frazier 8-21-1869 (8-23-1869)
Smith, Mattie to Annias Bond 3-15-1873
Smith, Mildred to John Smith 12-29-1868 (12-31-1868)
Smith, Minerva to Antelpes? Bond 5-5-1871 (5-7-1871)
Smith, Minnie E. to E. McDaniel 2-26-1874
Smith, Minnoy? to William McIntosh 7-29-1865
Smith, Namie to J. A. Owen 12-4-1866
Smith, Nancy A.? to James S. Clark 2-6-1869 (2-10-1869)
Smith, Nancy S. to Fred Marion Miller 11-4-1850 (11-6-1850)
Smith, Nancy W. to Jame J. Clements 3-6-1871 (3-16-1871)
Smith, Nancy to Henry Y. Billings 8-1-1855
Smith, Nancy to Saml. Robert Smith 1-13-1844 (1-14-1844)
Smith, O. to William Hetawer 4-29-1867 (4-13?-1867)
Smith, Polly L. to Dolphus Brown 9-23-1867
Smith, Polly to David H. Smith 2-4-1841
Smith, Rosana to J. A. T. McAfee 9-14-1864 (9-15-1864)
Smith, Safroney to Landon Bradford Yarbrough 6-2-1853
Smith, Sallie to Charles Barman? 7-8-1867 (7-9-1867)
Smith, Samuella to Charles A. Yarbro 3-10-1869
Smith, Sarah F. to Chas. F. Griffin 12-27-1871 (1-25-1872)
Smith, Sarah F. to Thomas A. Wood 1-3-1874 (1-4-1874)
Smith, Sarah to B. F. Lock 3-1-1860
Smith, Sarah to Ben F. Locke 3-1-1860 (3-3-1860)
Smith, Sarah to Casper M. Smith 2-27-1844
Smith, Sarah to Henry Haley 12-27-1872
Smith, Sarah to John McDaw 9-1-1867 (9-12-1867)
Smith, Susan Giles to Jessee Strange 11-17-1842
Smith, Susan W. to C. C. Carr 5-26-1866 (5-29-1866)
Smith, Susan to Edward Thomas 3-31-1870
Smith, Susan to James S. McIntosh 9-14-1867 (9-15-1867)
Smith, Susan to John H. Smith 12-22-1858 (12-23-1858)
Smith, Susan to William Smith 1-15-1868
Smith, Sylva to Sandy Smith 9-6-1869 (9-7-1869)
Smith, Tebitha Emaline to Robert Sevier Williams 2-13-1854 (2-15-1854)
Smith, Virginia E. to George W. Smith 10-30-1867
Smith, Winnie to John Johnson 3-1-1871 (3-2-1871)
Smith, Winnie to John Stevens 9-17-1866
Smitheal, Narcissa Caroline to William Hamelton 9-11-1867
Sneed, Lucinda F. to Robt. Bayley 1-10-1872 (1-11-1872)
Snider, Jane to James A. Whitmore 7-24-1856
Solomon, Martha to Thos. H. Wilson 2-13-1861 (2-14-1861)
Solomon, Mary E. to J. C. Mills 9-2-1872 (9-6-1872)
Somervell, Emma to Jacob Hurt 12-8-1866 (12-9-1866)
Somervell, Hannah to Jack Robinson 12-8-1866 (12-9-1866)
Somervill, Catherine T. to T. W. Green 10-26-1869 (10-27-1869)
Somervill, Eliza to Bill Robertson 12-16-1865 (12-25-1865)
Somervill, Grace to Saml. Rhodes 9-30-1869
Somervill, Gussie M. to W. M. Tarvoaler 10-27-1859 (11-17-1859)
Somervill, Kysiah to Boston Coats 7-2-1866
Somervill, M. B. to A. C. Somervill 10-10-1859 (10-11-1859)
Somervill, Margaret to William Jackson 12-29-1866 (12-31-1867?)
Somervill, Mary Hillen to Thos. W. Roane 11-13-1858 (11-17-1858)
Somervill, Renetta to Gilbert Vaughan 3-24-1869
Somerville, Annie E. to J. N. Harris 1-18-1869
Somerville, Eleanor H. to Willia Macon 12-25-1843
Somerville, Ellin G. to John M. Somerville 8-3-1868 (8-4-1868)
Somerville, Fannie M. to R. J. Black 4-12-1869 (4-14-1869)
Somerville, Kate Aubry to S. P. Green 10-13-1869 (10-20-1869)
Somerville, Lizzie to Lorenzo Dowell 12-25-1871
Somerville, Mary T. to Frank J. Whitley 4-5-1874 (4-13-1874)
Somerville, Mary to Nelson Sanford 3-30-1867 (3-31-1867)
Sommervill, Ann F. to Geo. Ardmore? Taylor 11-16-1852
Sommervill, Mary to W. F. Sommerville 12-28-1865 (12-30-1865)
Spencer, Emeline to Isaac Wiseman 9-25-1866
Squiers, Martha to Thomas White 9-5-1872
Squires, Martha to Thomas White 9-5-1872 (9-13-1872)
Sraynie?, Addie to Jas. L. Stitt 9-12-1860 (9-13-1860)
Stafford, Eliza to Pomp Newman 5-6-1867 (5-30-1867)
Stafford, Mary Thomas to Daniel W. Paremore 8-8-1871
Stake, America to James Coffman 11-17-1874 (11-18-1874)
Stallins, Nancy to Calvin Mackado 5-16-1871
Stanley, Martha E. to Martin McCool 2-5-1844 (2-7-1844)
Starnes, Amanda to R. G. Ensley 10-23-1869 (10-24-1869)
Starnes, Maria Amanda to David Davenport 4-25-1849 (4-26-1849)
Starnes, Martha to William H. Selfridge 10-2-1849 (10-3-1849)
Starnes, Mary Catharine to Hiram Malachi Yount 3-12-1851 (3-13-1851)
Starnes, Rebecca to Alexander Dacus 8-15-1850 (8-18-1850)
Starnes, Sarah E. to James Ewart 6-30-1857
Starr, Malinda to Zachariah Reese 10-13-1841 (10-15-1841)
Steele, Miss Fannie to Wm. H. Wall 11-28-1864 (11-29-1864)
Steele, Sarah A. to Harry McGuiver? 10-29-1869 (11-13-1869)
Stephens, Jane to George Weatherly 9-22-1866 (9-30-1866)
Stephens, Sarah M. to William F. McGuire 4-7-1858
Stephenson, Mary J. to J. C. Wilkins 2-22-1871 (2-25-1871)
Stevens, Caroline to Alfred McCall 10-16-1869
Stevens, Eliza to Thomas J. Oates 6-8-1846
Stevens, Elizabeth Winney to William Henry Harrison 11-22-1845
Stevens, Elizabeth to W. H. Mason 2-25-1870 (2-27-1870)
Stevens, Elizabeth to W. R. Evans 12-27-1865 (12-28-1865)
Stevens, Evaline to David Combs 3-2-1869
Stevens, L. to James Lewis 11-16-1864 (11-17-1864)
Stevens, Louiza to Haywood Cannon 10-29-1856
Stevens, Martha Ann to Joel Stevens 8-18-1852 (8-19-1852)
Stevens, Mary to Alexander Sears 7-31-1869
Stevens, Mildrid C. to Alfred Broomly 12-23-1868 (12-24-1868)
Stevens, Nancy to Jacob M. Brodnax 12-7-1874
Stevens, Susan Ann to John J. E. Bryant 8-1-1853 (8-3-1853)
Stevens, Susan Ann to Robert Searcy 8-3-1851 (8-10-1851)
Stevens, Susanah to James Home 9-25-1857
Stevens, Viney to John Sharp 9-15-1866 (9-22-1866)
Stevenson, Margaret E. to John J. Templeton 3-12-1866 (3-14-1866)
Stevenson, Nancy to George McCam 10-1-1870
Steveson, Martha to E. W. Hill 9-5-1870 (9-7-1870)
Steviss?, Susan to Jas. R. Shepard 9-13-1871
Stewart, C. C. to J. C. Batey 1-2-1871 (1-5-1871)
Stewart, Henrietta to Saml. Henry Hughes 7-15-1850 (7-16-1850)
Stewart, Mary E. to James J. Culbreth 1-22-1844 (1-?-1844)
Stewart, Virginia to James Arnold 10-6-1845
Still, Tucy to Hally? McCullough 12-28-1871
Stitt, A. E. to R. S. Hall 11-10-1858 (11-11-1858)
Stitt, Mary to Thomas Rice 9-26-1873 (10-6-1873)
Stitt, Mollie to Lafayett Whitis 12-22-1869 (12-23-1869)
Stitt, Nancy to Anderson Wellingham 3-19-1869 (4-11-1869)
Stockley, Emaline to David Williams 11-10-1870 (12-14-1870)
Stockley, Jane to William Mitchell 5-27-1872 (6-14-1872)
Stokes, Catharine Murphy to Willia Anthony Crouch 4-12-1845 (4-15-1845)
Stokes, Elizabeth to Sampson Rogers 11-7-1853 (11-15-1853)
Stokes, Emily A. to James E. Crouch 1-14-1846 (2-24-1846)
Stokes, Frances to Thos. J. Baugh 7-26-1854 (1-?-1854)
Stokes, Jenny to Benjamin Cobb 5-25-1841 (5-27-1841)
Stokes, Josephine to J. R. Starnes 7-20-1853 (7-21-1853)
Stokes, M. E. to J. M. Stevens 2-26-1872
Stone, Laura A. to Nat Tipton 11-21-1850
Stone, Martha Hill to Edwin James Morgan 8-10-1852 (8-11-1852)
Strain, Jane to John J> Faulkner 11-8-1871 (11-9-1871)
Strange, Anne Belle to James Clement 10-29-1874
Strange, Charity to Thos. Green 2-18-1873 (3-25-1873)
Strawn, Mary to William Addison Kirk 10-24-1848 (11-1-1848)
Strayhorn, Julia Ann to M. Drennon 12-17-1861 (12-22-1861)

Street, Charlotte M. to A. A. Yarbro 3-20-1872 (3-21-1872)
String, Jane E. to Jno. D. Banks 12-13-1864 (12-14-1864)
String, Margaret E. to John Adkinson no date (with 1862)
Strong, Eliza to Lewis Caroway 1-27-1872 (2-6-1872)
Strong, Elizabeth to L. McCain 9-23-1865
Strong, Frances to H. O. Banks 4-25-1871 (4-26-1871)
Strong, George A. to Wallace Kitchen 3-27-1869 (3-30-1869)
Strong, Lotty to Archibald M. Simonton? 2-19-1842 (3-3-1842)
Strong, Louisa Elmira to Ro. M. Banks 1-10-1853 (1-12-1853)
Strong, Margaret E. to John Atkison 3-18-1862 (3-20-1862)
Strong, Martha L. to David Moffett 10-23-1867 (10-24-1867)
Strong, Mary A. to John McLoughland 12-8-1860 (12-12-1860)
Strong, Milley to Richard Adams 9-30-1865 (10-28-1865)
Strong, Sarah J. to John G. Mathews 12-23-1850
Stroud, Martha H. to John W. Akin 11-21-1870 (11-23-1870)
Stroud, N. J. to A. J. Fisher 10-7-1874 (10-8-1874)
Sulfrick, Martha to David Loovell 3-3-1859 (3-9-1859)
Sullivan, Dicy A. to James L. Burdick 5-10-1861 (5-14-1861)
Sullivan, Mary J. to William Wright 6-28-1871 (7-2-1871)
Sullivan, Mary R. to Saml. M. Yarbro 12-26-1870 (12-29-1870)
Sullivan, Mattie P. to J. F. Benton 12-22-1874 (12-23-1874)
Sullivan, Namie? to W. C. Davis 3-12-1866 (3-15-1866)
Sullivan, Nancy Wade to Benjamin C. Bailey 12-8-1845 (12-10-1845)
Sullivan, Nancy to Gabriel McCraw 6-29-1841
Sullivan, Susan Ann to David Fletcher Moore 9-17-1844 (9-19-1844)
Sumervill, Tinah to Charles Somervill 12-27-1867
Swayne, Bettie T. to A. L. Elcan 11-3-1869 (11-4-1869)
Sweeney, Mary to Peter Owen 1-5-1867 (1-6-1867)
Sweney, Frances Jane to George W. Gorin? 4-19-1842 (5-2-1842)
Sylvester, Malvina to John Ligon Ralph 9-24-1851
Tacket, E. J. to Jno. Edwin Baxter 11-13-1872
Talley, Arrianna Pernett to Milton Jackson Ballard 4-5-1848
Talley, Emily Mildred to Joseph Elder 7-2-1849 (7-5-1849)
Tally, Sarah E. to Chas. W. Fallon 10-6-1840
Tally, Urilda C. to John W. Rose 4-25-1867
Tam?, Frances Jane to Neapolheo? D. Byrd 12-24-1846 (12-30-1846)
Tamey?, Louise to Edward Davis no date (with 12-1874)
Tarbish, Margaret A. to Wm. M. M. Drappin 5-13-1856 (5-14-1856)
Tarry, Lucey to Riland Day 4-15-1867 (4-27-1867)
Tarry, Lutia to Lewis Williamson 3-21-1866
Tate, Amanda J. to G. L. Barker 4-29-1871 (4-30-1871)
Tate, Mary E. to W. C. Nowel 1-15-1866 (1-17-1866)
Tate, Sarah E. to E. A. Weatherford 12-11-1866
Taylor, Ann to Wilkins Smithin 12-22-1868
Taylor, Bettie to William Johnson 5-20-1869
Taylor, Camdis D. to Alexander Carroll Wood 4-10-1854 (4-12-1854)
Taylor, Charlotte to Caleb Jacobs 12-24-1866 (12-25-1866)
Taylor, Chatherine to Henry Towns 3-6-1871
Taylor, Duley to William Alston 5-6-1867
Taylor, Easter Jane to Fred Augustus Mill 7-24-1867 (7-25-1867)
Taylor, Ellen to John Upchurch 1-20-1866 (1-21-1866)
Taylor, Eudora to Paul Macklin 6-21-1867
Taylor, Fannie to Frank Lewis 3-15-1873
Taylor, Fanny to James Taylor 2-11-1869
Taylor, Frances A. to James Allan Taylor 2-6-1843 (2-8-1843)
Taylor, Hamar to George Bean 1-1-1872 (1-7-1872)
Taylor, Hellen to J. Baylam? 2-26-1869
Taylor, Henrietta to Milton Jett 5-26-1866 (6-2-1871?)
Taylor, Hester Ann to Ras.? Terry 4-7-1866 (4-29-1866)
Taylor, Isau? to Jackson Walton 12-15-1874
Taylor, Jane Eleanor to Edwin Robert Peete 10-21-1851 (10-22-1851)
Taylor, Jennie to Wm. Winn 1-17-1866 (1-20-1866)
Taylor, Judith to David Woodard 8-8-1864 (8-10-1864)
Taylor, Laura to Ruffin Jackson 11-11-1871
Taylor, Levinia to Sam Taylor 1-25-1868
Taylor, Lucy Jane to Loyd Robertson 12-28-1868
Taylor, Lutish to Nowell Taylor 1-9-1869
Taylor, Margaret to Jim James 7-4-1868
Taylor, Martha H. to Edward Braden 11-7-1871
Taylor, Mary Ann to Billey Bullock 2-27-1868
Taylor, Mary L. to Andrew J. Douglas 12-17-1866
Taylor, Mary Lucy to Phillips Peete 6-5-1867 (6-8-1867)
Taylor, Mary to J. Jackson 5-16-1872 (7-24-1872)
Taylor, Mary to Richman Saunders 1-7-1872
Taylor, Mary to Willis Rhodes 8-30-1870
Taylor, Mollie Bet. to William F. Brodnax 12-24-1862 (12-25-1862)
Taylor, Nancy to Nathaniel Taylor 1-2-1866
Taylor, Pamiel? to Alex Nelson 4-28-1866
Taylor, Parthena Ann to George Butler 3-13-1856
Taylor, Philis to Albert Taylor 5-6-1867
Taylor, Sallie H. to Richard T. jr. Brodnax 1-18-1867 (1-23-1867)
Taylor, Sallie to Caldwell Taylor 2-20-1866
Taylor, Sarah H. to Frederick N. Muehler 1-20-1844
Taylor, Sue M. to Ben J. Sanford 10-29-1873 (10-30-1873)
Taylor, Susan A. to Sipio Tumer 12-20-1872 (12-26-1872)
Taylor, Vergun to Albert Maclin 12-24-1869
Taylor, Victoria to Ned Cook 8-1-1868
Taylor, Virginia Triplett to Richard B. Somervill 3-13-1847 (3-16-1847)
Taylor, Virginia to William Robinson 12-8-1845 (12-17-1845)
Taylor, 'Bettie to Harvey Maclin 1-14-1868
Templeton, Maggie E. to Henry J.W. Mayo 2-24-1868 (2-26-1868)
Tenant, Mary to Joseph H. Walker 1-12-1850
Tennant, Jane W. to James S. Smith 8-5-1858
Tennant, Margaret to Jefferson Elam 1-21-1852 (1-25-1852)
Tennant, Mary to John McCullough 4-8-1851 (4-9-1851)
Tennant, Purlina M to Smith M. Feezor 3-5-1849 (3-8-1849)
Ternas, Ellen C. to David Goss 9-6-1873 (9-11-1873)
Thacker, Ellen to John P. Hutchinson 8-5-1867 (8-6-1867)
Thomas, Angeline to William Coward 1-7-1874 (1-8-1874) B
Thomas, C. S. to Robert R. James 10-19-1874 (10-21-1874)
Thomas, Carolin to James M. Beson 12-22-1869 (12-25-1869)
Thomas, Caroline to George Washington Sherrill 12-26-1866 (12-27-1866)
Thomas, Eulah H. to Richard H. Rives 11-15-1873 (11-18-1873)
Thomas, Fannie to Burril Boyd 12-22-1866
Thomas, Lucy to Napolian William 8-1-1867 (8-2-1867)
Thomas, Susan A. to William A. Pullen 2-20-1868
Thomas, Susan M. to Josiah Home 10-16-1848 (10-18-1848)
Thompson, Caroline to J. Taylor 12-3-1874
Thompson, Dorcus Melissa to Wm. Thos. Ford 1-28-1851
Thompson, Harriet to A. B. Hill 1-23-1865 (1-24-1865)
Thompson, Julia M. to Francis Wylie 12-12-1854 (12-13-1854)
Thompson, Lennie to Saml. Will Adkins 12-29-1870
Thompson, Lue to James B. Shelton 10-30-1867 (10-31-1867)
Thompson, Margaret C. to Christopher A. Simonton 2-5-1848 (2-10-1848)
Thompson, Margaret Jane to Hemphill Smith 11-13-1867
Thompson, Maria to Lewis Cowan 9-18-1872
Thompson, Mary C. to Peter D. Ennis 2-8-1871 (2-9-1871)
Thompson, N. E. to C. J. Simonton 7-24-1865 (7-25-1865)
Thompson, Nancy to James Huffman 11-12-1857
Thompson, Sarah to William J. Marshall 5-31-1847 (4?-?-1847)
Ticon, Elisabeth to L. Flerms? 7-7-1856
Tilley, Nancy E. M. to Nathan Petty 10-22-1860
Tilman, Frances to Wm. Hughes 10-23-1873
Timens, Susana to Wm. Glidewell 11-6-1861 (11-7-1861)
Timms, Ellen to Silas Johnson 12-21-1864 (12-22-1864)
Timms, Josephine to James Wilkins 4-21-1868 (4-23-1869?)
Timms, Lydia A. to C. E. Lee 8-27-1874
Timms, Mary T. to M. C. Timms 12-28-1871 (12-29-1870?)
Timms, Nancy to Wm. Starnes 7-9-1860 (7-12-1860)
Timms, S. F. to C. C. Byrd 8-11-1874 (8-13-1874)
Timms?, Sarah Ann to Francis Marion Pennell 1-1-1851 (1-4-1851)
Tims, Catherine A. to L. A. Barker 6-3-1871
Tims, Irena E. L. to Nathaniel Tims 2-15-1871
Tims, Lucinda to thomas Davidson 11-2-1847 (11-3-1847)
Tims, Nancy to John Hammers 5-22-1867
Tinnan, Malina to Saml. D. Mitchell 9-5-1855 (9-8-1855)
Tinnen, Elizabeth Jane to Nathaniel C. Hoffler 12-12-1853 (12-13-1853)
Tinnen, Isabel to William Stanford 5-18-1867 (5-19-1867)
Tinsley, Emma to George Bell 9-7-1872
Tipton, Ann D. to James R. Sanford 2-9-1859
Tipton, Frankie to Guy Bynan 11-4-1872 (11-5-1872)
Tipton, Indy to Ephraim Morgan 1-11-1866
Tipton, L. J. to Thos. S. Lauderdale 1-30-1861
Tipton, Mary to Amos Jay Matthews 10-29-1846 (11-?-1846)
Tipton, Rozelle to Saml. W. Sanford 12-2-1874
Tipton, Sallie to Albert Morgan 7-26-1866

Tipton, Seraphina C. to LaFayette Hill 11-15-1855
Titus, Sarah to James Matthews 10-8-1866
Tivool?, Synthia to Alexander Gaines 9-4-1872
Toddy, Mary Louisa to Wm. Jefferson Donelsen? 11-13-1855 (11-15-1855)
Tool, Ann to Shed Richardson 9-5-1871
Totty, N. Catharine to Wm. H. Fuller 7-9-1855 (7-19-1855)
Towell?, Mattie V. to R. H. Harrison 5-5-1856
Townsend, Caroline Elizabeth to William Goodrum 7-12-1849
Townsend, Emeline S. to Jos. C. Hindman 2-2-1870
Townsend, Frances E. to Oliver B. Farris 12-29-1865 (12-31-1865)
Townsend, Louisa to Robt. Thompson Foster 12-1-1851 (12-4-1851)
Townsend, Lucetta P. to P. E. Tisdale 10-10-1857 (10-15-1857)
Townsend, Lucy A. to John S. McNeal 11-23-1857 (11-26-1857)
Townsend, Maria Ketuna to Peter Townsend 2-6-1850 (2-7-1850)
Townsend, Mary Jane to Daniel Mordecai Rhodes 8-11-1846 (8-?-1846)
Townsend, Miss Mary Ann to Adam Rode 5-20-1874
Townsend, Nancy E. to George W. W. Townsend 8-2-1865
Townsend, Sarah ANn to James Cicero Rhodes 7-23-1844 (7-?-1844)
Townsend, Sarah E. to Anderson J. Anderson 7-12-1869 (7-13-1869)
Townsend, Sarah E. to Andrew J. Anderson 7-12-1867
Townsend, Susanna W. to Aaron S. Bell 2-11-1851 (2-13-1851)
Trantham, Melissa to West Wilkins 5-19-1840
Trayler, Pamelia to George Jamison? 10-20-1855 (10-25-1855)
Traylor, Ann to W. W. Galbreath 5-6-1867 (5-7-1867)
Traylor, Sarah L. to James M. Curlin 4-10-1861
Treadaway, Caroline to Willis Davis 10-24-1874 (10-25-1874)
Trentham, Nancy to Richard Martin 10-30-1872 (10-31-1872)
Trigg, Caroline to Frank Sexton 9-18-1871 (9-25-1871)
Trigg, Charlett to Daniel Pews 7-2-1872 (7-13-1872)
Trigg, Claricy to Phill Smith 7-2-1872 (9-30-1872)
Trigg, Famy to Matt Archey 7-2-1872 (7-13-1872)
Trigg, Phebe to Aaron Kelly 11-27-1872 (12-16-1873?)
Trim, Louisa to R. M. Prater 9-12-1868 (9-15-1868)
Trimm?, Mary to G. W. Redden 9-?-1874 (9-22-1874)
Trobaugh, Elizabeth to M. A. Slone 12-22-1874 (12-23-1874)
Trobough, D. R. to J. G. McBride 2-22-1869 (2-27-1869)
Trobough, D. W. to D. L. McBride 6-16-1866 (6-20-1866)
Trobough, Elizabeth J. to Jacob Sullivan 12-21-1842 (12-23-1842)
Trobough, Elizabeth to Albert Adkins 4-14-1866
Trobough, Jiffy R. to J. C. Goforth 1-3-1866 (1-1?-1866)
Trobough, Mary E. to N. M. Lindsey 2-28-1862
Trobough, Nancy to Newman Bland 12-9-1865
Trobough, Nancy to Willis Morrow? 10-8-1873
Trosdale, L. A. to Ned Crenshaw 9-8-1874
Trousdale, Mailsey Jane to Wm. Montgomery no date (with 11-1874)
Truitt, Agnes to Wesley H. Lauderdale 3-26-1869 (4-4-1869)
Trusdale, Martha Ann to Mansfield Rhodes 11-6-1869 (11-7-1869)
Trusdale, Sina Ann to Moses Weathers 12-30-1873 (12-3?-1873)
Trusdile, Mary to Danil Branch 11-4-1871 (11-5-1872?)
Tucker, Allice A. to Thomas P. Edings 10-15-1859 (10-18-1859)
Tucker, Eliz. Murphy to Henry M. Turnage 10-14-1850 (10-16-1850)
Tucker, Elizabeth O. to Jas. A. Harris 12-15-1866 (12-6?-1866)
Tucker, Frances E. to Joseph S. Tucker 8-23-1869 (8-24-1869)
Tucker, Frances M. to John G. Mears 6-18-1860 (6-29-1860)
Tucker, Frances V. to W. F. Bowers 11-24-1856 (11-25-1856)
Tucker, Helen to Cannon Smith Wooton 9-28-1843
Tucker, Hulen H. to William A. Tucker 12-20-1867 (12-23-1867)
Tucker, Mary E. to Y. B. Turner 11-19-1866 (11-20-1866)
Tucker, Nancy Jane to Henry J. Mailey 1-23-1851
Tumage, Jane to Alfred Richard 1-14-1871
Turnage, Bettie to Ephran P. Fletcher 5-27-1867 (6-2-1867)
Turnage, E. M. to J. S. Bowles 3-21-1871 (3-23-1872?)
Turnage, Elizabeth W. to George W. Rogers 1-11-1841 (1-12-1841)
Turnage, Henrietta to Mark Grizzard 3-10-1873 (3-13-1873)
Turnage, Julia Catharine to James N. Smith 4-17-1850
Turnage, Margaret C. to William Delashmet 12-1-1840 (12-2-1840)
Turnage, Margaret to John Boyd 8-13-1873 (8-14-1873)
Turnage, Mary Amanda to Albert Gallatin Lanton 12-16-1843 (12-22-1843)
Turnage, Miss L. G. to M. L. Delashmit 12-16-1874 (12-17-1874)
Turnage, N. W. to J. D. Smith 1-7-1861 (1-10-1861)
Turnage, S. to Henry Thomas 12-24-1873 (12-27-1873)
Turnage, Sarah P. to Solomon R. Forbess 1-26-1870 (1-27-1870)
Turnage, Verlinske B. to George W. Delashmet 12-7-1867 (12-10-1867)
Turner, Callie to Charles Jones 10-21-1874
Turner, Easter to Thomas Lee 12-30-1873 (12-3?-1873)
Turner, Eveline to Tillman Duncan 7-27-1874
Turner, Fannie C. to James S. Maley 12-31-1866 (1-1-1867)
Turner, Mary to Robert Holland 11-6-1867
Turner, Sallie B. to B. D. Burch 5-12-1860
Tweedle, Sophronia to Peyton Hall 12-29-1874 (12-28?-1874)
Twisdale, A. E. to Henry Holoway 12-26-1859 (12-28-1859)
Twisdale, Ann Eliza to Henry Halaway 12-26-1859
Twisdale, Fannie to C. Malone 1-3-1870
Twisdale, Martha Ann to John Calvin Settle 6-22-1850 (6-25-1850)
Twyman, Mima to H. H. Walker 2-11-1873
Tyree?, Mary Louisa to Jas. W. Trobough 10-24-1856 (10-25-1855?)
Upchurch, Adaline to Henry Jones 7-14-1872 (7-15-1872)
Upchurch, Elizabeth C. to Joseph A. Dacus 7-25-1866 (7-26-1866)
Upchurch, L. A. to A. M. Owen 1-15-1862
Upchurch, Mrs. Sarah to Thos. B. Walk 1-5-1865
Upchurch, S. J. to Vincent P. Kelley 12-30-1858
Upchurch, Sarah J. to Vincent P. Kelley 12-30-1858
Valley, Kate to Solaman Howard 3-20-1867 (3-21-1867)
Vanderver, Margaret to P. R. Mitchell 1-4-1873 (1-5-1873)
Vaughan, Ann to Edward G. Allen 12-14-1844 (12-19-1844)
Vaughan, Claricy J. to James Young 1-13-1857
Vaughan, Mary J. to Thomas C. Howard 4-28-1852
Vaughan, Mary to Archer Lampkin 6-4-1870
Vaughan, Rebecca to Carlton Allen 4-3-1843 (4-4-1843)
Vaughn, Elizabeth A. to E. M. Downing 6-10-1868
Vaughn, Kate to Henry Allison 9-21-1867 (9-21-1867)
Veneer, Susan to Dick Richardson 5-9-1874
Verser, Ann to W. A. Chaney 12-5-1857 (12-6-1857)
Vertun?, A. to Gabril Granbury 12-28-1869 (12-30-1869)
Vincent, Mary Jane to James Byers 5-15-1851
Wade, L. L. to James M. Watson 11-24-1868 (11-26-1868)
Wade, Maggie E. to William E. Turner 1-3-1866
Wade, Manerva C. to J. L. Grigg 1-26-1858
Wade, Margaret J. P. to Alexander Timms 12-17-1873 (12-23-1873)
Wade, Peggy to A. R. Hicks 12-25-1873
Wages?, M. L. to C. C. Cannon 3-13-1873
Waggoner, Lizzie to Jessee Patten 10-12-1867 (10-13-1867)
Wagner, Sina to John Smith 1-15-1874
Walk, Alcy to William Lauderdale 5-24-1867 (5-26-1867)
Walk, Alice to Joseph M. Yarbro 1-2-1867
Walk, Amanda to John Loyd 10-19-1869
Walk, F. M. to Jno. M. Shelton 11-27-1873
Walk, Jane to Richmond Cotherum 12-7-1869 (12-8-1869)
Walk, Lucy A. to Jas. S. McIntosh 7-21-1866
Walk, Miss Lucy to James S. McIntosh 4-9-1862
Walk, Nancy to Henry Tornton 8-18-1870 (8-19-1870)
Walk, Sarah to Howard Houlsouser 12-29-1858 (12-28?-1858)
Walk, Susan Ann to Charles W. Archer 6-20-1855
Walker, Adaline to George Homan 8-1-1867 (8-9-1867)
Walker, E. J. to Chas. Thos. Oldham 3-18-1842
Walker, Elizabet J. to John B. Walker 3-4-1852
Walker, Emily R. to Charles D. Walker 3-3-1847 (3-4-1847)
Walker, Jane L. to George W. Billings 11-6-1847 (11-18-1847)
Walker, Jane to John Kirkpatrick 7-30-1849 (8-14-1849)
Walker, Jerusah D. to John A. Smith 10-25-1859 (10-28-1859)
Walker, Judia to Saml. Admas? 3-17-1866
Walker, Lusinda to Henry Brandon 3-23-1867 (3-24-1867)
Walker, Margaret to Dave Coldwell 10-5-1872 (10-6-1872)
Walker, Martha Agnes to Charles Webster Hoffler 8-7-1849
Walker, Martha M. to James A. Joodard 3-13-1861
Walker, Martha to Peter Strain 12-25-1866
Walker, Mary Jane to George Washington Manasker 12-19-1848 (12-7?-1848)
Walker, Mary to Jessee Grayham 5-5-1873 (7-4-1873)
Walker, Mary to Russell Moore 3-20-1854 (3-21-1854)
Walker, Mary to Wm. Delashmet 2-14-1855 (2-15-1855)
Walker, Mrs. Salina to Albert Roane 7-19-1867 (7-21-1867)
Walker, N. C. to W. T. Ward 11-26-1873
Walker, Nancy to James Drummons 1-15-1842 (1-16-1842)
Walker, Paulina S. to Jesse R. Haynie 8-13-1850
Walker, S. E. to John E. Wood 8-3-1874 (8-6-1874)

Walker, Sarah Elizabeth to Henry Harrison 1-2-1842 (1-3-1842)
Walker, Sarah F. to G. W. Billings 12-11-1865 (12-19-1865)
Walker, Sarah to Benjam. Timms 8-31-1869 (9-1-1869)
Wallace, Elizabeth to John Mayberry 11-15-1866 (11-18-1866)
Waller, Anna Reid to John J. Bolton 11-10-1874 (11-11-1874)
Waller, Catharine to C. Crenshaw 2-18-1874 B
Waller, Emma to John Talley 11-21-1874
Wallis, M. J. to J. H. Baskins 7-13-1864 (7-14-1864)
Wallis, Mary to Spencer Wilson 10-1-1866 (10-5-1866)
Walton, Amanda A. to William H. Dillahinty 12-17-1866 (12-18-1866)
Walton, Becka to Needham Smith 4-14-1874 (4-15-1874)
Walton, Bettie to Solaman Haynes 12-11-1866 (12-13-1866)
Walton, Mary M. to John W. Rose 4-21-1858
Walton, Minerva to Jerre Ford 1-20-1870
Walton, Sarah E. to J. C. Kinney 2-20-1873
Walton, Sarah F. to Richard B. Owen 12-18-1867
Ward, Luiza to Richard Shelton 12-27-1871 (12-28-1871)
Warmack, Mollie to Becton Eckford 12-12-1866
Warmath, Annie to W. W. Eckford 12-12-1865
Warthwait?, Catherine to Thomas Busic 7-20-1872 (7-21-1872)
Waters, Margaret S.? to G. P. Atkins 12-13-1871
Watson, L. P. to J. A. Ford 2-3-1873 (2-5-1873)
Watter, Emerlin to Sandy Alsten 1-10-1867
Watts, J. D. to N. H. McFadden 11-27-1873
Weatherford, Ellen L. to James A. Williams 9-20-1859
Weatherford, Lucy E. to John L. Pollard 11-18-1867 (11-19-1867)
Weatherford, Mary H. to Wm. R. Tate 11-18-1867 (12-19-1867)
Weatherford, Sarah E. to Elihu Morse 12-13-1865 (12-14-1865)
Weatherington, Harriet to William Beauty 1-19-1860
Weathington, Ann to Anthony Bledsoe 2-26-1857
Weathington, L. P. to James Murrin 2-11-1860
Weaver, Martha to Charles Adkins 7-26-1852 (7-27-1852)
Weaver, Sarah to Nathan Rachels 8-19-1852
Weaver, Susan to Berry Stubbs 3-9-1866
Weaver?, Clarinda A. to Ag? D. Hunter 10-19-1841 (10-21-1841)
Webb, Easter to Alexander Dennis 10-14-1871
Webb, Emily to James Manasco 6-21-1859 (6-23-1859)
Webb, Hester to Davy Fields 6-15-1867 (6-18-1867)
Webb, Jane to Burrel Anderson 12-24-1869 (12-25-1869)
Webb, Lowrana? to Benj. Franklin Pace 1-26-1856 (1-29-1856)
Webb, Lucinda to Wm. Jas. Roberts 4-11-1855
Webb, Sophia C. to Mason Moss 7-3-1858 (7-4-1858)
Weller, Elizabeth E. to Benj. Haskins Ligon 12-30-1846 (12-31-1846)
Weller, Mary S. to James Allen McLeary? 7-17-1855 (7-18-1855)
Weller, Sarah A. to Saml. D. McLeary 10-11-1841 (10-?-1841)
Wells, Elizabeth to Wesley Jones 12-31-1873
Wells, Mary to Peter Johnson 1-12-1874
Wenstram?, Jane E. to Francis Trice 10-22-1855 (10-23-1855)
West, Lizzie to James P. Kincaid 3-3-1874 (3-4-1874)
West, Percilla to Buck Williams 6-8-1867 (6-11-1867)
Wetherington, Cornelia to Wilson Byrnes 8-17-1867 (8-18-1867)
Wham?, Nancy Jane to David Hemphill McQuerter 5-6-1853
White, Caroline to Jack Blackwell 6-22-1868 (6-25-1868)
White, Drucilla to Edward A. McMillan 7-28-1841
White, Ellen Ann to Martin Harvey Kurts? 9-24-1853 (9-28-1853)
White, Josey to John Wells 4-19-1873 (4-20-1873)
White, M. E. to J. S. Waller 8-1-1870 (8-5-1870)
White, Margaret M. to Zachariah J. Doyle 11-11-1868 (11-12-1868)
White, Margaret to Ben Jones 1-11-1871
White, Marie to Martin Van Buren 8-12?-1868
White, Mary Ann to Edmond J. Booker? 8-3-1842 (8-4-1842)
White, Mary Ann to William P. Simpson 12-11-1858 (12-13-1858)
White, Mary L. to Augustus W. Walk 8-?-1866 (8-30-1866)
White, N. E. to W. J. Ragens 10-5-1868 (10-8-1868)
White, Nancy J. to James H. Bringle 11-11-1868 (11-12-1868)
White, Nancy to John McLaughlin 10-11-1854 (10-12-1854)
White, Sarah C. to Sam Long 8-21-1861
Whitley, Ann E. to John S. Peete 10-21-1844
Whitley, K. to Isaac Shaw 12-22-1870
Whitley, M. A. to James L. Cooper 5-21-1867 (5-23-1867)
Whitley, Patsey to James Foster 11-15-1870
Whitley, Polly to Henry Thompson 8-31-1866
Whitley, Sallie M. to Joseph Peete 10-3-1864 (10-5-1864)
Whitley, W. S. to W. J. McCall 11-1-1873 (11-7-1873)
Whitlock, Eliz. Ann to George Croghan Pinkston 3-19-1850
Whitlock, Eliza to Josiah Goforth 1-7-1850 (1-16-1850)
Whitlock, Mary C. to Granderson Sharp 2-4-1868 (2-5-1868)
Whitlock, Susan to John T. Brown 4-16-1857
Whitly, Patience to Dempsy Hunt 11-18-1865 (12-10-1865)
Whitman, Jane to Alexander Jones 11-30-1843
Whitson, Eliza to Obediah McGuire 88-7-1846 (8-13-1846)
Whitson, Susanah to Robert H. Owen 2-16-1859
Whitson, Susanah to Robert H. Owen 7-16-1859
Whitten, Harriet to William Hicks 12-29-1873
Whitworth, Mattie to Henry Hill 12-14-1870 (12-15-1870)
Wilbanks, Elisabeth Nancy to Miles Wade Kerr 4-22-1865
Wiley, Jane to Henry Baily 12-24-1872
Wiley, N. E. to P. H. Wilson 12-17-1872
Wilkins, Josephine to John F. Hammers 1-24-1871
Wilkins, Mary Catharine to Robt. Alex Williams 2-18-1861 (2-19-1861)
Wilkins, Nancy Jane to John E. Harrison 5-17-1853 (5-?-1853)
Wilkins, Sarah to Robert Lessley Dicus? 6-21-1853
Willhellmis, Nancy Jane to James B. Breck? 3-20-1873
Williams, Abigail to James Hartsfield 3-12-1849
Williams, Alice to Moak? Ealver? 12-27-1869
Williams, Amanda Jane to A. M. Overall 11-15-1869 (11-16-1869)
Williams, Amanda to John Bray Knox 8-8-1851 (8-17-1851)
Williams, Amanda to W. J. Rogers 5-11-1865 (5-12-1865)
Williams, America to Elijah Tilson? 6-23-1863
Williams, Angeline to W. J. Berry 12-21-1868 (12-23-1868)
Williams, Ann Henry to Charles A. Clements 12-21-1847 (not executed)
Williams, Anna Lee to Willis Peeler 3-13-1874 (3-4?-1874)
Williams, Annie to Nelson Sherrell 12-11-1871 (12-14-1871)
Williams, Charity to Anthony Dickens 12-23-1872
Williams, Eliza to Henry M. Ballard 7-16-1861 (8-17-1861)
Williams, Elizabet M. to George F. Monroe 12-24-1873 (1-5-1874)
Williams, Elizabeth Ann to Edward Thomas Harris 1-6-1849 (1-7-1849)
Williams, Elizabeth to Andrew McGowan 8-4-1866 (8-7-1866)
Williams, Elizabeth to Farris Hall 1-16-1874
Williams, Elizabeth to Martain Hall 10-8-1870
Williams, Emmer to Alexander Williams 12-27-1870 (12-28-1870)
Williams, Jane to Saml. Allen 12-28-1870
Williams, Katy to Jas. W. Trigg 2-20-1869 (3-1-1869)
Williams, Liller to Lane Warren 8-4-1870 (8-7-1870)
Williams, Lukky to Bedford Jackson 12-27-1869
Williams, Manerva Ann to Patrick Lavell 12-12-1859 (12-13-1859)
Williams, Margaret to Alexander Cassan 10-12-1867
Williams, Martha E. to David M. Billings 1-13-1866
Williams, Martha Jane to William H. Odam 12-16-1848 (12-20-1848)
Williams, Mary Margaret to Jesse Byrd 6-14-1855
Williams, Mary to J. A. Johnson 1-13-1873 (1-16-1873)
Williams, Mary to John B. Stevens 3-22-1850
Williams, Mary to Samuel B. Scott 12-17-1845 (12-19-1845)
Williams, Mary to W. R. Harvell 9-7-1874 (9-9-1874)
Williams, Mary to William Shaw 5-8-1871 (5-11-1871)
Williams, Mary? A. to _____ Trobough 4-18-1863 (4-21-1863)
Williams, Millie to Charles Rutherford 11-13-1873
Williams, Missouri A. B. to James J. Williams 6-22-1857
Williams, Mollie M. to Saml. O. Lemons 9-18-1871 (9-21-1871)
Williams, Nancy to Tom McAdams 2-19-1867 (2-10-1867)
Williams, Nancy to Wm. Johnston 6-9-1866 (6-12-1866)
Williams, Rosa to George Mitchell 8-9-1871 (8-10-1871)
Williams, Sallie to Frank McCraw 1-17-1874 (1-18-1874)
Williams, Sarah O. to John C. Williams 11-5-1868
Williams, Susan to Thomas Sale 12-19-1870 (12-25-1870)
Williams, Victoria A. to John D. McKnight 3-9-1867 (3-14-1867)
Williamson, Easter to Lamb Wilkerson 3-12-1870
Williamson, Elizabeth to Saml. Rhodes 10-27-1866 (12-1-1866)
Williamson, Fathy to Robert Macklin 1-29-1866
Williamson, Frances to Chas. Turner 4-17-1866
Williamson, Juda to Henry Wood 1-20-1874
Williamson, Patsey to Alexander Taylor 2-27-1867
Williamson, Penny to Peter Thompson 2-13-1867 (2-15-1867)
Williamson, S. P. to J. E. Wilson 9-14-1874 (9-17-1874)
Willis, Mary J. to James Dill 3-27-1874 (11-29-1874)
Willson, Jane to James Henderson 4-21-1870 (4-23-1870)
Wilson, Amanda to Governor Weaver 10-14-1874

Wilson, Annie to John Oglesby 11-4-1867 (11-5-1867)
Wilson, E. S. to William Cates 8-29-1871 (8-30-1871)
Wilson, Elizabeth to John Sullivan 1-9-1855 (1-11-1855)
Wilson, Emina to Barney Alexander 12-7-1874?
Wilson, Emma L. to H. M. Houston 7-9-1868
Wilson, Jennet to William Kidd 1-2-1866 (1-10-1866)
Wilson, Margaret E. to James A. Moore 5-14-1864 (5-16-1864)
Wilson, Margaret L. to John Steele 1-6-1845 (1-9-1845)
Wilson, Margaret to William Wood 12-23-1870
Wilson, Martha E. to R. C. Simonton 9-5-1859
Wilson, Martha Jane to Wm. S. Moffatt 4-16-1856 (4-17-1856)
Wilson, Martha to Anderson Adams 9-21-1870 (9-22-1870)
Wilson, Martha to E. L. Hatchel 9-6-1871 (9-12-1871)
Wilson, Mary to James Holton 5-7-1841 (5-8-1841)
Wilson, Mary to Simeon Richardson 5-8-1874
Wilson, Nancy to John P. Erwin 12-24-1866 (12-25-1866)
Wilson, Ruth to Essex Williams 10-20-1871
Wilson, Sarah E. to Josiah A. Morrow 7-8-1847
Wilson, Sarah to Mat Alston 1-16-1871
Wilson, Sarah to William H. McQuiston 9-26-1855
Wilson, Susan to Jorden Henderson 11-9-1866
Windham, Martha to John Tilmon 10-13-1842 (10-17-1842)
Winford, Alice to Paul Clements 8-31-1866 (9-13-1866)
Winford, Louisa to Andrew Smith 4-27-1870
Winford, R. C. to Richard A. Blalock 12-10-1870 (12-14-1870)
Winford, S. V. to Andrew Winford 7-25-1865? (7-26-1866)
Winn, Iva Ann to Joseph Dearing 6-24-1856
Winn, Mariah to James Devaughn 11-1-1873 (11-5-1873)
Winn, Mary to Pelly Hill 12-24-1873 (12-25-1873)
Winn, Miss M. E. to H. H. Wiseman 12-27-1860
Winn, Rhoda to Wm. Gatewood 10-17-1866 (10-20-1866)
Winn, Sarah Jane to Elias O. Yarbre? 10-25-1855
Winn?, Amand to Edmond Stevens 1-27-1873 (1-28-1873)
Winston, Permelia to Ira Harris 5-5-1874 (5-6-1874)
Winston, Sarah to Ira Adams 11-4-1865 (11-14-1865)
Winston?, Angelin to William Smith 7-9-1869
Wiseman, Amand L. to Henry K. Farmer 9-21-1867 (9-24-1867)
Wiseman, Elanor to Jacob Smith 8-17-1841
Wiseman, Frances to Thos. H. Tillman 1-1-1862
Wiseman, Julia Ann L. to James O. Mailey 3-27-1853
Wiseman, M. E. to Wm. A. Kinney 2-29-1860
Wiseman, Margaret to Geo. Tillman 2-27-1871 (2-28-1871)
Wiseman, Mary E. to George Nobles 7-18-1866 (7-19-1866)
Wiseman, Mary E. to Wm. A. Kinney 2-29-1860
Wiseman, Mary S. to William A. Kiney 2-29-1860
Wiseman, Matilda Elizabeth to Alfred B. Owen 3-15-1849
Wiseman, Matilda to Noah Brown 12-26-1865 (12-28-1865)
Wiseman, Sallie to L. L. Warr 9-9-1868
Wiseman, Sallie to William Brown 1-7-1874 (1-10-1874)
Wiseman, Sarah to J. W. Best 2-5-1868
Wiseman, Sarah to Wiley Stevens 3-18-1865 (3-21-1865)
Wiseman?, Frances Jane to John Carr Myers 2-25-1858
Wissen, Caroline L. to Joseph J.? Talley 4-22-1840 (4-23-1840)
Witherington, Louisa Jane to Thomas D. Wood 7-1-1842
Witherington, Martha to John Billings 12-5-1846 (12-6-1846)
Witherington, Mary to Aaron Bledsoe 9-11-1854
Withington, Sarah Ann to Wm. Porter Burgitt 12-17-1855 (12-20-1855)
Wolen, Lousella to David Hindman 2-26-1870
Wood, Amanda C. to Saml. Roe 1-4-1869 (1-5-1869)
Wood, Amanda to Joseph Maxwell 11-28-1861
Wood, America J. to Jas. Henry Tillman 1-8-1872 (1-11-1872)
Wood, Amy to Robt. Shepard 11-4-1865 (11-6-1865)
Wood, Ann to Andrew Robinson 9-7-1866 (9-16-1866)
Wood, Cordelia to Robert Elam 3-29-1858 (4-1-1858)
Wood, Eliza to Talbert Thompson 3-6-1871 (3-8-1871)
Wood, Lavicey Ann to Anderson Mailey 3-16-1848
Wood, Luciller to Moses Hay 12-10-1870 (12-11-1870)
Wood, Margaret J. to J. H. Hill 3-12-1866
Wood, Margaret to George Manual 10-18-1872 (10-19-1872)
Wood, Martha to William H. Ligon 9-12-1842 (9-20-1842)
Wood, Mary F. to Jordan C. Wood 12-16-1868
Wood, Mary Jane to Henry B. Ligon 1-4-1848 (1-5-1848)
Wood?, Laura to Andrew Strong 10-26-1869
Woodley, Catharin to Wesley Eldridge 7-1-1869
Woods, C. C. to Wm. E. Briseman 6-21-1859 (6-22-1859)
Woods, Cordia to William Dreums? 5-10-1873
Woods, Narcissus to Joseph H. Webster 1-17-1851 (1-19-1851)
Woods, Sarah to John C. Cocrum 2-23-1867 (3-11-1867)
Woods, Scyntha to Newt Coats 1-15-1866
Wooten, Athey to Burrell Warf 1-3-1850
Wooten, Lidia A. to Home? Dedrick 12-24-1866 (12-27-1866)
Wooten, Lola to G. B. Sale 11-16-1869 (11-17-1869)
Wooten, Mary F. to Jacob A. Sullivan 9-7-1869 (9-8-1869)
Wooten, Mary to Anthony B. Coward 12-14-1841 (12-15-1841)
Wooten, Matilda to James Brooks 3-16-1861
Wooten, N. A. to Richard Pullin 2-4-1867 (2-15-1867)
Wooton, Harriet L. to Charles Howell Adkins 9-11-1853 (9-13-1853)
Wormick, Susanna to E. Richardson 11-29-1866
Wormik, Sallie to James C. Rice 1-5-1872 (1-10-1872)
Wortham, Ellen to Jack Dyson 8-28-1869
Wortham, Indiana to Spencer Cannon 1-10-1870
Wortham, Mary to Billy Dyer 8-9-1869
Wright, Catherine to John Moore 11-12-1869
Wright, Cynthia Jane to Aganza? Benton Brooks 11-27-1848 (11-30-1848)
Wright, Elisabeth to Robt. H. Drappin 7-17-1856
Wright, Elizabeth A. to Prichard Cowser? 3-25-1843
Wright, Elizabeth A. to S. K. Drummonds 2-22-1871 (2-23-1871)
Wright, Elizath. A. to William H. Yancy 12-21-1867 (12-22-1867)
Wright, Jennie T. to Saml. S. Craig 3-13-1862
Wright, Lucinda to Jordan Weathers 2-23-1874
Wright, Margaret to David H. McQuistin 4-8-1843 (4-11-1843)
Wright, Margaret to Lawson Lane 1-26-1870
Wright, Martha P. to Isaac M. Miller 7-25-1855 (7-26-1855)
Wright, Mary A. H. to Ezekiel Smith Williams 1-29-1855 (1-31-1855)
Wright, Mary to Isaac S. Hill 6-10-1867 (6-11-1867)
Wright, Matilda to Monroe Bumphass 2-16-1874 (2-24-1874)
Wright, Nancy C. to Samuel K. Horning? 9-21-1842
Wright, Nancy M. to Banyan Tayne? 7-22-1841
Wylie, Mary E. to Abner J. Hanner 1-3-1857
Yarbro, Amanda to Coleman Hall 10-15-1873 (10-16-1873)
Yarbro, Amanda to Gobe Wilson 8-11-1874 (8-12-1874)
Yarbro, Ann Liza to Frank Fortune 11-21-1867
Yarbro, Ann to Henry Millen 11-19-1868
Yarbro, Anna to F. F. Davis 7-15-1874
Yarbro, Anna to Wm. Wright 5-7-1873
Yarbro, Caroline to Lippman jr. Howsar 8-27-1867 (8-29-1867)
Yarbro, Charletta to Saml. Strong 12-11-1867
Yarbro, Charlotte to Zack Williams 4-18-1873 (4-13?-1873)
Yarbro, Elizabeth to S. H. Brown 6-5-1856
Yarbro, Freesave? to Granderson Bledsoe 3-10-1873 (3-11-1873)
Yarbro, Louisa to Washington Goodram 11-20-1867 (11-21-1867)
Yarbro, M. B. to G. T. Smith 11-19-1872 (11-20-1872)
Yarbro, M. J. to W. A. Max 8-19-1868 (8-26-1868)
Yarbro, Mary E. to James L. Ayers 5-12-1858
Yarbro, Mary to George W. Walton 6-8-1870 (6-9-1870)
Yarbro, Mary to Isaac Payne 4-17-1869 (6-9-1869)
Yarbro, Sophronia to James K. Kinney 1-24-1861
Yarbro, Susan to Lymas Lauderdale 12-18-1872
Yarbroh, Harriet E. to Jas. M> Smith 2-7-1864
Yarbroh, Mary to Pompey Calhoun 9-29-1866 (10-29-1866)
Yarbroh, R. V. to John W. Morton 3-21-1865 (3-22-1865)
Yarbroh, R. V. to John W. Moton 3-21-1865
Yarbroh, Sallie J. to James W. Upchurch 2-18-1861
Yarbrok, Catharine to Robert W. Warmouth 2-3-1858 (2-4-1858)
Yarbrough, Mary E. to Augustus W. Smith 9-29-1845 (10-2-1845)
Young, D. E. to H. D. C. Baker 9-9-1867 (9-11-1867)
Young, Ellen to Anderson Edward 2-18-1868
Young, Harriet to Joseph Jorden 10-29-1867 (10-30-1867)
Young, Jane to Geo. Chambers 11-30-1872 (12-1-1872)
Young, Julia C. to John W. Jackson 1-12-1867 (1-13-1867)
Young, M. J. to John H. Goad 12-17-1874
Young, Martha Ann to Luby? Demar 12-20-1873
Yount, Mary to Alexander Murphey 1-12-1874 (1-13-1874)
Yount, Sarah A. E. to Peter L. Feezor 7-27-1854
Yunt, Eliza to Sterling Pinner 12-31-1847 (1-7-1848)
Zimmermann, Caroline to John Schmeller 11-19-1858
_____, Josephine to Anthony Dover? 4-24-1873
_____, M. J. K. to James C. Nelson 3-20-1860 (3-22-1860)

_____, Maria to Isaac Trigg 7-2-1872
_____, Mary to Johnb Randolph 5-20-1869
_____, _____ to Isaac Wilson 12-20-1869

www.ingramcontent.com/pod-product-compliance
Lightning Source LLC
LaVergne TN
LVHW061257100826
845148LV00008B/1156
* 9 7 8 1 5 9 6 4 1 0 5 6 5 *